THE PSYCHOLOGY OF VANDALISM

THE PLENUM SERIES IN SOCIAL/CLINICAL PSYCHOLOGY

Series Editor: C. R. Snyder

University of Kansas
Lawrence, Kansas

Current Volumes in this Series:

AGGRESSIVE BEHAVIOR
Current Perspectives
Edited by L. Rowell Huesmann

THE ECOLOGY OF AGGRESSION
Arnold P. Goldstein

EFFICACY, AGENCY, AND SELF-ESTEEM
Edited by Michael H. Kernis

HUMAN LEARNED HELPLESSNESS
A Coping Perspective
Mario Mikulincer

PATHOLOGICAL SELF-CRITICISM
Assessment and Treatment
Raymond M. Bergner

PROCRASTINATION AND TASK AVOIDANCE
Theory, Research, and Treatment
Joseph R. Ferrari, Judith L. Johnson, and William G. McCown

THE PSYCHOLOGY OF VANDALISM
Arnold P. Goldstein

SELF-EFFICACY, ADAPTATION, AND ADJUSTMENT
Theory, Research, and Application
Edited by James E. Maddux

SELF-ESTEEM
The Puzzle of Low Self-Regard
Edited by Roy F. Baumeister

A Continuation Order Plan is available for this series. A continuation order will bring delivery of each new volume immediately upon publication. Volumes are billed only upon actual shipment. For further information please contact the publisher.

THE PSYCHOLOGY OF VANDALISM

ARNOLD P. GOLDSTEIN
Syracuse University
Syracuse, New York

PLENUM PRESS • NEW YORK AND LONDON

Library of Congress Cataloging-in-Publication Data

Goldstein, Arnold P.
The psychology of vandalism / Arnold P. Goldstein.
p. cm. -- (The Plenum series in social/clinical psychology)
Includes bibliographical references and index.
ISBN 0-306-45140-9
1. Vandalism--Psychological aspects. 2. Vandalism--Prevention.
I. Titie. II. Series.
HV6666.G65 1996
364.1'64--dc20 95-44578
CIP

ISBN 0-306-45140-9

A Division of Plenum Publishing Corporation
233 Spring Street, New York, N.Y. 10013

10 9 8 7 6 5 4 3 2 1

Printed in the United States of America

To Lauren Noe and Rachel Akie

PREFACE

Vandalism is a serious and growing problem in the United States and beyond. Schools, parks and playgrounds, mass transit vehicles, city streets, museums, libraries, and numerous other venues are its common targets. As higher and perhaps more dramatic expressions and concomitants of aggression—fights, assaults, gangs, guns, the drug trade—have grown and increasingly commanded public and professional attention, focus on its less damaging expressions has diminished. Vandalism is one casualty of such diminished attention. For reasons made clear in Chapter 1, society pays a handsome price for its relative ignoring of low levels of aggression expressiveness. In this book, I seek to remediate this absence of concern through a comprehensive presentation and examination of the status, causation, prevention, and remediation of vandalistic behavior.

In telling the "story" of vandalism, I begin (Chapter 1) with an exploration of its importance, consequences, frequency, and costs. This exploration shows vandalism to be a serious societal problem. In Chapter 2, I attempt to bring some clarity to the confusing array of definitions that have been offered over the years for *vandalism*, a term variously employed both too restrictively and too inclusively. Further in this chapter, I examine demographic information in order to begin painting an approximate profile of both the "typical" vandal and his or her frequent targets. Why such behavior occurs is addressed in Chapter 3, primarily a consideration of the several typologies of vandalism motivation and the small but pregnant number of theories of its etiology.

The book's remaining chapters deal with intervention. With "strategies" representing schema, plans, or perspectives, and "tactics" the concrete means for implementing such plans, Chapters 4 and 5 deal, respectively, with vandalism intervention strategies and tactics. Environment-oriented and vandal-oriented strategies are described and evaluated, and a strong case is made for the value of a dual, person–environment strategic intervention orientation. The several dozen tactical procedures for actually intervening are catalogued and listed in Chapter 5 by subtypes so as to facilitate such person–environment intervention. This facilitation effort expands in Chapter 6, where approaches to selecting and combining single interventions into intervention programs of probable effectiveness are described. A series of additional effectiveness-enhancing characteristics of intervention efforts are also described and examined, toward the goal of maximizing their vandalism prevention and reduction impact. Do such programs actually succeed? Vandalism intervention research, unfortunately, has not been frequently conducted and, when it has, has frequently not been of rigorous quality. Chapter 6 concludes with a presentation of research design and measurement alternatives and suggestions offering the potential of enhancing the quality of such needed investigative effort. The book's text (Chapter 7) concludes with a brief, but important, journey to the topic of ecovandalism—the many individual and organized sources of damage and destruction to our macroenvironment. Here I briefly describe the large number of beginning efforts by psychological researchers to better understand the role of human behavior as it relates to ecovandalistic damage, as well as possible means for altering such behavior in prosocial directions. This expansion of the domain of vandalism studies appears to be an especially worthwhile advance for psychological inquiry.

What is known today about the causes and reduction of vandalism rests far too extensively on a shaky foundation of anecdote, experience, and speculation, and far too little on rigorous research. However, a small amount of such investigative inquiry, both quantitative and qualitative, does exist. The final section of this book, a research appendix, consists of a small group of exemplary studies focused upon one or another significant aspect of vandalism. I include them here as both information and example, in the hope of stimulating further high-quality empirical efforts by other investigators.

CONTENTS

CHAPTER 1

WHY STUDY VANDALISM?

DOWNSIZING DEVIANCE

A major part of my early preparation for the writing of this book involved a broad and deep literature search on the topic of vandalism. Several databases were searched, including education, psychology, criminology, environmental science, sociology, and more. These searches went back 20 years. The product of this energetic effort was curious. While the total number of relevant articles, books, dissertations, and commentaries was large, their appearance by year departed substantially from my initial expectations. As described later in this book, because the problem of vandalism seems to have grown and even accelerated over this 20-year span, I thought there would be a corresponding increase in writings about it. Examination of the collected references, however, revealed a steady buildup through the late 1960s and the 1970s that was not followed in the 1981–1983 period by a continued increase, or a leveling off, or even a steady decline. Instead, theoretical, research, and speculative writing about the nature of vandalism and its reduction virtually ceased in these several bodies of literature in the early 1980s!

My hypothesis regarding this abrupt near-cessation of written evidence of professional interest in vandalism as a focus of inquiry rests on the notion of downsizing deviance. This is the creeping indifference to lower levels of a given transgressive behavior as higher levels of such behavior become more frequent and, hence, more salient. It is a phenomenon I have observed in other contexts. The concern of law enforcement personnel with smoking on the New York City subway, or jay walking in Philadelphia, or other now "low-level" transgressions fades as concern and thus attention refocuses on assaults, robbery, and the like. This also, I believe, is the case with vandalism. As school personnel, for example, become increasingly preoccupied in the early 1980s with drug sale and use, gangs, student fights, weapons, assaulted teachers, and similar "high-level" aggression, "mere" vandalism could no longer command center stage—either in one's workday or in the professional writings of educators, school psychologists, criminologists, or the other contributors to the flood of vandalism articles during the 1970s.

While drugs, gangs, guns, and the like certainly deserve our attention, we downsize lower levels of deviance at a substantial cost. Aggression, whether toward persons or property, is primarily learned behavior. Youngsters break windows or break noses because, through either direct or vicarious (modeling) experiences, they have learned that such behaviors are likely to be rewarded and unlikely to be punished. Behaviors rewarded are likely to recur and often do so in an ever-escalating manner. Thus, just as the oppositional child may (via the success of his or her oppositional behavior) grow into the conduct-disordered preadolescent and the juvenile delinquent adolescent, so, too, may the successful, chronic vandal evolve into the assaultive youth. I assert that such developmental patterns are not inevitable, but merely likely. If peer adulation follows vandalistic feats, striving for more adulation through the same or escalated means is thus made more probable.

Our attitude toward vandalism is much the same as that toward other low levels of aggressive enactment, such as refusal, disruptiveness, bullying, cursing, and harassment. Namely, if one successfully seeks to diminish their occurrence, higher levels of aggression also become less likely. *Catch it low to prevent it high*. As evidence examined in this book will make clear, a vandalized neighborhood not only is promotive of additional, same-level incivilities but also encourages a progression toward more severe levels of infraction. Downsizing deviance has its costs, and they are not minor. We study vandalism here, and urge others to resume doing so, toward the dual goal of reducing both it and its more severely aggressive descendants.

FREQUENCY OF OCCURRENCE

Broken windows, walls covered with graffiti, a building destroyed by arson, initials carved in a park picnic table, a treasured painting slashed in a museum, mutilated library books, road signs obliterated through target practice, a rural fence knocked over, a city phone booth incapacitated, and public bathroom fixtures ripped from a wall—how frequent are such products of vandalism? For several reasons, firm approximations are not

In a grisly act of school vandalism, scores of pets at the elementary school in Wynnefield were killed by vandals who broke into the school over the Memorial Day weekend. They killed all the school pets, including gerbils, hamsters, goldfish and birds, in more than 25 of the 40 classrooms. They uprooted dozens of houseplants, rifled teachers' desks, ransacked supply closets, destroyed a television set, broke windows and stole thirty cassette tape recorders, an adding machine and $35 in cash.

Source: J. R. Ban and L. M. Ciminillo (1977). *Violence and vandalism in public education.* Danville, IL: Interstate Printers & Publishers, p. 3.

easily arrived at, and when they are, they are likely to be serious underestimations. Our society's collective downsizing of deviance, discussed above, is one basis for such underreporting. A substantial portion of the victims of vandalism also fail to report its occurrence, in the apparently accurate belief that little will follow from their act of reporting—only an estimated 3%–4% of vandalistic acts lead to prosecution (Anon., 1980b; Coffield, 1991; Walden, 1980).

Much of the difficulty in estimating the extent of vandalism in the United States and elsewhere follows from the sheer variety of definitions regarding what in fact constitutes a vandalistic act. How inclusive should an optimal definition be? What is vandalism versus "normal" wear and tear? What is vandalism versus damage occurring in the course of a burglary or theft? Beyond definitional concerns (examined in depth in the next chapter), there is apparent underreporting as a result of the perception of many who are responsible for public property (e.g., schools and parks) that the occurrence of vandalism in their domain somehow reflects poorly on their management skills. Hence, substantial denial often occurs. For those administrators who do attempt to keep records of occurrence, the criteria and means of recording are exceedingly diverse—and often far too inadequate and lacking in uniformity across sites—for meaningful compilations of incidence data to be possible. In addition, as Coffield (1991) observed, many victims elect not to report vandalistic acts because they view such behavior as trivial, or have not themselves witnessed the act, or do not believe the police will act if a report is made.

Yet, all of these obstacles not withstanding, some reasonable estimations are possible. One basis for such an effort is financial costs. These are considerable in magnitude and will be presented in this chapter's next section. A second source of incidence information derives from the fact that some (probably the more serious) acts of vandalism often do lead to arrest, and these arrest data are regularly included in the Federal Bureau of Investigation's annual *Uniform Crime Report*. Thus, the incidence of such vandalism—judged from arrest statistics—can be reported. If these are, in fact, statistics of arrests for more serious (more costly, more damaging) vandalistic acts, it is probably reasonable to assume that, as levels of such serious transgression vary upward and downward, so, too, in parallel do more minor vandalistic behaviors. Though arrest data are often as much a measure of police decisions regarding which crimes to pursue, and how energetically, as they are of actual crime levels, they are at least a rough, satisfactory index of criminal behavior.

To get a sense of vandalism arrest levels, and of the changes in such levels, over both the short term and across longer gaps of time, incidence information for 1983, 1992, and 1993 are of interest. Respective vandalism arrest-frequency data for these years are 175,981 (1983), 234,483 (1992), and 261,282 (1993).[1] For long-term comparisons in particular (1983–1993), the increase in the incidence of arrests for vandalism substantially exceeds the corresponding increase in the size of the population in the United States.

While these police arrest data are of value in providing a general sense of the serious levels of vandalism in the United States, they must be viewed as severe underestimates. As Coffield (1991) noted, and as Sturman (1980) demonstrated, "official statistics on vandalism which at first sight appear objective, accurate and convincing can be quickly shown to be patchy, imprecise and misleading" (Cobblefield, 1991, p. 41). Indeed, in the study by Sturman (1978), vandalism across a number of public locations was shown to be 14 to 15 times greater than that reported to police!

In addition to these arrest data pointing to substantial levels and upward trends in vandalism, what other sources of national incidence may be drawn upon? As will be seen throughout this book, vandalism is often targeted toward schools. Thus, one might expect that, if a reliable data source does exist, it would be school-focused. Such, however, is not the case. Surprising as it may seem, vandalism data (frequency or costs) are not compiled by the U.S. Department of Education, the National Education Association, the National School Boards Association, the American School Health Association, the Parent Teachers Association, the National Associa-

[1]These figures, as noted, are *actual* arrest incidence data for vandalism. The FBI also provides *estimated* arrest data, combining incidence from both those criminal justice agencies reporting such information and estimates for those not reporting. Total actual plus estimated arrests for vandalism were 323,100 (1992) and 313,000 (1993).

At 5:11 A.M. on October 1, 1963, the duty man at fire alarm headquarters in Saugas, Mass., answered the telephone and heard a frantic voice reporting an apparently serious fire.

While the alarm operator was trying to get an address from the incoherent caller, a street box alarm sounded—from the local junior high school. The fire, which had originated in the school auditorium, spread upward to the attic of the two- and three-story brick building. When firemen arrived, they found flames spreading throughout the undivided attic to other sections of the building and downward through combustible fiberboard ceilings to the second story corridors.

Because the school had no automatic fire detection or sprinkler system, delayed discovery allowed the flames to penetrate deep into the building's nonfirestopped concealed spaces—attic, ceilings, walls—and firemen couldn't control it. Lost: one junior high school building valued at $1.2 million.

That was the beginning.

Investigation led authorities to suspect that the fire was a touch off by person or persons unknown. The school board declared a four-day holiday....

On October 22 at 2:35 A.M. an unidentified person telephoned the fire department to report a fire in the senior high school. This time, fire heavily damaged three classrooms and a corridor and made 11 additional classrooms inaccessible—along with an entire wing of the high school, including the general science, biology, physics, and chemistry laboratories.

Once again, suspicion of a touch off. Once again, the loss of classrooms—at $250,000—and still only part of the story. Another four-day holiday—this time to make stop gap alterations to put the high school building in some kind of operating condition....

Two months later. Early morning hours. Fire. At Veterans Memorial School. This time, however, the blaze was discovered and extinguished before it could spread from the classroom in which it had started.

Another touch off, but not another dead end. A pattern of evidence had taken shape and investigators arrested a 14 year old junior high school boy who confessed to setting all three fires (he was trying to destroy records of his failing grades).

Source: E. E. Juillerat, Jr. (1972). Fires and vandals: How to make them both unwelcome in your schools. *The American School Board Journal, 159*, 23–24.

tion of School Safety and Law Enforcement Officers, or any other of the several relevant national-level agencies which I queried energetically. A small number of states do maintain school vandalism incidence data—New Jersey (Anon., 1992b) reporting a modest recent decrease; California (Anon., 1990), Michigan (Anon., 1991), and Kansas (Anon., 1992a) each showing moderate to substantial increases. Ample national statistics are readily obtainable regarding drug utilization in schools, the presence of weapons, the existence of gangs, the frequency of student–student and student–teacher assaults, and the incidence of yet other expressions of high levels of violence—but not regarding school vandalism. The downsizing-of-deviance hypothesis may well explain this phenomenon.

Nonetheless, the absence of (especially) national incidence data notwithstanding, there have been numerous survey and anecdotal reports during the past 25 years which support the contention that school vandalism levels are both absolutely high and still growing in the United States (Casserly, Bass, & Garrett, 1980; Dukiet, 1973; Goldstein, Harootunian, & Conoley, 1994; Meany, 1987; Rubel, 1977; Sadler, 1988; Schumacker & Leitner, 1979; Thomas, 1981; Tygart, 1988). Because school property is such a frequent target of vandalism, and school-aged children are so commonly its perpetrators, much of this book is devoted to both likely sources of, and promising interventions for, school vandalism.

Several other frequent targets of vandalistic acts exist and equally deserve our attention. Their consideration not only will illustrate the breadth or generality of such aggression toward property but will also contribute to our understanding of its diverse motivations. Davis (1971) described a large and varied array of acts of vandalism directed toward university libraries as part of the student protest movement of the 1960s. Incidents included the destruction of catalog drawers, the slashing of furniture, arson, books scattered randomly throughout the building (a "book-in"), glue poured into card trays, clogged toilets, broken windows, and more. In less dramatic ways, but perhaps frequently with rather similar academic consequences, university library vandalism has continued. Martin's survey (1972) indicated that 80% of university libraries experienced serious mutilation problems. Gouke and Murfin (1980), Hendrick and Murfin (1974), Pederson (1990), and Weiss (1981) each reported substantial levels (between 10% and 15%) of periodical mutilation by the students they surveyed, as well as similar levels of book theft. In America's forests and national parks, there reportedly are growing levels of damage or destruction of both the natural environment and campground facilities, as well as the cutting of trees for firewood, garbage dumping, littering, the theft of cultural artifacts ("pot hunting"), soil erosion from all-terrain cycles, cut fencing, grazing violations, spray-painted graffiti ("piecing"),

> The Intervale Avenue stop in the South Bronx has been closed since March 15, 1989, when the station was set on fire by three youths frustrated in their attempts to rob the token booth: the mezzanine was destroyed. The numbers 2 and 5 trains of the Interborough Rapid Transit system still roll along the elevated tracks at the corner of Intervale and Westchester Avenues, but don't stop at Intervale Avenue anymore, the first subway station shut down by the TA [Transit Authority] because of vandalism.
>
> *Source*: Anon. (1990, July–August). Transportation blues. *Metropolis*, p. 17.

gunshot destruction of signs, and arson fires (Anson, 1987; Clark, 1971; Doolittle & Lightsey, 1979; Harris, 1991; Simmons, 1979).

Vandalism on America's farms and, more generally, in rural areas is also a common event. It most certainly is not only an urban phenomenon. Phillips's (1982) victimization survey of rural vandalism in Ohio yielded 38% of the respondents reporting that their property had been targets. Cleland (1990) conducted a similar inquiry in Tennessee, and 24% of his respondents indicated vandalism to their farms during the preceding 12 months. In both rural and urban settings, sign vandalism appears to be particularly frequent. Chadda and Carter (1983) reported that, according to Federal Highway Authority estimates, vandalized traffic signs cost states, counties, and cities $50 million per year. Their 1980 survey of 30 states revealed that 1.2 million signs had been replaced that year, approximately 28% because of vandalism. Harris (1991) observed that, in many rural areas, "a legible five-year old sign is unusual." He estimated two years as the average lifetime of a sign.

Where else may the vandal strike? Museums and public art galleries are frequent targets. Cordess and Turgen (1993) and Freedberg (1985) have described a long history of such "iconoclastic" events. In a recent survey of directors of 92 such institutions, 67% reported some vandalism (Cordess & Turgen, 1993). Most acts were minor (e.g., scratching and graffiti); 10% were major (e.g., smashing sculpture or vases, slashing or shooting canvasses, and arson). Instances of art vandalism, they assert, are increasing in frequency. Public transportation—trains, buses, and stations—are also common vandalism sites (Bennett, 1977), as are public telephones (Jamieson, 1987), university dormitories (Anon., 1983b; Bowles, 1982), privately owned stores, and even homes (Phillips & Donnermeyer, 1982).

Selected List of Well-Known Artworks Attacked, with Location and Year of Attack

1. *Portrait of the Artist Jacob Cornelisz and His Wife*, by Dirck Jacobsz; Museum of Art, Toledo, Ohio (date unknown).
2. *The Nightwatch*, by Rembrandt; Rijksmuseum, Amsterdam (1911 and 1975).
3. *The Toilet of Venus* ("The Rokeby Venus"), by Velasquez; National Gallery, London (1914).
4. *Martyrdom of St. James*, by Mantegna; Ovetari Chapel, Eremitani, Padua (1944).
5. *Mona Lisa*, by Leonardo da Vinci; Louvre, Paris (1956).
6. *Sposalizio*, by Raphael; Brera Palace, Milan (1958).
7. *Fall of the Damned*, by Rubens; Alte Pinakothek, Munich (1959).
8. *The Virgin and Child with St. Anne and St. John*, by Leonardo da Vinci; National Gallery, London (1962 and 1987).
9. *Christ of St. John of the Cross*, by Dalí; Glasgow Art Gallery (1965 and 1980).
10. *Virgin with the Innocents*, by Rubens; Louvre, Paris (1968).
11. *Pietà*, by Michelangelo; St. Peter's, Rome (1972).
12. *The Adoration of the Magi*, by Rubens; King's College, Cambridge (1974).
13. *Guernica*, by Picasso; New York Museum of Modern Art (1974).
14. *Archduke Albert*, by Rubens; Kunstakademie, Düsseldorf (1977).
15. *Berceuse*, by Van Gogh; Stadelijk Museum (1977).
16. *Christ Appearing to the Magdalene*, by Drost; Gemaldegalerie, Kassel (1977).
17. *Goldfish*, by Klee; Kunsthalle, Hamburg (1977).
18. *Jacob Blessing Ephraim and Menasseh*, by Rembrandt; Gemaldegalerie, Kassel (1977).

COSTS AND CONSEQUENCES

Monetary Costs

For all of the several reasons that reliable vandalism incidence data are difficult to obtain, accurate estimates of monetary costs are also hard to locate. In addition, those estimates which have been offered sometimes do not include the same categories of events. As my later discussion of the various definitions of *vandalism* will highlight, there is far from a consensus

19. *Martin Luther*, by Cranach; Hanover (1977).
20. *Massacre of the Innocents*, by Di Giovanni; Pinacoteca, Museo Nazionale di Capodimonte, Naples (1977).
21. Self-portrait, by Rembrandt; Gemaldegelarie, Kassel (1977).
22. *Self-Portrait in Gray Hat*, by Van Gogh; Van Gogh Museum, Amsterdam (1977).
23. *Adoration of the Golden Calf*, by Poussin; National Gallery, London (1978).
24. *Lady Diana Spencer (Princess of Wales)*, by Bryan Organ; National Portrait Gallery, London (1981).
25. *The Marriage of Isaac and Rebecca (The Mill)*, by Claude Lorrain; National Gallery, London (1982).
26. *Sun Rising through Vapour*, by Turner; National Gallery, London (1981).
27. *Who's Afraid of Red, Yellow and Blue IV?* by Barnett Newman; Berlin (1982).
28. *Polaris*, by David Mach; exhibited outside Hayward Gallery, London (1983).
29. *Christ Appearing to St. Peter on the Appian Way*, by Carracci; National Gallery, London (1985).
30. *Danae*, by Rembrandt; Winter Palace, Leningrad (1985).
31. Henry Moore sculpture; Harlow, Essex (1988).
32. Paumgartner Alte Triptych, *Our Lady of Sorrows*, and *Lamentation of Christ*, by Dürer; Alte Pinakothek, Munich (1988).
33. *Madonna and Child with St. Joseph and the Infant Baptist*, by Barocci; National Gallery, London (1990).
34. *David*, by Michelangelo; Piazza della Signoria, Florence (1991).

Source: C. Cordess & M. Turgen (1993). Art vandalism. *British Journal of Criminology, 33*, pp. 101–102.

on the definitional inclusion and exclusion of damage due to wear and tear or faulty design and the cost of theft, arson damage, inflation, insurance, and so forth. Further, as Vestermark and Blauvelt (1978, p. 137), suggested in their discussion of the hidden monetary costs of school vandalism, the following expenses ought legitimately to be included:

1. The cost of the supervision of the workers doing the repair work.
2. The costs of operating the vehicles needed to transport workers and materials to the job site.

Four strategically placed fire bombs ignited a fire that raged out of control at Truman Junior High School causing an estimated $260,000 worth of damage. Administrative offices, a science laboratory and several classrooms were destroyed causing classes to be cancelled. Two junior high school students were arrested and charged with arson. They claimed they wanted to get even with the principal.

Source: J. R. Ban & L. M. Ciminillo (1977). *Violence and vandalism in public education*. Danville, IL: Interstate Printers & Publishers, p. 3.

3. The clerical cost of the preparation of work orders and of the ordering of materials.
4. The difference between the replacement cost of equipment and the original purchase price.
5. The cost of custodial labor to clean up the debris of the vandals.
6. The costs associated with the security investigation of the act.

In school settings, a number of additional hidden costs of vandalism were suggested by Grimditch (1973):

1. The destruction of valuable and irreplaceable records.
2. The cost of transporting students to other schools.
3. The loss of classroom availability during repairs.
4. The loss of specialized teaching facilities (e.g., laboratories and gymnasiums).
5. The loss of income from canceled athletic events.

With these several caveats in mind, comprehensive monetary cost estimates of vandalism have been put forth and collectively illustrate—as was true of the available incidence data—that the expense of vandalism is both absolutely high and increasing. In America's approximately 84,000 schools, for example, monetary vandalism-cost estimates over the past 25 years show a nearly linear upward trend, as Table 1.1 reveals.

In an article aptly subtitled "The Billion Dollar Prank" (1973), Kobetz estimated that the loss to America's businesses from vandalism was indeed close to that figure, an amount which can only have grown substantially in the two-plus decades which followed. In fact, Coffield (1991) reported a series of estimates suggesting that total current vandalism costs in the United States may well exceed $1 billion. Vandalism, of course, is a phe-

TABLE 1.1. Monetary Cost of School Vandalism

Year	Estimated cost	Source
1969	$100 million	Casserly, Boss, and Garrett (1980)
1970	200 million	National Education Association (1973)
1972	260 million	Dukiet (1973)
1979	500 million	School Violence Prevention Manual (1980)
1987	500 million	Sadler (1988)
1990	600 million	Stoner, Shinn, and Walker (1991)

nomenon experienced in almost all societies, at least to some extent.[2] Batiste (1991) reported that on their respective mass transit systems, the annual monetary cost of vandalism is $35 million in Germany, $30 million in the Netherlands, $20 million for the London underground, and $14 million for the French National Railways. Dahlstrom (1980) reported a slow but steady climb in the incidence and cost of vandalism in Sweden in recent years, as did Coffield (1991) for England and Wales, and Wiesenthal (1990) for Canada. The monetary costs of vandalism are high indeed.

Social Costs

The costs of vandalism are not only monetary but social as well, as perhaps explicated best by Vestermark and Blauvelt (1978) in the context of school vandalism:

> By limiting criteria of vandalism's impact to only monetary costs, we overlook those incidents which have low monetary cost but, nevertheless, tremendous impact upon the school. The impact of a seventy-nine cent can of spray paint, used to paint racial epithets on a hallway wall, far exceeds the monetary cost of removing the paint. A racial confrontation could result, which might force the closing of the school for an indefinite period. How does one calculate that type of expense: confrontation and subsequent closing of a school? (p. 138)

Reilly (1978) asserted the same perspective vis-à-vis neighborhood vandalism:

> There is also an enormous human cost. The victim of vandalism experiences a sense of having been singled out by an unkind fate, a heightened sense of vulnerability, of not being safe even on his own grounds; there is a sense of impotent rage and a desire for revenge ... but often, as most vandals are never

[2]But not quite all. At least as of 1988, Wilson (1988), in a discussion of the cultural factors influencing vandalism, reported a virtual absence of such behavior in Moscow and Tokyo.

Well it's really hard to say what caused the two boys to do what they did. Both of them are not what you would call the ideal kind of student. Both of them had been in trouble with the law outside of school.... What happened was they broke in one night and they totally vandalized the new wing that we just finished in our building. They got a hold of a BB gun or several BB guns and shot out every plate glass window, put holes in every plate glass window that went to the outside. And then they broke into the library and knocked over all of the shelves. And then they went down into the kitchen and vandalized the cafeteria.... The staff, because of the mess that we had, wanted to call out school. But I said I wouldn't dignify the action or the people who did it with the satisfaction.... The staff all pulled in.... I said get your kids in your classroom and let's just try to get class and school going as though it's a normal everyday situation. As soon the first bell rang I got on the P.A., notified the students what had happened and what we were going to do, and the fact that the library would be closed that day, and that the cafeteria would serve food but it would not be the type A lunch that we normally had.... By 9:00 I had the names of the two boys who were responsible for the vandalism. The staff all pitched in and got everything cleaned up so that we could have lunch in the cafeteria. Our library was down for about a week. You can imagine the mess having thousands of books scattered all over the floor.... The total cost was somewhere in the neighborhood of $20,000.... We contacted the juvenile authorities, had both boys arrested.

Source: A. P. Goldstein, J. Palumbo, S. Striepling, & A. Voutsinas (1995). *Break it up: A teacher guide to student aggression*. Champaign, IL: Research Press, p. 128.

> caught, without a specific target of blame. The victim of vandalism becomes more alienated from his neighbors ... more fearful ... and more hostile and suspicious of strangers, especially young people. (p. 1134)

In the field of environmental regulation, the term *social impact* is typically employed to describe the economic and community lifestyle consequences of new housing, new businesses, new land-use schemes, or other displacements and relocations (Shields, 1975). Extending the range of events categorizable as having "social impact," and in clear support of Reilly's (1978) and Vestermark and Blauvelt's (1978) positions, a number of studies have convincingly demonstrated the considerable social impact or social cost of vandalistic behavior on its victims. LaGrange, Ferraro, and Supanic (1992) demonstrated the stress-enhancing effects of vandalism and related incivilities, and Lavrakas (1982) showed it to increase victim feelings of abandonment and insecurity. The presence of vandalism gives rise to concern that more of the same will follow. Such concern, it should be noted, is well placed, as several investigators have shown that incivility leads to more incivility (Finnie, 1973; Krause, Freedman, & Whitcup, 1978; Miethe & Meier, 1994), and that litter, broken windows, stripped automobiles, abandoned buildings, and the like communicate a sense of "disorder and decline" (Skogan, 1990) which may lower the inhibition level of both residents and passersby (Wilson & Kellog, 1982) and thus permit and in a sense release or encourage further such deteriorative behavior. As Skogan (1990) aptly commented, "Once a community slips into a cycle of decline, feedback processes rapidly take control" (p. 12). Vandalism, especially in the context of more general levels of neighborhood social and physical incivility, has also been demonstrated to be associated with higher levels of both fear of crime and the rate of actual crime (Skogan, 1990; Wilson & Kellog, 1982). As I observed elsewhere:

> Incivility does relate to crime, and it is likely to do so in a cause-and-effect manner. The mediating processes connecting the two may be contagion (Lewis & Salem, 1986), an array of sociodemographic neighborhood characteristics (Taylor & Gottfredson, 1986), diminished sense of control (Janowitz, 1975), neighborhood residents' "sense of unworthiness" (Rainwater, 1966), and/or the reduced interactions and surveillance associated with the perception of the neighborhood as, first, an inhospitable and, later, a dangerous place (Skogan, 1990). Whatever its mediation of crime, incivility appears to be a significant physical ecological characteristic of many problem neighborhoods. (Goldstein, 1994, p. 47)

In the school setting, Vestermark and Blauvelt (1978) suggested that the social cost of vandalism is the summation of three components: (1) its impact on the school's educational program; (2) its psychological impact on both students and adults; and (3) its degree of disruptiveness of group or intergroup relations. I have long asserted that optimal interventions for transgressive and disturbed behaviors should be offered *prescriptively*, so that they match characteristics of the behavior to be changed with qualities of the intervention to be offered (Goldstein, 1978; Goldstein & Stein, 1976). In this same tailored, differential, or prescriptive spirit, Vestermark and Blauvelt (1978) offered a matrix (see Figure 1.1) of four types of vandalism. The matrix arrays high and low monetary costs against high and low social costs, yielding four categories of vandalism and its consequences.

I do not wish in the present discussion to anticipate too greatly the

	SOCIAL COST	
	High	**Low**
MONETARY COST **High**	*Type I Vandalism* Incidents having both a high monetary cost as well as a high social cost. *Examples* 1. Destruction of school media center. 2. Destruction of school records. 3. Vandalism which closes the school	*Type II Vandalism* Incidents having a high monetary cost but a low social cost. *Examples* 1. Large number of broken windows. 2. Cherry bomb dropped in a toilet. 3. Vandalism to vending machines.
Low	*Type III Vandalism* Incidents having a low monetary cost but a high social cost. *Examples* 1. Racial graffiti. 2. Systematic vandalizing of minority-owned property. 3. Killing of classroom animals	*Type IV Vandalism* Incidents having both a low monetary cost as well as a low social cost. *Examples* 1. Tire tracks in the lawn. 2. Cutting of the flag-pole rope. 3. Painting of names on the bleachers. 4. Single broken windows.

FIGURE 1.1 Types of Vandalism. SOURCE: From Vestermark and Blauvelt (1978, p. 140). Reprinted by permission of Parker Publishing Co., Inc., West Nyack, NY.

later in-depth consideration of vandalism intervention (see Chapters 4–7), but I do want to make an important point regarding the value of a prescriptive intervention strategy. My primary purpose in including Figure 1.1 here is to highlight the significance of the social costs associated with vandalism:

> When faced with declining resources, you may find that your control and repair priorities run in rank order as follows: Type I, Type III. Type II, Type IV. Where vandalism is just beginning, Type III and Type IV acts may take almost all your attention. Type III acts can provoke other acts that carry very high

> monetary costs. Relatively harmless Type IV acts can be a cue to kids that the system can't control their pranks, much less their serious acts. Don't fall into the trap of equating the cost of vandalism with money alone. Except where you have a true Type I case, requiring urgent and expensive repairs, as well as binding up whatever social wounds have been inflicted, take a hard look at what you *really* have to do. Type II acts can be expensive and look bad—but they really may not be all that important. Always ask: What are the social costs? You will usually find that when you have high social costs, they represent more real damage to the educational process than can ever be measured in monetary terms. Dealing with high social costs will be, almost always, your first priority in vandalism control. (Vestermark & Blauvelt, 1978, pp. 146–147)

Thus, I come full circle and return to this chapter's central question: Why study vandalism? The answers have been both several and substantial. Vandalism ignored (as it often is) encourages its continuation and escalation. Vandalism is a frequent event in widely diverse venues: schools, libraries, museums, home, neighborhoods, forests, parks, farms, transportation facilities, and more. Vandalism is a costly phenomenon—monetarily, socially, educationally, and in the encouragement of further incivility, the fear of crime, and actual criminal behavior. The reasons to study vandalism are indeed several and substantial.

CHAPTER 2

DEFINITIONS AND DEMOGRAPHICS

BACKGROUND AND CURRENT CONCEPTS

In the fifth century A.D., a fierce Germanic tribe, the Vandals, plundered Gaul, North Africa, Rome, and other conquered territories. Their heavy destruction of buildings and works of art lent their name in perpetuity to the behaviors of concern herein. Perhaps then, which particular behavior could be called *vandalistic* was clear. That is certainly not the case now. Like many other behavior-descriptive terms (e.g., *stress, anxiety, dependency, aggression*), behaviors contemporaneously subsumed under the term *vandalism* are many and varied. So, too, its very definitions. In the present chapter I will seek to bring a beginning sense of order to what Christensen, Johnson, and Brookes (1992) correctly asserted has become a "hodgepodge concept," Levy-Leboyer (1984) termed a "ragbag" of meanings, and Rubel (1980) called a "catch-all."

The definition, sources, and remediation of vandalism have long been a concern in American society. Note the dates, sources, and concerns of the following articles:

Eddy, G. (1909, October). American vandalism. *Travel*, p. 41.
Barnes, W. C. (1913). Modern Goths and Vandals. *Technical World Magazine, 19*, 505–506.
Anon. (1916). Bury or burn. *Spectator, 117*, 232–233.
Hynds, H. D. (1941). Prevention of vandalism in school buildings. *National Association of Public School Business Officials*, 199–203.

Now of course everybody's memory of school includes reminiscences of school vandalism. Stanley Hall, the famous American psychologist (who was born in 1846), wrote in his autobiography, "In the treatment of the schoolhouse and its surroundings we were vandals. The first schoolhouse I attended is still standing as it was. The desks were carved by the jack-knives of generations of pupils, especially on the boys' side. There were rude initials deeply indented, and the walls had to be whitewashed often to obliterate pencil marks and drawings. At the end of the term the rounded ceiling of the room was covered with chewed paper wads which it was a favorite deversion to throw and make stick there. We tore up the floor in the wood-house and raised havoc in the cellar, while the outhouses, both that of the girls and boys, were indescribable."

Source: C. Ward (1973). *Vandalism*. New York: Van Nostrand, pp. 292, 294.

Maslow, A. H. (1942). A comparative approach to the problem of destructiveness. *Psychiatry, 5*, 5–12.

Gingery, S. L. (1946). School vandalism is not decreasing. *School Management, 16*, 5.

Alexander, P. W. (1948). "What's this about punishing parents?" *Federal Probation, 12*, 23–29.

Bachrach, W. (1949). Vandalism, a big business in public schools. *American School Board Journal, 119*, 33.

Otwell, F. (1951). What price vandalism? *Bus Transportation, 30*, 27–29.

Booth, C. E. (1952). Christmas vandalism in our forests. *Nature Magazine, 45*, 538–539.

Anon. (1952, July 5). Vandalism: Rehearsal for sabotage? *Business Week*, 72–74.

Clark, W. H. (1952). Sex differences and motivation in the urge to destroy. *Journal of Social Psychology, 36*, 167–177.

Park Association of the City of New York. (1952). *Vandalism in city parks*. New York: Author.

Fox, J. G., & Lazes, A. H. (1953). Children, spare that window. *Clearing House, 29*, 288.

Usher, A. (1953, November). Vandals, or just kids? *Better Homes and Gardens, 31*.

Bristow, W. H., & Lazes, A. H. (1954). Vandalism is minimized by a continuous program of constructive citizenship. *Nations Schools, 52*, 43–46.

Lippman, H. S. (1954). Vandalism as an outlet for aggression. *Federal Probation, 7*, 5–6.

Dauw, B. (1956). High cost of vandalism. *Safety Education, 24*, 2–7.

Clinard, M. B., & Wade, A. L. (1958). Toward the delineation of vandalism as a sub-type in juvenile delinquency. *Journal of Criminal Law, Criminology and Police Science, 48*, 493–499.

Colney, J. W., & Valentine, T. W. (1960). Stop vandalism with parent responsibility laws. *American School Board Journal, 141*, 9–11.

Bates, W. (1962). Caste, class and vandalism. *Social Problems, 9*, 62–69.

Ehrlich, H. J. (1962). The swastika epidemic of 1959–1960: Anti-semitism and community characteristics. *Social Problems, 9*, 13–19.

Taylor, L., & Walton, P. (1971). Industrial sabotage: Motives and meanings. In S. Cohen (Ed.), *Images of deviance*. New York: Penguin.

These several citations illustrate the 75-year-long stream of articles (becoming a trickle in the 1980s) which have dealt with diversely targeted vandalism, diversely conceptualized vandals, and diversely promoted interventions. From these and later sources there emerged equally numerous and diverse definitions of just what vandalism is:

- Hostility to, or willful destruction or defacement of, things of beauty, as works of art, literature, historical monuments, etc. (*Webster's*, 1984).
- Intentional hostile behavior aimed at damaging environmental objects (Feshbach, 1964).
- The dilapidation or destruction of an environmental object (Christensen et al., 1992).
- An intentional act aimed at damaging or destroying an object that is another's property (Moser, 1992).
- A willful act of physical damage that lowers the aesthetic or economic value of an object or area (Harrison, 1976).
- A voluntary degradation of the environment with no motivation of profit whatsoever, the results of which are considered damage by the actor(s) as well as the victim in relation to the norms that rule the situation (Christensen, et al., 1992).
- All forms of property destruction, deliberate or not (Baughman, 1971).
- Any destructive behavior ranging from littering to arson (Ducey, 1976).
- The willful or malicious destruction, injury, disfigurement, or defacement of property without the consent of the owner or person having custody or control by cutting, tearing, breaking, marking,

Vandalism of city trees is probably as old as the first public park. Vandalism has plagued Boston Common (which Bridenbaugh says is the first public park in the United States) ever since it was set aside as a common field in 1640. Town meetings of the seventeenth and eighteenth centuries record both the incidence of vandalism and the steps taken by the town to prevent and punish such acts. In 1764 the selectmen levied fines for breaking down the posts between the common and adjacent Tremont Street and proceeded against citizens who persisted in driving their carriages and horses on the Common. To prevent further incursions, the town meeting in 1771 ordered that the Common be enclosed by a fence. In that same year a private citizen offered a reward for the identification of the person who "hacked" down a tree bordering the Common, and two years later two vandals went to jail for destroying trees on the Common.

Source: A. W. Spirn (1984). *The granite garden*. New York: Basic Books, pp. 178–179.

painting, drawing, covering with filth, or any such means as may be specified by local law (FBI *Uniform Crime Report*, 1975).

- The wanton and apparently motiveless destruction, or damage to, property without any clear advantage accruing to anyone, least of all the perpetrators (Cross, 1979).

Though varying in inclusiveness, these several definitions collectively highlight *intentionality*, *destructiveness*, and *property ownership*[1] as the central features of a definitional constellation. These features form a good beginning, but only a beginning, in shaping a comprehensive and utilitarian (for intervention purposes) definition of vandalism. Such a definitional quest is aided further by restrictions on inclusiveness, that is, by identifying those additional features of a destructive act which often lead to the act normatively not being considered vandalistic.

Cohen (1974) pointed to three widely accepted exculpating circumstances:

[1]Ownership is clearly one defining consideration, as a number of the foregoing definitions suggest. Nicholson (1975), for example, commented, "If a stranger enters a garden and destroys a tree which is a delight to passers-by, he would be called a vandal. If, however, the owner chops down a tree, he is exercising his right as a property owner, but the effect for the on-looker is no different" (p. 14).

> The illegal destruction or defacement of property belonging to someone else … does not invariably lead to its classification as the deviant act, vandalism. The behavior can be institutionalized under at least the following conditions: *ritualism*: on certain ritual occasions, such as November 5th, New Year's Eve, property destruction is expected, condoned, or even encouraged; *protection*: certain groups, particularly of high social status, such as students, are given some sort of collective license to engage in property destruction; *play*: in certain areas, or among certain groups such as very small children, the rule breaking is not regarded as deviant or problematic because it is recognized as local tradition, part of a game, or the targets—say windows of derelict houses—are simply regarded as expendable. (pp. 39–40)

Pitt and Zube (1991), who defined vandalism as "otherwise acceptable behavior in an inappropriate context" (p. 1031), made a similar point regarding the central role of setting beliefs in shaping definitions:

> At the same time that society carefully preserves the cliff inscriptions of American Indians, publicly supports the reshaping and preservation of Mount Rushmore's cliffs, marvels at a human-made tunnel cut through a giant sequoia tree, it also becomes outraged when rock outcrops are defaced by a spray paint artist or trees are initialed by knife-wielding whittlers. Indeed, the Boston Tea Party, a vandalistic foray aboard British merchant ships, is celebrated as a harbinger of the American Revolution (Wells, 1971). The felling of a tree for winter firewood in an established fuelwood cut area involves the same set of overt behaviors as does the felling of the same tree in a park. In one context, the behavior is permitted and even encouraged, whereas in another context [it] may result in incarceration. Thus, in the right context, what might otherwise be considered appropriate behavior, becomes an act of vandalism. (p. 1031)

In addition to group or community norms and traditions setting the limiting parameters for a definition of vandalism, individual norms operate similarly. The tagger or "street artist" may be creating—in his or her view—an affirmation of self, a mural, a work of art, or attractive decoration. To the property owner, community residents, and the police, the same "art" will be viewed as defacement, invasion, disfigurement, or, more generally, vandalism. Similarly with destructive events occurring in industrial contexts, which may be labeled sabotage, illegal and vandalistic, by management and owners, and justified protest, just deserts, and "giving notice" by worker-perpetrators.

Christensen and Clark (1978) aid us further in delimiting which events may or may not appropriately be classified as vandalism by drawing clear distinctions between vandalistic and depreciative behavior: A path worn in a campus lawn by students creating and repeatedly taking a shortcut; a chipped corner to a hallway wall, banged time and again by workers

> It's a good feeling—like being an outlaw. Out there in the night with a couple of friends on your own. You're creating something wonderful and beautiful for others to enjoy. I understand that British Rail don't want to see murals on their walls, but I don't look upon it as vandalism. It's a popular art. Unfortunately a majority of people are ill-informed and don't understand what the culture is about. It's all about self-expression. We are adding something colourful to a bland, blank surface which others will see and admire. It may not be fully appreciated at the moment, but in due course I believe it will be recognised as an art form (*The Guardian*, 21 January 1991).
>
> *Source*: F. Coffield (1991). *Vandalism and graffiti: The state of the art*. London: Calouste Gubbenkian Foundation, p. 67.

pushing loaded carts; park playground equipment broken as a result of long and often overly energetic use—these are depreciative behaviors. Christensen and Clark (1978) suggested that such behaviors differ from vandalism[2] in intent, awareness, and responsibility:

> The first distinction is the matter of intent. Depreciative impacts [are] unintended, vandalism impacts are intended. From this, follows the second distinction concerning awareness of the consequences of one's actions. Individuals who engage in depreciative behavior are unaware of the consequences of their behavior.... Vandals, in contrast, are aware of the consequences for their actions. The final distinction, then, is one of responsibility. People who behave depreciatively do so because they are uninformed about the consequences of their actions. In that sense, they are not responsible for them. Vandals, however, are responsible for their behavior—they know what they are doing. (p. 65)

Vandalism is an intentional act of destruction or defacement of property not one's own. Considerations of tradition, ritual, play, awareness, and responsibility may—individually and collectively—appropriately restrict an act of destruction or defacement from being so classified.

I have thus far in this chapter sought to begin establishing what vandalism is, and what it is not, by examining an array of its definitions, and exclusions thereto. In the following section, to further this parameter-establishing purpose, I explore the who, where, and when of vandalistic

[2]Though, to add to the definitional confusion, Madison (cited in Peuleche, 1976) termed such behavior "erosive vandalism."

G. M. in Kansas City Charges "Sabotage"

DETROIT, JUNE 19—The General Motors Corporation reported that "sabotage" had recurred today at the Fisher Body Division plant in Kansas City.

The company said its Fisher Body Assembly Plant and its Chevrolet Plant in Kansas City were forced to close earlier than usual yesterday after unidentified employees "inflicted severe damage to painted surfaces of forty-five finished bodies."

Today, the company said, thirteen more bodies were damaged, but it was possible for the plant to continue operations.

A spokesman for the United Automobile Workers, currently seeking a new contract with General Motors, denied that the union was in any way responsible for the damage. There was no allegation by the company that the U.A.W. was involved.

Source: J. M. Martin (1961). *Juvenile vandalism: A study of its nature and prevention.* Springfield, IL: Charles C Thomas, p. 89.

acts. I will examine person characteristics held to characterize individuals prone to vandalism, preferred timing, and likely targets.

THE VANDAL

Vandalism is motivated behavior. Who engages in such behavior in any given instance is in substantial part a function of motivation. In an industrial setting, it may be a disgruntled middle-aged worker who sabotages company machinery in reprisal for real or imagined grievances, or perhaps a dishonest businessman who torches his firm's building in order to collect insurance monies. In a forest campground, the vandal may be an adult damaging a tree to obtain firewood for cooking, or a teenager using the campground sign for rifle-shooting target practice, or a group of preadolescents clogging a comfort station toilet to make it overflow. In a school context, it may be a youngster who feels particularly alienated from the school, or unjustly placed in detention, or the recipient of what he or she deems to be an unfair grade. Across settings, and across age levels, the vandal is considerably more likely to be male than female, and white rather than nonwhite (Anon., 1978c; Goldmeir, 1974; Howard, 1978; McQuoid,

McKibben, & Heaney, 1989; Phillips, 1982). Vandalistic acts perpetrated by children are quite typically committed in small groups (Clark, 1971; McQuoid et al, 1989; Peuleche, 1976). In public school settings, according to Tygart (1988) and Zweig and Ducey (1978), vandalism reaches its peak frequency in seventh grade and then progressively decreases with each succeeding grade. The typical school vandal is as likely socioeconomically to be a middle-class youth as one from a low-income background (Howard, 1978), is no more disturbed emotionally than are youngsters less apt to vandalize (Richards, 1976), is someone likely to have been retained (Nowakowski, 1966), often is truant (Greenberg, 1974), or is suspended from school altogether (Yankelovich, 1975).

Youngsters prone to vandalism appear to have a poor understanding of the impact of their behavior on others and are primarily concerned with the consequences of such behavior for themselves, such as getting caught. In their view, public property in a real sense belongs to no one. In contrast, for boys less prone to vandalism, such property belongs to everyone—reflecting their greater sense of themselves as part of a larger community (Anon., 1978c). As is true for all forms of aggression, the single best predictor of future vandalistic behavior is engaging in similar past behaviors (Tygart, 1988).

At the university level also, males are more vandalistic than females. Freshmen commit more vandalism than upper classmen or women, and regardless of class levels, alcohol consumption is a frequent concomitant of such behavior (Bowles, 1982). Other person and setting vandalism-associated variables observed in this context include academic and social stress on students, the presence of nonstudents on campus, inadequate lighting, poor security, inadequate dormitory supervision, and overcrowded dormitories (Anon., 1983b).

Arson is a particularly costly form of vandalism. Karchmer (1982) estimated that 25%–50% of all fires begin by arson. As with other forms of vandalism, perpetrators here tend to be young–66% aged 20 or under (FBI *Uniform Crime Report*, 1993)—Caucasian, and male (Canter, 1980; Rider, 1980; Riopelle, 1978). As seems to be occurring for other forms of aggression, however, the relative male–female incidence rate for arson is changing. Akiyama and Pfeiffer (1984) noted that in 1965 there were 12 male arson arrests for every female arrest. By 1983, reflecting a trend that continues to date (FBI *Uniform Crime Report*, 1993), the ratio had dropped to 8 males for every female. In 1993, the ratio was 6 to 1. Herbert (1990) and Vernon (1979) described two types of young fire setters: the child under 10 whose arson typically occurs out of play or experimentation, and the adolescent whose more complicated motivation may relate to life crises, peer or family

A writer gains respect from other writers through the actual physical placement of graffiti. Hip hop graffiti written on places difficult and dangerous to access (such as building roofs, train tunnels, freeway overpasses, and signs high above the ground), property of authority figures (such as police cars), or obscure or unlikely targets (such as remote parks), if ever noticed, attest to the writer's ingenuity, courage, and mobility.

Source: D. D. Brewer, H. H. Christensen, & M. L. Miller (1992). Hip hop graffiti writers: Ethnographic observations on an urban youth subculture. In H. H. Christensen, D. R. Johnson, & M. Brookes (Eds.), *Vandalism: Research, prevention and social policy*. Portland, OR: U.S. Department of Agriculture Forest Service, p. 23.

concerns, independence and power issues, revenge motivations, or attention-seeking.

Rider's (1980) review of the arson research literature led him to offer a psychological profile of the typical fire setter as an individual of below-average intelligence, with a history of poor academic achievement and significant school failure. He or she comes from a large family and a harsh and unstable home environment and displays a clearly troubled and inadequate social, marital, and employment history. Sexual and alcoholism problems are common, as is frequent prior difficulty with the criminal justice system. Others (e.g., Rothstein, 1963) quite properly wonder whether a "typical" arsonist exists other than as a profiling abstraction. Indeed, the variety of alleged types of arsonists is quite substantial, to wit, arson-for-profit fire setters, solitary fire setters, group fire setters, the revenge fire setter, the would-be-hero fire setter, the fire "buff" fire setter, the pyromaniac, the excitement fire setter, the pathological schizophrenic fire setter, the child fire setter, the adolescent fire setter, and the "general arsonist"! In Bradshaw and Huff's (1985) interview study of 90 arsonists in California and New York, 52% reported setting their fire(s) for revenge, 12% for excitement, and others to cover a crime, for profit, or for no apparent reason.

FBI *Uniform Crime Report* (1993) information is a further valuable source of vandal-specifying information. In 1993, of the 235,170 acts of vandalism for which an arrest took place, 206,389 were by males, and 28,781 were by females. Vandalism arrest data by perpetrator race are white (194,140), African-American (59,820), American Indian (2,890), and Asian

> A wide variety of medical, criminological and fire publications have dealt with the psychopathology of firesetting over a long period of time. There were, for example, at least 130 articles on the subject prior to 1890. It is perhaps not a little surprising that, with such an early start in research, we still know very little about the aetiology of firesetting and even less about its treatment.
>
> *Source*: R. G. Vreeland & B. M. Levin (1980). Psychological aspects of firesetting. In D. Canter (Ed.), *Fires and human behavior*. New York: Wiley, p. 31.

(3,074). Arrestee age data show a clear linear upward trend in incidence to age 13–14, followed by an equally clear linear decrease through age 65+. Thus, representative incidence figures by age are 442 (under 10), 1,626 (10–12), 3,778 (13–14), 2,021 (15), 1,919 (16), 1,655 (17), 1,405 (18), 1,109 (19), 961 (20), 1,018 (22), 932 (24), 3,788 (30–34), 1,180 (40–44), 272 (50–54), and 61 (60–64).

THE ECOLOGY OF VANDALISM: CONTEXT AND TARGET

Having provided at least a partial sense of who the vandal is, I wish now to turn to the "where" of vandalism. "Where" concerns two closely related ecological matters: (1) the setting or contexts shown to be promotive of, or at least frequently associated with the occurrence of, vandalism and (2) the specific targets of such behavior. I believe that *all* acts of aggression are person–environment events. Whether murder, mayhem, or marking of a school corridor wall, aggression derives in part from in-the-person (perpetrator) motivations and predispositions and in part from characteristics of the physical and social context in which the aggression occurs.

> Our perspective is responsive to one of the most significant developments in the study of human behavior in recent decades—the ascendance of interactionism. Broadly defined, interactionism is a philosophical stance toward understanding and predicting human behavior which holds that such efforts will be optimized when they reflect both intraindividual (e.g., trait) qualities and relevant characteristics of the individual's environment. These latter ecological features may be other people (e.g., victims, fellow group members) or qualities of the immediate or larger physical location in which the perpetration occurs. In recent years, this interactionist perspective has been brought to bear upon a wide range of behaviors, and aggression is certainly among them. (Goldstein, 1994, p. VII)

In this chapter's previous section, I described the vandal demographically, on such static bases as age, gender, and social class. Note how much fuller and richer one's understanding of the vandal and her or his behavior can be when vandalism is viewed as a person–environment interactional event. Vandalism, as noted earlier, is quite typically a group phenomenon (Peuleche, 1976; Truckenmiller, 1982). In the quotation which follows, the centrality of the group context and its dynamics to the emergence of vandalistic behavior is made salient:

> The first stage is that of "waiting for something to turn up." A group of adolescents may be sitting around talking or playing when the idea of destruction comes up. This may occur as part of a game of skill: who has the best aim in rock throwing. At this point the second stage develops, the "removal of uncertainty" or "the exploratory gesture." The act of destruction suddenly becomes interesting and everyone thinks about participating.... The third stage, "mutual conversion," happens almost simultaneously with the removal of uncertainty. The group becomes convinced to join in the act because of peer pressures. "Joint elaboration of the act" then follows as the spirit of the activity takes hold of the participants. The excitement is contagious and often as the momentum builds, destruction far exceeds expectation. Here the idea of group participation is particularly important. It gives a sense of anonymity and group solidarity; the responsibility is diluted and no one feels guilt or fear. Stage five, "aftermath and retrospect," takes over as the destruction ends. The group looks back at the "fun" and neutralizes guilt by saying that nothing was stolen and no one was hurt. (Peuleche, 1976, p. 37)

In addition to such peer facilitation, other social ecological forces (the people in the context and their behavior) have been shown to impact on vandalism—for better and for worse. In school settings, for example, vandalism has been shown to be associated with autocratic or laissez-faire versus "firm but fair" school administration; inconsistent or weak administrative support and follow-through (Casserly et al., 1980); school governance which is too impersonal, unresponsive, nonparticipatory, overregulated, oppressive, arbitrary, or inconsistent (Greenberg, 1969; Ianni, 1979); high teacher turnover rates (Leftwich, 1977); such teacher inadequacies as disrespectfulness, callousness, lack of interest, and middle-class bias (Bayh, 1978; Rubel, 1977); overuse of punitive control methods; and inadequate clarity of school and classroom rules and discipline procedures (Mayer & Sulzer-Azaroff, 1991). In contrast, aggression toward property in schools is lower in those venues whose social ecology is characterized by high levels of teacher identification with the school, evenhanded rule enforcement, parent support of school disciplinary policies, teacher avoidance of use of grades as disciplinary tools, and teacher avoidance of use of

They smashed every inside window on the fifth floor and threw paint on the ceiling. In room 400 they destroyed a typewriter and a duplicating machine. All the keys to the entire school were stolen. They also stole a sterilizer and instruments and medical supplies from the medical room. Two fires were also set, but they weren't too bad. One on the second floor and one on the fourth floor. The estimated cost of the material stolen and damaged, plus the cost of repairs, was $1,970.

It was a gang affair. There were at least six or seven boys involved. The red-headed ring-leader went to St. James' school. He had been having a good deal of trouble with our custodian. He wanted to "get back" at him. He didn't attend this school and had no loyalties toward it. At the time this happened, no one who was involved had gone to this school—just Eddie F__________. Perhaps one other. Most of them went to St. James'.

Source: J. M. Martin (1961). *Juvenile vandalism: A study of its nature and prevention*. Springfield, IL: Charles C Thomas, p. 98.

hostile or authoritarian behavior toward students (Bayh, 1978; Goldstein, 1992).

The school's physical ecology equally bears importantly upon its frequency as a context for vandalism. Noteworthy here is its age as reflected in the obsoleteness of its facilities and equipment (Greenberg, 1969; Howard, 1978); its size—the larger having more incidents per capita (Garbarino, 1978; Goldman, 1961; Kingston & Gentry, 1977; Stefanko, 1989); its physical appearance (DeBunza, 1974; Pablant & Baxter, 1975); its density (little space per student; Stefanko, 1989); and the fact that it is often unoccupied, is easily accessible, and is a public place owned by no one in particular (Vestermark & Blauvelt, 1978). Regarding physical ecological correlates of *low* school vandalism levels, Pablant and Baxter (1975) constituted 16 pairs of schools—one having a high vandalism rate, the other low—and matched them within each pair for size, ethnic composition, grade level, and location. The schools with lower rates, as the authors had predicted, (1) were characterized by better aesthetic quality and maintenance of school property; (2) were located in more densely populated areas with higher activity levels; (3) permitted a more unobstructed view of school property by surrounding residents; and (4) were located in better-illuminated neighborhood areas.

Schools are a prime ecological context for vandalism not only due to the presence of large number of youths at a highly vandalism-prone age

Site Characteristics

Certain physical characteristics of cultural resource sites and their environmental settings have been found to be important attributes in overall vulnerability to theft and defacement in the southwestern United States.... Examples of variables of this type which have been utilized to analyze vulnerability are the following:

1. Site density, usually quantified as the number of sites per square mile or square kilometer.
2. Site visibility, in terms of the obviousness of physical features.
3. Site type, such as a village site with remains of houses versus a quarry and tool manufacturing site where only stone artifacts are present.
4. Types of artifacts present, for example, sites with decorated and undecorated pottery as opposed to those with only undecorated ceramics.
5. Types of features present, including items such as houses, storage facilities, ceremonial structures, and graves or burials.
6. Site accessibility, for example, distance to trails, roads, private property, and towns.

Source: H. H. Christensen, K. Mabery, M. E. McAllister, & D. P. McCormick (1988). *Cultural resource protection*. Denver: Rocky Mountain Forest & Range Experiment Station, p. 63.

(the person component), but also because of a number of real and symbolic qualities of the school itself (the environmental component). Its size, age, aesthetic appearance, public ownership, maintenance level, and location vis-à-vis possible sources of surveillance have been mentioned. Community characteristics are also often important influences upon in-school events. School vandalism tends to be correlated with community crime level and the degree of nonstudent (intruder) presence in the school (Casserly et al., 1980; Irwin, 1976).

Several of the vandalism-relevant physical ecological characteristics of the school site and its community location also appear to constitute a relevant context for vandalism elsewhere. Note the several common targets of destruction and defacement described in the previous chapter: libraries, museums, highway signs, trains, buses, mass transit stations, and public telephones. Each of these is a public site, easily accessible, often with

Signs are vandalized all year, but experience indicates that vandalism becomes more pronounced during certain months, seasons, and community festivals. The following are typically high periods for sign vandalism:

1. Summer months when schools are closed,
2. Graduation time and the end of school year,
3. Hunting season,
4. Election time,
5. Halloween time,
6. First warm day of spring, and
7. Holiday periods.

Source: H. S. Chadda, & E. C. Carter (1983). Sign vandalism: Time for action-now. *Institute of Transportation Engineers Journal, 53*, pp. 17–18.

low levels of formal or informal surveillance, many of which, because of low maintenance effort, display the already vandalized "releasor cues" that permit and encourage further destruction. They each are, in addition, "symbols of the social order" (Zimbardo, 1969) and hence handy targets of dissatisfaction or frustration. The ecology of vandalism also has a temporal dimension: When does it occur? For many of the same contextual reasons that contribute to site determination—especially accessibility and presence or absence of surveillance—a high proportion of vandalism (of schools and elsewhere) occurs before and after school hours, at night, on weekends, during vacation periods, later in the school week, and later in the school year (Andersen, 1977; Casserly et al., 1980; Massucci, 1984; McPherson & Carpenter, 1981; Rautaheimo, 1989).

I have sought in this chapter to identify the defining characteristics of vandalistic behavior by examining both what it is and what it is not. Such behavior, from our interactionist perspective, is a joint outcome of both person and environmental considerations. A focus on the vandal herself or himself—both static demographic qualities and more dynamic interactional features—constituted the person component of this effort. The social and physical ecological contexts of the vandalistic act comprised the environmental component. Having thus explored the "who" and "where" of vandalism, I will now turn to its roots. In the chapter which follows, the question of "why" it occurs is explored, as I examine both motivational typologies and formal theories of vandalistic behavior.

CHAPTER 3

CAUSATION

Both a number of vandal demographic characteristics, as well as qualities of the social and physical context in which vandalism occurs, were examined in the previous chapter as they are associated with the occurrence of vandalistic behavior and, perhaps, its initiation. I view these several correlational and perhaps etiological findings and speculations as prefatory to the primary concerns of the present chapter, "Causation." What are the roots of vandalism, its sources, its antecedents? The answer will rely on two types of information. The first is a presentation and examination of the several typologies of vandalism which have been put forth. With the exception of Vestermark and Blauvelt's (1978) approach, which, as noted earlier, focused on the *consequences* of vandalism (monetary and social costs), these several schemata are each *motivational* typologies. As such, they collectively provide an array of cogent suggestions for the multiple sources of such behavior. Our second informational source is the set of informal and formal theories of vandalism causation that have been put forth. Some of these, as will be seen, are complex, elaborate, and heuristically framed for purposes of evaluation regarding their adequacy. Other theoretical offerings are better described as informal partial theories or theoretical beginnings. These, too, will be considered.

MOTIVATIONAL TYPOLOGIES

We begin chronologically with the work of Martin (1959, 1961), who proposed a tripart typology, derived from "assorted incidents of vandalism reported in the daily press," "case material available in the literature," and "other [unspecified] sources" (1959, p. 73).

1. *Predatory vandalism.* Here the perpetrator's motivation is material gain. The destruction or damage involved is attendant on burglary or theft and, at times, the effort to cover up the act. Smashing a parking meter or public telephone is an example of such predatory behavior.
2. *Vindictive vandalism.* The goal of vandalism motivated in this manner is to express animosity or anger toward, and perhaps to intimidate, a particular individual or group. Martin (1959) provided the example of "spiteful damage to property to settle a grudge" (p. 148).
3. *Wanton vandalism.* Perpetrator motivation here is less clear or obvious and appears to be "without reason" (Howard, 1978). Destruction accompanying play and "malicious destruction for the sheer joy of annoying [unspecified] others' are the examples offered by Martin (1959, p. 149).

Vandalism of these three types may, in turn, be perpetrated by three types of vandal according to Martin (1961). The *disturbed* vandal engages in destructive behavior as but one manifestation of more encompassing emotional problems. The *law-abiding* vandal enacts so-called incidental vandalism in response to (temporary) anger or need to retaliate. Finally, the *subcultural* vandal performs vandalism as part of a formal gang or delinquent youth group activity.

Weinmayr's (1969) core belief regarding the roots of vandalism is that its sources reside not in the vandal himself or herself, but in the nature and quality of the buildings, park equipment, public facilities, and other targets of vandalism. He asserted:

> The real vandals in our society are the designers, specifiers, and installers who provide the opportunity for so-called "vandalism" to occur. Ninety percent of what is labelled vandalism can be prevented through design, the remaining 10 percent is malicious and unaccountable.... Vandalism happens because a hypocritical generation presents opportunities for misuse, then shifts the blame for deterioration to vandalous youth. (p. 286)

The typology of vandalism following from this singularly ecological view of its causes includes the following categories:

1. *Vandalism of overuse,* such as the chain on the park swing which wears out.
2. *Conflict vandalism,* for example, breaking a tree branch which is too low to walk around but low enough to swing on.
3. *Curiosity vandalism,* for example, a damaged drinking fountain after a youth jams a stick in its opening to see how high the water will squirt.

Portrait of Ike Slashed in Club

HOUSTON, MARCH 10 (AP)—A portrait of President Eisenhower, hung in the exclusive Houston Club, was found slashed last night. A note tacked to the frame said: "We don't like Ike in Texas."

The oil painting by Boris B. Gordon was about a year old. It had been in the club 10 days and was valued at $1,000. Club manager Henry O. Barbour said the painting was to be sent to the Texas Capitol in Austin. Police had no suspects.

Source: J. M. Martin (1961). *Juvenile vandalism: A study of its nature and prevention.* Springfield, IL: Charles C Thomas, p. 77.

4. *Leverage vandalism*, which would occur from trying to pry open a hole or slot with a bat or hockey stick.
5. *Deleterious vandalism*. For this category, Weinmayr (1969) cited as an example damage to a concrete trash can "which couldn't possibly be stolen" (p. 286).
6. *Irresistible temptation vandalism*, a common example of which Weinmayr suggested is graffiti, that is, "writing on a shiny painted surface with a magic marker" (p. 286).
7. *No-other-way-to-do-it vandalism*, such as that from leaning a bicycle against a tree when there is no bicycle rack.

Cohen's (1971, 1974) vandalism typology, clearly the most frequently utilized in the vandalism literature, consists of six subtypes:

1. *Acquisitive vandalism*. The same as Martin's (1961) predatory type, this is damage committed in order to obtain property or money, for example, stripping lead or wire from buildings and breaking open gas or electric meters.
2. *Tactical vandalism*. Here the perpetrator's motivation is to employ vandalism as a purposeful tactic to accomplish other goals, such as sabotaging a factory machine to facilitate a longer rest period of "downtime" or breaking a window in order to get arrested and thus secure a prison bed and meals.
3. Ideological vandalism. This is similar to tactical vandalism but is oriented toward a social, political, or similar cause or message. Cohen (1971) cited, for example, breaking an embassy window or chalking political slogans on walls.

The data support the proposition that carving impacts are related to environmental conditions surrounding the picnic table. The occurrence of new carving on tables was significantly related to the presence of previous carving, for tables with previous carving had two and one-half times more new carving than did tables without previous carving. This relationship did not disappear under controls for salience of authority, screening, or color of the table, suggesting that the relationship is not spurious. Previous carving was viewed as a releasor cue that defined carving as an acceptable action for that particular setting.

Source: D. M. Samdahl & H. H. Christensen (1985). Environmental cues and vandalism: An exploratory study of picnic table carving. *Environment and Behavior, 17,* p. 454.

4. *Vindictive vandalism*. This is damage done in order to gain revenge. The student who torches the school principal's office after perceiving he was unjustly punished exemplifies such vandalism.
5. *Play vandalism*. This is destruction or disfigurement in the course of play: Who can break the most windows or shoot out the most street lamps?
6. *Malicious vandalism*. Cohen (1971, 1974) described this last subtype as damage used to express rage or frustration, often directed at symbolic middle-class property, for example, urinating in public elevators or breaking lights on buses or trains.

Thaw (1976) described:

1. *Hostility-directed acts,* having as their purpose "revenge, change, or gain."
2. *Acts of thoughtlessness*, characterized primarily by play with little regard for its destructive consequences.
3. *Acts of carelessness*, exemplified by littering and similar behaviors.

Zeisel (1977) offered:

1. *Malicious vandalism*, as described above by Cohen (1973, 1974).
2. *Misnamed vandalism*, that is, damage due more to poor design planning than destructive intent, for example, a basketball court placed too close to the windows of the school hallway.
3. *Nonmalicious property damage*, for example, youths painting lines on a wall or elsewhere to define a goal or playing boundaries.

4. *Hidden maintenance damage*, that is, gradual property defacement as a result of poor planning of location, materials, or design.

Coffield (1991) suggested four central motivational bases for vandalistic behavior:

1. *Financial gain*, as occurs in association with vandalism attempts directed to meters, telephone coin boxes, and the like.
2. *Peer-group pressure*, held by several observers (e.g., Gladstone, 1978; Wade, 1967) to be a substantial contributor to acts of vandalism. In a group context, vandalism may be viewed as a game in which all participants win (Gladstone, 1978), and as an activity frequently initiated in and by the group, acting as an "antiboredom committee" (Coffield, 1991).
3. *Pleasure*, a source of destructive behavior central to the two formal "enjoyment" theories of vandalism examined later in this chapter (Allen & Greenberger, 1978; Csikszentmihalyi & Larsen, 1978).
4. *Excitement*, described by Coffield (1991) as often sought in the form of a kind of "manufactured malice" by youths with few other satisfactory (to them) opportunities for self-expression.

How are we to evaluate these several motivational typologies? All appear to have been derived by informal and largely unsystematic means, using to varying degrees "armchair" speculation, intuition, and informal observation. None seems rooted in formal theory, or systematic observation or in the use of survey, factorial, cluster-analytic, or other relevant research means.[1] To point out these deficiencies is not to single out typologies as the only weak point in the vandalism literature. An absence of formal research—for intervention generation or evaluation purposes or otherwise—is singularly characteristic of the vandalism literature.

Instead, I view these several typologies collectively as a substantial beginning creative effort. One cannot answer the question: Are they any more than that? They seem comprehensive (again, collectively, and Cohen's 1971, 1974, in particular), but the satisfactoriness of their span of coverage is a yet-to-be-answered, yet-even-to-be-asked research question. The reliability with which raters can categorize a pool of vandalism acts into any given set of typological categories is unknown, and largely unestimable at this point. So, too, is the potential of any of the foregoing category sets for

[1]An interesting survey research effort by Prewer (1986), while not yielding a formal typology of vandalism, is relevant here. He interviewed a consecutive sample of 98 men, each of whom had been arrested for breaking a window. Their causal explanations included accident, prelude to smash-and-grab theft, revenge, to "get under care" (shelter and meals in jail), to draw attention to a grievance, despair, frustration, excitement, symbolism, desire for punishment, and pleasure.

Boy, 11, Cripples 5 School Buses

DAYTON, OHIO, March 12 (AP)—A fifth-grade boy has admitted that he cut the hydraulic brake lines on five Centerville school buses over the weekend because he was "angry" with a bus driver.

Police said the 11-year-old boy admitted cutting the lines with a pair of snippers because the driver had disciplined him last Wednesday. The vandalism, which knocked out half the fleet of school buses, was discovered Monday during a routine check of the lights and brakes."

Source: J. M. Martin (1961). *Juvenile vandalism: A study of its nature and prevention*. Springfield, IL: Charles C Thomas, p. 78.

generating meaningful research about either the nature of vandalism or its prevention and reduction. On one criterion, however, these approaches can be further examined and evaluated, namely, their potential utility for vandalism intervention purposes.

It appears to me that where several of the category systems described above are strong is in their collective attempt to suggest interventions optimally matched to particular vandalism subtypes. This prescriptive stance, the opposite of a one-true-light or one-size-fits-all intervention perspective, is likely to be an especially productive orientation to vandalism prevention and reduction. It is an orientation with ample successful precedents in the context of efforts to alter other, related forms of disturbed and disturbing behavior, for example, Kiesler's (1969) grid model, Magaro's (1969) individualization model, and my own prescriptive psychotherapy orientation (Goldstein, 1978; Goldstein & Stein, 1976). Its differential intervention spirit also lies at the heart of Keller's (1966) personalized instruction, Cronbach and Snow's (1977) aptitude-treatment interactions, and Hunt's (1972) teacher–student matching model.

Thus, with reference to the vandalism typologies presented, we see a substantial effort to propose *differential* interventions by subtype or groups of subtypes. On Cohen's (1974) typology, for example, Bowles (1982) commented:

> One would hypothesize that certain types of destructive behavior (play, vindictive, tactical, and ideological vandalism) have a higher probability of being affected by appropriate intervention techniques than others. It is felt that in instances where these types of behavior occur, there is a greater degree

> of evaluation of risk and higher likelihood that the actor will have a positive perception of the environment. Strategies aimed at increasing risk and increasing positive perception of the environment could, therefore, make a difference. On the other end of the continuum, malicious vandalism and acquisitive vandalism are probably less likely to be affected by any means other than "technical strategies." In either case, it is postulated that it is unlikely that risk factors or environmental perceptions will make much of a difference in the actions of the vandal because malicious vandalism probably occurs with the greatest degree of spontaneity, is usually unleashed by a high level of frustration and anger, and usually involves a great deal more violence. Since the motive in acquisitive vandalism is theft, it is also hypothesized that the vandal would be minimally effected by anything other than a technical strategy designed to keep him or her away from the article that is to be stolen. (p. 18)

With a very different view of the roots of vandalism (recall his "The real vandals in our society are the designers"), Weinmayer (1969) similarly proffered a prescriptive intervention schema for his typology and its illustrations:

1. For vandalism of overuse: provide sufficient equipment.
2. For conflict vandalism: build the path where the kids walk.
3. For curiosity vandalism: unlock the gate so it won't be torn down.
4. For leverage vandalism: remove loose boards used as levers or hammers.
5. For deleterious vandalism: mount trash can on poles; replace when damaged.
6. Irresistible temptation vandalism: use timbers difficult to write on.
7. No-other-way-to-do-it vandalism: install bicycle racks.

The point is taken. Typologies of vandalism have been put forth and seem reasonable but remain largely untested as to comprehensiveness, reliability, and descriptive adequacy.[2] Regarding their utility for vandalism prevention and reduction purposes, however, their prescriptive framing appears to be a valuable, intervention-efficacy-enhancing first step.

[2]With the exception of Weinmayer's (1969) effort, existing categorizations almost singularly avoid inclusion or consideration of sociopolitical motivational antecedents for and types of vandalism. It is one thing to omit from inclusion defacement or destruction due to accident, or that incurred attendant on theft or burglary. It is quite another matter to leave out damage due to intentional environmental design, corporate greed, careless or avaricious developers, or political chicanery. Such "pinstripe vandalism" (Downes, 1974), Coffield (1991) correctly asserted, has "damaged our cities and landscapes a thousand times more permanently and irreversibly than all the vandals without power rolled into one" (p. 11). I will consider such ecovandalism further in Chapter 7.

THEORIES OF CAUSATION

The central behavior constituting vandalism is aggression toward property, *aggression* being defined in its usual manner as intentional physical or psychological injury. Therefore, one would guess that at least some of the several extant theories of aggression have already been brought to bear in efforts to better understand and explain vandalism. Unfortunately, such is not the case. Indeed, a wide and fruitful array of psychological and sociological theoretical perspectives on aggression currently exists: social learning theory (Bandura, 1973, 1986), social interactional theory (Patterson, 1982; Patterson, Reid, & Dishion, 1992), developmental-organizational theory (Greenberg & Speltz, 1988), social information-processing theory (Dodge, 1980, 1993), cognitive script theory (Huesman, 1988), subcultural theories (e.g., Sutherland & Cressey, 1974), strain theories (e.g., Cloward & Ohlin, 1960), control theories (e.g., Hirschi, 1969), labeling theories (e.g., Lemert, 1967), and more (see Goldstein, 1990, and Pepler & Slaby, 1994, for reviews). Surprisingly, and disappointingly, the general ignoring of vandalism as a topic worthy of inquiry also extends to the near absence of efforts to apply existing psychological and sociological theories of aggression toward its elucidation.

Though the observation by Richards (1976a) that "the vandalism literature consists of informal discussions of the problems it presents and speculation about their causes" (p. 482) is still largely accurate, the good news is that the relevant theoretical landscape is not entirely barren. Some partial, and some elaborate, efforts have been mustered to view vandalism in meaningful theoretical contexts. The partial perspectives are theoretical fragments or beginnings. Some focus on the uniquely ambiguous position in our society of that most common of vandals, the adolescent. Included here are the beginnings of what some day may be called *adolescent marginality theory* (Scott, 1954), *half-culture theory* (Ducey, 1978), and *age-inequality theory* (Richards, 1976b). Central to these perspectives are adolescents' need to deal with subordination by adults, mastery strivings, and inequality, all in a context of ambiguous marginality. In the person–environment perspective on vandalism adopted in this book, such core person characteristics must be accorded theoretical centrality. The theoretical speculations regarding vandalism and blocked opportunity (Agnew, 1985; Tygart, 1988), routine activity (Miethe, 1994), and political-economic forces (Shaw, 1973) each exemplify initial thinking vis-à-vis necessary environmental components of a causation framework.

Three formal theories of vandalism have been put forth, and will be considered here. In contrast to the beginning offerings cited above, each is a grounded, systemic, and, at least in substantial part, empirically evaluated theoretical position. The first has as its core process the role of intrinsic rewards in fostering vandalistic behavior.

Enjoyment Theory

Csikszentmihalyi and Larsen (1978) suggested that high levels of vandalism in school settings may grow from a combination of three circumstances: (1) the extrinsic reward system (e.g., grades) that encourages compliance and the extrinsic punishment system that seeks to compel it have become less effective; (2) the means–ends relationship between complying with school demands in order to receive an education and be successful in future life goals has become less believable; and (3) the "schools are less fun, ... intrinsic motivation for becoming educated is decreasing, ... 'criminal' activities are providing more enjoyment than what schools have to offer" (p. 7). Their theory centers on this third source, the relative intrinsic reward or enjoyment of vandalism and other antisocial behaviors in a context in which many of the demands made are intrinsically unenjoyable. Csikszentmihalyi and Larsen's (1978) position grows jointly from earlier work on optimal arousal levels in human functioning (Berlyne, 1960; Hebb, 1965; Hunt, 1965) and on intrinsic motivation research showing the positive consequences for personal competence following from control over one's own behavior versus the perception of being controlled by outside agency (deCharms, 1968, 1976; Deci, 1975):

> An activity seems to be enjoyable when a person perceives that his or her capacity to act (or skills) match the opportunities for action perceived in the environment (or challenges). In this balanced state of interaction—which appears to be the subjective counterpart of the optimal arousal state—people find themselves in a peculiar dynamic experience which we have called the flow state. (Csikszentmihalyi & Larsen, 1978, p. 13)

Flow, in their view, is impeded—and boredom encouraged—when activities lack graduated challenge, predictability, feedback, and clear goals. For many youths, especially those who find schools lacking in these qualities,

> violent confrontations provide the most clearly understood match between challenges and skills, the clearest goals, the most immediate feedback.... It is for this reason, presumably, that so many young children's flow experiences involve violent or destructive acts. Children who learn no other skills or see no other opportunities for action find violence and destruction a ready source of enjoyment.... Unfortunately, school activities often fail to provide flow experiences, so students do not get intrinsically motivated to take part in them. (pp. 18–19)

The "fusion of versatility and malice" (as sociologists have more prosaically described delinquency) has always been taken as the characteristic of vandalism. Thrasher's classic study of delinquency in the Twenties contains the following example:

> We did all kinds of dirty tricks for fun. We'd see a sign, "Please keep the street clean," but we'd tear it down and say, "We don't feel like keeping it clean." One day we put a can of glue in the engine of a man's car. We would always tear things down. That would make us laugh and feel good, to have so many jokes.

Examples of this sort could be multiplied: pouring acid on car roofs; pulling out all the flowers of floral clocks; strangling swans in ornamental lakes; slashing the tyres of all the cars in a car park; stripping the insulation round water mains; dumping the manhole covers in a sewerage farm; putting matches in the tyre valves of police cars (which causes the tyre to leak, and when it gets hot, the match ignites); throwing life belts into the sea; placing sleepers on railway lines; throwing stones at the drivers of passing trains; urinating in public telephone receivers; defecating in the lifts of council flats; pouring dye or acid into swimming baths; sabotaging the engines of children's miniature trains; ripping out lavatory chains in public conveniences; placing bicycle chains on railway overhead wires to cause short circuits....

Source: S. Cohen (1974). Breaking out, smashing up and the social context of aspiration. *Working Papers in Cultural Studies, 5,* pp. 55–56.

Indeed, in their own studies, teenage students rated themselves as more bored in school than in any other setting (Csikszentmihalyi, Larsen, & Prescott, 1977), finding only 40% of the classes near the optimum level of balance between the challenges presented and the youths' skills (Mayers, 1977). Schools, as my later detailed examination of vandalism intervention procedures will highlight, have relied heavily on purported technological solutions to such behavior: alarms, lighting, fencing, and the like. In what should be taken as an apt warning, enjoyment theory suggests:

> More and more high schools are becoming mechanical systems ruled by constraints on timing, location, and behavior. The similarity between schools and jails is becoming ever more pronounced. In such a system, for many students the only way to experience the self-determining state necessary for enjoyment is to disrupt its rules (p. 23)

Alternatively, suggest Csikszentmihalyi et al. (1977), it is desirable that schools seek a more optimal match between challenges and skills, and thus more intrinsically motivated and more intrinsically enjoyable participation. In their words:

> If strict schedules, unbending rules, and impersonal teaching situations continue to prevail, schools will have to rely even more heavily on extrinsic contingencies to survive, and in the process they will breed new generations of bored, alienated adults for whom violence is a logical way to assert their existence. (p. 34)

Aesthetic Theory

Research in the field of aesthetics has identified a number of factors responsible for the pleasure that frequently accompanies aesthetic experiences. These include such qualities of the artistic object being enjoyed as, for example, its perceived complexity, predictability, novelty, intensity, and organization. Allen and Greenberger (1978) proposed that these very same variables are central not only to enjoyment of artistic creation, but also to its destruction. In this strictly environmental theory, an object's initial appearance and its expected appearance after being vandalized are held to serve as eliciting stimuli for destructive behavior. Thus, in a manner complementary to the approach of Csikszentmihalyi et al. (1977), this, too, is an "enjoyment" theory.

Its key constructs are defined as follows. *Complexity*, whether of a visual, auditory, or literary piece, increases directly with the number of independent elements involved and negatively with the similarity or redundancy among the elements. In general, people report greater liking for and interest in complex stimuli and, in fact, spend more time exploring complex patterns. *Predictability*, or expectation, refers to the individual's anticipation vis-à-vis a stimulus event. Violations of an expectation (i.e., unpredicted outcomes) have been shown to yield surprise and arousal, typically accompanied by positive affect. *Novelty* also elicits positive effect, and pleasure, arousal, and interest rapidly diminish with repeated exposure. Allen and Greenberger (1978) also offered, and reviewed studies showing, increasing levels of aesthetic enjoyment as *intensity* increases, to a point, as well as substantial influences upon perception and emotional response thereto as a function of stimulus *organization* (i.e., patterning, grouping, proportion, and symmetry).

In an interesting and, as we shall see, theory-supporting manner, Allen and Greenberger (1978) extrapolated these several findings from the domain of experimental aesthetics to the study of vandalism. Their research program consisted of a series of analog investigations of vandalismlike behaviors in a laboratory context, as well as retrospective interview studies of actual vandalistic behavior. The theoretical perspective from which their operational hypotheses followed is captured well in their statement:

> Three phases or stages of vandalism can be identified—before, during, and after destruction.... In the first stage (before destruction) variation in appearance may exist in terms of structural variables (such as complexity, novelty, and expectedness), psychophysical properties (size or intensity), and organization (patterning) of stimulus elements. These properties determine whether an object will be judged as interesting or dull, pleasing or displeasing, beautiful or ugly. If a person expects that altering the appearance of an object will make it more interesting or pleasing, an effort will be made to change its appearance even if it means resorting to socially disapproved methods such as vandalism.
>
> In the second phase (during an act of destruction) enjoyment derives primarily from the visual, auditory, and tactile-kinesthetic stimuli which arise during rapid transformation of an object.... Greater enjoyment should be derived from destroying an object if the process of breakage is, for example, more complex, unexpected, or novel....
>
> In the third phase (after destruction) ... the static appearance of the object after destruction, for example, may be very interesting or pleasing. The patterning and organization of the object also importantly affects its post-destruction appearance. (p. 52)

Thus, they hold, the initial (predestruction) appearance of an object, the expectation or predictions held by the individual regarding the manner in which it will break, and anticipation regarding its postdestruction appearance may each serve as an eliciting cue—held by the investigators to actually stimulate or evoke the vandalism—or as a discriminative cue, influencing the selection among potential vandalism targets.

For Allen and Greenberger's investigation predicting that initial (predestruction) complexity would serve as a discriminative cue for choice of vandalism target, three pairs of model buildings were constructed. One model in each pair was complex in its construction and materials; the other was of a simple initial structure. Initial complexity, reported the investigators, was operationally defined in three ways: (1) tall versus short buildings, with size of blocks and shape of building held constant; (2) irregular versus regular design, with size of blocks and height of building held constant; and (3) large versus small blocks, with design and building height held constant. Given the choice, 82% of their research subjects elected to destroy the complex structure within each pair: the tall building, the one of irregular design, and the one constructed of small blocks.

Complexity was similarly shown to influence vandalism in their second investigation, relating to the process of destruction and the complexity of its outcome. Subjects were shown a silent film showing 26 panes of glass being broken and were required to indicate how much they would like to break each one. As predicted, the rank order of desire to break each pane of glass was significantly related to the rank of its subjective complexity, that is, to the complexity of the manner in which it shattered and its post-destruction appearance.

As noted above, aesthetic theory also predicts that a destructive act will be enjoyed most when it disconfirms or violates what the individual anticipates will occur. Allen and Greenberger (1978) created two films, each showing a sequence of four panes of glass being broken. In both films, the first three panes of glass broke the first time they were hit. In one film (control condition), first-hit breakage also occurred for the fourth pane. In the other (experimental condition), however, the fourth pane did not break until the third time it was hit. After viewing one of the films, research subjects rated their degree of enjoyment. The experimental-condition enjoyment scores were significantly higher than those for control subjects, who, in contrast to their experimental counterparts, had not had their destruction-relevant expectations disconfirmed. Employing similarly structured experimental designs, Allen and Greenberger (1978) found evidence in support of their theory's predictions regarding the influence of novelty and organization on destruction-associated pleasure.

Beyond the laboratory, Allen and Greenberger (1978) conducted an open-ended interview study with 129 male subjects, inquiring into their recollections regarding actual vandalistic acts they had perpetrated. Incidents recalled were rated by respondents on an array of dimensions relevant to their perception and experience of destruction. Significant positive correlations were obtained between the degree of reported enjoyment during destruction and the complexity, interestingness, and unexpectedness of the destruction.

The investigators concluded:

> According to aesthetic theory, vandalism could be greatly reduced simply by making it a less enjoyable experience. Vandalism can be made less enjoyable by selecting structures, designs, and types of material which minimize complexity, unexpectedness, and novelty while reducing the temptation to "improve" the appearance of an object or its environment by defacement or destruction. (p. 62)

Equity-Control Theory

Fisher and Baron (1982; DeMore, Fisher, & Baron, 1988) proposed that the core motive underlying vandalistic behavior is perceived inequity (i.e., perceived violations of norms of fairness in social or environmental arrangements), and that the goal of vandalism is equity restoration. In this two-factor social psychological theory, perceived inequity interacts with perceived control. The latter is defined as the strength of a person's belief that he or she can effectively modify existing arrangements. Perceived control is determined by actual control opportunity, one's ability to use these opportunities, the person's ability to identify the source(s) of inequality, and her or his learned expectations for control in similar past situations. The theory's central prediction is that vandalism is most likely to occur under conditions of low perceived equity and low to moderate levels of perceived control. Persons perceiving high perceived control are likely to employ socially accepted means for restoring equity; those with very low perceived control may well be rendered inactive or helpless. With low to moderate perceived control, however, the person is "less apt to believe he or she can restore equity through socially acceptable means, [and] will look for a solution that is immediate, low cost, and difficult to thwart, e.g., vandalism" (DeMore et al., 1988, p. 82).

The theory also proposes that acts of vandalism can be arrayed along an instrumental-expressive continuum. It is predicted that malicious or vindictive vandalism—that is, the more expressive-cathartic forms of such behavior—will be used to seek to restore (psychological) equity when the individual perceives low control. The key feature of such vandalism is high levels of spontaneity, anger, and overt aggression. As perceived control increases, it is predicted that more instrumental forms of vandalism will be employed—acquisitive, tactical, or ideological, in Cohen's (1971, 1974) typology. In contrast to the vandalism expressions indicated above as prototypical for conditions of low perceived control, that described here may restore actual (not only psychological) equity. It is also likely to be less intense in its expressiveness.

Equity-control theory is also a person–environment theory. In addition to equity and control characteristics of the perceiver/potential vandal, physical and social qualities of the perceiver's ecology serve as moderator variables:

> These are sufficient but not necessary for its occurrence and affect the likelihood and intensity of certain types of vandalism. Aspects of the physical environment (e.g., whether targets are "hardened," the degree of surveillance, etc.) constitute one secondary moderating variable. Other secondary moderators include group variables. Two types are discussed: those associated with the target group (e.g., a strong, cohesive target group may be less likely to be vandalized), and those of the vandal group. Concerning the latter, peers may contribute to vandalism if they provide models of antisocial behavior and diffuse responsibility for it. (DeMore et al., 1988, pp. 82–83).

In a test of equity-control theory, DeMore et al. (1988) measured perceived equity, perceived control, and vandalism among a sample of university students residing in a dormitory. Results clearly supported the theory's predictions, as multiple-regression analysis revealed higher frequency of vandalism by students perceiving both low equity and low control. This perceptual status (and hence vandalism, too) was significantly more likely for male than female students. Such findings quite directly imply that inequity-reducing, control-enhancing student participation in dormitory and university administration and decision making has substantial potential for reducing vandalism. These correlational results were successfully replicated in a later study by Warzecha, Fisher, and Baron (1984). Further, in an experimental test of the theory's core predictions, Cassady (1985) was able to demonstrate a significant causal effect of the combination of high inequity and low control on overt vandalistic behavior. Further tests of this comprehensive and promising theory are clearly warranted.

The motivational typologies and theoretical explanations presented in this chapter collectively constitute a valuable beginning information base from which to view the causation of vandalism. It is an information base in marked need of both expansion and fuller evaluation. While full of seemingly useful descriptions and assertions, the utility of both—typology and theory—for more fully understanding and more adequately controlling vandalistic behavior is largely yet to be determined.

CHAPTER 4

INTERVENTION
ALTERNATIVE STRATEGIES

I believe that every act of aggression—toward persons or property—is a person–environment event. Thus, all acts of vandalism in my view are a combined result of qualities of the vandal and characteristics of the physical and social environment in which the vandalism occurs. In this chapter, I will elaborate on this "interactionist" perspective and examine the several strategies for vandalism intervention which have been put forth as they do or do not accord with such person–environment causal thinking. As will be seen, while some perspectives indeed capture this central interactionist quality, many others are much more fully oriented toward *either* environmental solutions or person-focused (vandal-focused) solutions. These latter strategies—based only on environment *or* person—are in my view equally limited when enacted alone. Both are necessary; neither is sufficient. I will describe each strategic orientation and, in the next chapter, present in considerable detail the specific intervention tactics which have been employed to enact each strategy. I do so in the spirit of providing the strategic and tactical environment-and-person building blocks toward effective interactionist interventions.

Since the joint goals of this book are elucidation and optimizing application, in Chapter 6 following the present consideration of strategies and tactics, I will explore means of meaningfully combining intervention tactics into person- *and* environment-oriented operational programs, and of evaluating their effectiveness for both immediate and long-term change.

THE PERSON–ENVIRONMENT DUET

The central tenet of the interactionist perspective on human behavior is captured well in the following quotation from two of its energetic proponents:

> The trait model and the psychodynamic model propose that actual behavior is primarily determined by latent, stable dispositions. Both assume that the sources for the initiation and direction of behavior come primarily from within the organism. The situational model assumes that the sources for the initiation and direction of behavior come primarily from factors external to the organism. The interactional model assumes that the sources for the initiation and direction of behavior come primarily from the continuous interactions between the person and the situations that he or she encounters. (Endler & Magnusson, 1976, p. 960)

Person–environment interactionism had its early roots in the works of Lewin (1935, 1936) and Murray (1938). In Lewin's well-known formula, $B = f(p,e)$, not only was behavior considered a function of both the person and the environment, but the environment most influential in its behavioral consequences was considered subjective in nature, that is, the environment-as-perceived (also termed the *phenomenal field* or the *psychological situation*). Murray (1938) took a similar position, in his description of behavior as a joint outcome of both the individual's needs (the person variable) and environmental press or need-satisfying potential (the situation variable). Others followed Lewin's (1935, 1936) and Murray's (1938) early theorizing. Murphy's (1947) organism-field perspective, Rotter's (1954) and Mischel's (1968) social learning positions, and Angyal's (1959) phenomenological theory emphasizing the inseparability of organism and environment and the subjectivity of environment in shaping human behavior are major examples of this interactionist theme in psychological theory. In addition to the phenomenologists and social learning theorists, a third view advancing interactionism emerged, variously called *ecological psychology* and *environmental psychology*. Roger Barker and his research group's (Barker & Gump, 1964; Barker & Wright, 1954) studies of the "stream of behavior" in a variety of field settings were the pioneering works in this context. Their investigations were a major clarification of the effects of diverse real-world "behavior settings" on behavior, as well as a significant step forward in determining how environments might be optimally defined, classified, and measured. Both the spirit and the substance of the interactionist perspective have continued to grow and find empirical support in modern psychological theory and research (e.g., Altman, Brown, Staples, & Werner, 1992; Goldstein, 1994; Little, 1987; Pervin, 1986; Stokols & Altman, 1987).[1] Further, directly to the point of this book, investigative support for a person–environment stance regarding the sources and reduction of aggressive behavior has also been amply forthcoming (Campbell, 1986; Cordilia, 1986; Forgas, 1986; Gibbs, 1986; Goldstein, 1994; Page & Moss, 1976; Rausch, 1967, 1972).

I have titled this section "The Person–Environment Duet" as a means of proposing that the person and context interactions at the heart of the interactionist position taken here are both probabilistic and reciprocal. Probabilism contrasts with both determinism and possibilism. Determinism views the environment as the shaper of human behavior and the individual as the passive responder, inexorably led, with little ability or opportunity to select or alter his or her environment. Possibilism, alternatively, sees the person as acting upon the environment, but an environment which provides opportunities to grasp but which does little or no selecting or shaping of its own. Probabilism views the environment as neither determining nor merely providing possibilities. Instead, it makes certain choices more likely, enlarges, and reinforces, and in Krupat's (1985) view:

> The relationship of person to environment is dynamic, rather than static. There is a give and take, with each part of the system providing reciprocal influences on each other. We shape our environments and in turn are shaped by them in a never-ending cycle of mutual influence. (p. 12)

As we now turn to consideration of vandalism intervention strategies, it will become clear that some are deterministic in their orientation, holding that the physical and social environment determines vandalistic behavior, and hence, it is environmental changes that will reduce it; other strategies are possibilistic, asserting person qualities as the single influences upon vandalistic behavior and its remediation; and still others are probabilistic and interactionistic, calling for both person and environment means for altering vandalistic behavior.

[1]Parallel theoretical movement toward a person–environment perspective has also occurred simultaneously in sociology and criminology. In sociology, it is captured in differential association-differential reinforcement theory (Akers, 1985), social development theory (Hawkins & Weiss, 1985), social disorganization theory (Kornhauser, 1978), and Hogan and Jones's (1985) socioanalytic theory. Criminology, in turn, has offered integrated learning theory (Feldman, 1977), criminal opportunity theory (Cohen & Land, 1987), and routine activity theory (Cohen & Felson, 1979; Cohen, Kleugel, & Land, 1981).

VANDALISM INTERVENTION STRATEGIES

Changing the Physical and Social Environment

This deterministic perspective on vandalism control and reduction has appeared and reappeared under a variety of rubrics: utilitarian prevention (Cohen, 1973), deopportunizing design (Wiesenthal, 1990), architectural determinism (Zweig & Ducey, 1978), crime prevention through environmental design (Andel, 1968; Wood, 1991), situational crime prevention (Clarke, 1992), and environmental criminology (Brantingham & Brantingham, 1991).

Unlike the person-oriented strategies, all of which in a variety of ways seek to reduce the potential or actual vandal's *motivation* to perpetrate such behavior, the environment-oriented strategies seek to alter the physical setting, context, or situation in which vandalism might occur so that the potential or actual vandal's *opportunity* to perpetrate such behavior is reduced. This ecological strategy, of altering the physical or social environment to prevent or reduce the occurrence of vandalism, has been an especially popular choice—particularly in a society as technologically oriented as the United States. Thus, venues as diverse as school districts, mass transit systems, museums, shopping malls, national and state parks, and many others have time and again opted for target hardening, access controlling, offender deflecting, entry–exit screening, surveillance increasing, inducement removing, and other similar tactical concretizations of an environment-altering intervention strategy as their first, and often only, means of defense against vandalism. In the next chapter, I will enumerate and catalog the several dozen specific means by which this strategy has been implemented. I suspect the reader will respond (correctly) to this lengthy, technology-oriented enumeration with the sense that we certainly love our hardware in America! Yet, paradoxically, very little other than anecdotal, impressionistic, or testimonial "evidence" exists for the actual vandalism control effectiveness of this widely held strategy. Further, the very scope of its implementation (in extremis, the "Bastille response"—Ward, 1991—or the "crime proof fortress"—Zweig & Ducey, 1978) has in some settings served to impact quite negatively on the very mission for which the setting was created in the first place. In schools, for example, one finds "More and more high schools are becoming mechanical systems ruled by constraints on timing, location, and behavior. The similarity between schools and jails is becoming ever more pronounced" (Csikszentmihalyi & Larsen, 1978, p. 23).

Not only may the setting's mission be compromised, but as a sort of paradoxical self-fulfilling prophecy, the environmental alterations put in place to *reduce* vandalism may be experienced by the vandal-to-be as an inviting, potentially enjoyment-providing challenge to his or her vandalistic skills and thus may serve actually to *increase* such behavior (Wise, 1982; Zweig & Ducey, 1978). The fence around the school, the graffiti-resistant wall surface, the theft-proof parking meter, the slash-proof bus seat, toughened glass, the aisle store cameras—each is a possibly, opportunity-reducing deterrent and each a challenging invitation to vandalism.

Thus, the "downside" of reliance on alterations in the physical environment as *the* means of vandalism control and reduction is not inconsiderable. Yet, an important "upside" also exists. First, without concurring with a position as extreme as Weinmayr's (1969) assertion that "ninety percent of what is labeled vandalism can be prevented through design" (p. 286), one may still accept and act on the belief that venue changes can be a significant component of an effective person–environment intervention. First, design innovations may be relevant to deopportunizing vandalism in more than one way. Wiesenthal (1990), for example, observed that "property damage can be avoided by design elements that do more than resist attack; design can be used to subtly steer the user away from destruction or defacement" (p. 289). Wise (1982) suggested that design may be employed to channel attention away from potentially damaging activities, to reduce the effects of natural processes (e.g., erosion and weathering) which vandals may augment, and to eliminate or reduce the type of environmental feedback which may serve to reinforce vandalistic behavior. Thus, plywood road signs, which "thunk" when hit by a target practice bullet, may be less attractive vandalism targets than signs made of metal, which yield a louder noise when so hit.

Levy-Leboyer (1984) augmented the case for design-as-intervention by noting that some locations are more prone to be vandalized than others, a view also put forth by Christensen, Mabery, McAllister, and McCormick (1988) in their call for a predictive framework for identifying various degrees of site vulnerability. The public, the newer, the previously vandalized, and the previously damaged by something other than vandalism, as well as location in "low-status" institutions and venues providing inadequate service, are each common targets—and thus desirable sites for environmental alteration. Wilson (1977), writing as an architect, succinctly summarized the case for design-as-intervention:

> The shape of buildings can dictate patterns of use and the circulation of people around them and hence help to structure the networks of social relationships that develop. In addition, buildings, by the amount of surveillance they afford, may prevent or offer opportunities for certain activities to take place unobserved. Finally, attrition and damage to buildings can be prevented to an extent by careful use of materials and finishes. It is eminently

Check Your Security Status

To deter vandals, ask local police, district security personnel, or commercial security firms for help identifying vulnerable areas of your schools and campuses and recommending security countermeasures.

Answer Yes or No to these questions to check your schools' security status:

- Are school entrances supervised during the day and locked after school hours?
- Are hallways, rest rooms, and other school areas supervised while students are in the building?
- Do police or security officers patrol the campus regularly at night and on weekends?
- Are fences used to keep vandals out of high-risk areas?
- Are school grounds clear of rocks?
- Is exterior lighting sufficient to serve as a deterrent?
- Are parking areas visible from the street and the school?
- Are windows properly secured? In high-risk areas, are windows constructed of vandal-resistant materials or protected by wire mesh?
- Are exit doors secured by deadbolt locks or chains and locks after hours? Can vandals open locks by breaking out glass?

> sensible to suppose that there is come connection between design and behavior, including vandalism (p. 795).

Individuals do or do not elect to engage in vandalistic behavior partially in response to characteristics not only of their physical environment but also of their social environment. This is purported to be the case at both micro and macro levels. At the micro, immediate level, the central, social-ecological intervention concept is surveillance, both perceived and actual. Vandalism, it is held, is less likely to occur if the potential perpetrator believes he or she will be observed and perhaps apprehended. Thus, for example, Blauvelt (1980) urged making the school "occupied":

> The key to controlling vandalism is to make the school a place that in some sense is continuously occupied by some form of human or mechanical presence, which will deter or respond to the vandal. The heart of any effective

- Are rooms secured, along with offices and other areas where vandalism would be especially costly?
- Are school files stored in vandal-resistant storage areas?
- Is the school protected by an intrusion-detection system?
- Can automobiles be driven onto lawns and athletic fields? Are these areas protected by fences?
- Are skylights or trapdoors on the roof sufficiently secured to prevent access to the building?
- Do trees and bushes offer hiding places for vandals?
- Are portions of the school hidden from the street? If so, are fences or other means used to protect these areas?
- Do garbage dumpsters or drainpipes provide access to the roof?
- Are trash cans securely anchored?
- Are break-resistant lenses used on exterior lights?
- Are doors and door frames constructed of steel or other vandal-resistant materials?
- Have local police or security personnel inspected the school for security problems?
- Have school neighbors been asked to watch the school?
- Are school grounds patrolled after hours? Do teachers patrol grounds during the day?

Source: D. Stover (1990, November 20–30). How to be safe and secure against school vandalism. *Executive Educator*, p. 21.

approach to controlling vandalism will be establishing that sense of "presence" which defines the building as no longer being an inert target. (p. 4)

A directly parallel conclusion emerges from Sturman's (1980) investigation of surveillance and bus vandalism. Comparisons of several arrangements of conductor presence revealed (1) that the greatest amount of vandalism occurred on buses with no conductor, and (2) that, across arrangements, the magnitude of vandalism was greatest in those bus locations (upper deck and back seat) with the least personnel supervision. Added bus conductors, real and dummy TV cameras in stores, neighborhood watch programs, improved neighborhood lighting, and an increased number of store employees are each examples of vandalism-opportunity-reducing, surveillance-increasing social-ecological interventions.

Blauvelt (1980) extended the notion of "presence" in his emphasis on

Although a single instance of off-trail hiking may be seen as minor rule-breaking activity, in the aggregate over an extended period, such behavior causes severe damage to fragile natural environments. Trailside signs at locations where off-trail hiking frequently occurs represent the final opportunity for managers to deter such activity. The sparse literature suggests that the use of such signs should reduce off-trail hiking rates and that alternative sign texts will have different effects. To test these and related hypotheses, an experiment was administered in a popular subalpine day-use area in Mount Rainier National Park. The behavior of more than 14,000 people was observed. The results of the research indicate that trailside signs reduce instances of off-trail hiking, and that effectiveness of sign texts differs significantly. Most effective was a sanction sign (OFF-TRAIL HIKERS MAY BE FINED), which reduced off-trail hiking by about 75 percent. The second most effective sign, an ethical appeal (STAY ON PAVED TRAILS and PRESERVE THE MEADOW), reduced off-trail hiking by 52 percent.

Source: D. R. Johnson & T. C. Swearingen (1992). The effectiveness of selected trailside sign texts in deterring off-trail hiking at Paradise Meadow, Mount Ranier National Park. In H. H. Christensen, D. R. Johnson, M. Brookes (Eds.), *Vandalism: Research, prevention and social policy*. Portland, OR: U.S. Department of Agriculture Forest Service, p. 104.

shared responsibility. The broader the responsibility within an institution for deopportunizing vandalism, the more likely its success. Thus, in a school setting, such matters are ideally not only the concern of security personnel or administration, but also all teachers, secretaries, custodians, kitchen personnel, and fellow students. Porter's (1980) "place defense model" suggests a taxonomy of means for citizens in general, and not only institutional personnel, to join the social ecological intervention effort against vandalism. Included are *incident-specific personal* confrontations, in which citizens are urged when appropriate to threaten transgressors and physically stop vandalistic behavior; *incident-specific appeals to authority*, requesting police or other authorities to confront transgressors; and *non-incident-specific social intervention*, such as forming a crime watch group or hiring security personnel. Ducey's (1978) call for heightening citizen involvement via antivandalism public relations efforts and Yambert and Donow's (1984) highlighting the need for enhanced "community instincts"

Schoolmen in Alpena, Mich. may be on the right track. They've turned the city schools—six elementary, one junior high—into community centers and, in so doing, have cut vandalism sharply.

Putting an end to vandalism wasn't the school district's only objective, or even its main objective. It was out to capture community support, to make its schools more accessible to parents and other community residents. It hoped to do this by throwing open the schools to children in the afternoons and to adults at night, for educational courses, arts and crafts and recreational activities.

How has this cut vandalism? Simply by having adults on the premises, after classes are dismissed, from 3:30 to 11 P.M.

Source: Anon. (1967, February). Putting an end to vandalism. *Workshop*, p. 25.

and "ecological commandments" are further, citizen-oriented, social-ecological calls for intervention.

Finally, and in quite a different manner, Shaw (1973) also accorded the vandal's social ecology a central intervention role with his macroenvironmental observation:

> Vandalism is a rebellion with a cause. To prevent it, we must combat social indifference, apathy, isolation and the loss of community, neighborhood and family values. We must reaffirm the principle that human rights are more important than property rights, and property rights are acknowledged by all only when all have a share in them. (p. 18)

Changing the Vandal

The other half of the person–environment duet will now be considered. In contrast to intervention efforts directed toward the actual or potential vandal's physical or social environment, here the intervention target is the vandal himself or herself. Cohen (1974) suggested three such person-oriented strategies:

1. *Education*. Here the effort is made to increase the potential vandal's awareness of the costs and other consequences of vandalistic behavior. These interventions assume that, once aware, such persons will consider such possible consequences and choose to refrain from perpetrating vandalism.

2. *Deterrence and retribution*. These strategies rely on threat, punishment, or forcing those committing vandalistic acts to make restitution.

Punishment strategies are especially widely employed. Ward (1973) commented:

> The most frequent public reaction to vandalism is "Hit them hard": all that is needed is better detection by the police and stiffer sentences by the court. The general tendency is to support heavier fines, custodial sentences.... Other, extra-legal sanctions include banning offenders from swimming baths, sports fields, youth clubs or play centers. Some local authorities have suggested the evicting of tenants whose children are responsible for vandalism. (p. 256)

3. *Deflection*. These strategies "attempt to understand and redirect the motivational causes of vandalism into non-damaging means of expression" (Cohen, 1974, p. 46). They include allowing controlled destruction, providing substitute targets, or other alternative outlets for energetic activity.

Koch (1975) reflected a parallel array of person-oriented strategies, employing either coercive controls, a system of indoctrination of information, legal regulations, or the substitution of functional equivalents.

> The first model has as its goal the total prohibition or elimination of some objectionable behavior. It implies strict enforcement and punishment of offenders. The second is an educational and/or propagandistic strategy. It has as its major goal the objective of changing behavior and attitudes. The third model is a regulative approach which utilizes rules or laws and prescribes allocations of time, space, age groupings, and monetary costs, in order to influence behavior.... The final alternative involves the substitution of some functional equivalent for an identified objectionable behavior. (p. 61)

To repeat an earlier-mentioned distinction, environmentally focused interventions target opportunity reduction; person-oriented efforts seek to alter motivation. While punishment, as noted above, appears to be an especially frequent person-oriented strategy implemented (Heller & White, 1975; Stoner et al., Walker, 1991), there is evidence that heavy reliance on such a strategy may not infrequently actually result in an increase, not a decrease, in the frequency of vandalism (Greenberg, 1974; Scrimger & Elder, 1981). These same investigators, as well as others, have reported a substantial decrease in vandalism as punitiveness decreased and such interventions as increased use of teacher approval for desirable student behaviors increased (Flaherty, 1987; Krause, 1985; Mayer & Butterworth, 1979; Mayer, Butterworth, Nafpaktitis, & Sulzer-Azaroff, 1983; Mayer, Nafpaktites, Butterworth, & Hollingsworth, 1987).

In contrast to such use of extrinsic rewards (i.e., teacher approval) targeted to altering vandal behavior, Csikzentmihalyi and Larsen (1978)—it will be recalled from our earlier discussion of their enjoyment theory of

Caning Sought as Punishment in Tennessee

NASHVILLE, FEB. 3 (AP)—Vandals, burglars and people who burn the American flag in Tennessee could be publicly beaten with a cane under legislation filed on Thursday by two state legislators.

"The public is interested in seeing crime punished," said one of the legislators, Representative Doug E. Gunnels, a Republican from Greenback. "I'm not an expert on crime, but people who are involved in more serious crime usually start out with crimes like this."

Under the bill, people convicted of certain misdemeanors could get 1 to 4 lashes, and people convicted of certain felonies would get 5 to 15, in addition to jail terms and fines. The offenses subject to caning would include vandalism, the defacing of government property, burglary and civil rights intimidation

Mr. Gunnels said his legislation was inspired by the case of Michael Fay, an American youth who was caned by the authorities in Singapore in May after he was convicted of vandalism.

Source: *New York Times*, February 4, 1995.

vandalism—focused more directly on a strategy calling for enhancement of intrinsic processes. Reliance on extrinsically provided rewards or reinforcement, they proposed, is cumbersome and cost-ineffective and, most significant in their view, functions to diminish the individual's intrinsic motivation not to engage in vandalistic behavior. A second vandal-oriented strategy, of which they were similarly critical on these very same grounds of diminished intrinsic motivation, is "strengthening the means-ends connection between adherence to school constraints and achievement of desired future goals" (p. 29). This is a difficult strategy to implement, as it requires a considerably closer correspondence between school performance and future rewards. For many youths, and in many schools, such a connection is not easy to perceive. And when perceived, it is a second instance of training youths to guide their behavior based on extrinsic, rather than intrinsic, motivations. As their recommended, alternative strategy, Csikszentmihalyi and Larsen (1978) suggested reorientation of school procedures and curriculum in a manner designed to stimulate and respond to youths' intrinsic motivation for challenge, for extension of their skills, for mastery, for growth, and for, in these authors' terms, the experience of flow:

Reasons for rock art vandalism range from appreciation of the artistic nature of the art, through a desire for financial gain, to a psychological drive to destroy or damage what others consider precious. Means of controlling the activity include scientific documenting of the rock art, public education, concealing rock art locations, and physically restricting access.

Source: H. C. Higgins (1992). Rock art vandalism: Causes and prevention. In H. H. Christensen, D. R. Johnson, & M. Brookes (Eds.), *Vandalism: Research, prevention, and social policy*. Portland, OR: U.S. Department of Agriculture Forest Service, p. 222.

> The authors propose that the state of enjoyment occurs when a person is challenged at a level matched by his or her level of skill.... Ideally, learning should involve systemic involvement in sequences of challenges internalized by students.... In the absence of such opportunities, antisocial behavior provides an alternative framework of challenges for bored students. Disruption of classes, vandalism, and violence in schools are, in part, attempts of adolescents to obtain enjoyment in otherwise lifeless schools. Restructuring education in terms of intrinsic motivation would not only reduce school crime, but also accomplish the goal of teaching youth how to enjoy life in an affirmative way. (p. 1)

My own strategic perspective regarding vandal-oriented intervention suggests that both externally imposed incentives *and* intrinsic motivators serve the cause of vandalism reduction well. Vandalism is a domain of interest resting on a remarkably meager research base. When rigorous and relevant research on aspects of this topic do exist, they need especially to be listened to. The Mayer et al. (1979, 1983, 1987) extrinsic reward studies, and the intrinsic motivation studies (deCharms, 1968, 1976; Deci, 1975) cited earlier, stand in support of the value of both orientations to enhancing vandal prosocial motivation.

One final point needs to be offered regarding vandal-oriented intervention strategy. In our Chapter 1 discussion of the Vestermark and Blauvelt (1978) matrix yielding four combinations of the financial and social costs of vandalism, I began urging the desirability of a prescriptive intervention response plan. There, it was held, different combined levels of the two cost categories were optimally dealt with by differing intervention priorities. This strategic point is, in my view, widely applicable. Both who the vandal is (Griffiths & Shapland, 1979) and the level of his or her

Maintaining attractive schools is extremely important. When buildings are in poor condition, the resulting attitude erodes discipline, morale and learning. Some schools have utilized students as student patrols or safety monitors, assigning these students such responsibilities as antilitter campaigns.

Included in such a program may be a pride flag, a pride trophy or other emblems, badges or plaques which positively reinforce the importance of student participation. A great deal of positive peer pressure is utilized and delinquent behavior is not acceptable. Other components might include:

- School spirit days
- Bumper sticker contests
- Slogan contests
- School assemblies
- Media campaigns
- Speeches
- Buttons
- Field trips
- Celebrity awareness programs
- School beautification programs

Source: G. C. Scrimger & R. Elder (1981). *Alternative to vandalism—Cooperation or wreckreation*." Sacramento: California Office of the Attorney General School Safety Center, p. 10.

vandalistic behavior (Hauber, 1989) will ideally, in part, determine the nature of the intervention implemented. Griffiths and Shapland (1979) correctly asserted that vandal motives and the very meaning of the act itself change with age and context:

> The preventive measures that need to be taken to make any given environment vandal-proof may be different according to the nature of the vandal.... As an example of this, look at how a window in a deserted house may be broken. This may have been done by kids getting in to play; by older children as a game of skill; by adolescents or adults in order to remove the remaining furniture or fittings; by someone with a grudge against the present or previous landlord; by a pressure group to advertise the dereliction of empty property; or by an "old lag" to gain attention or to doss for the night. (pp. 17–18)

Person–Environment Strategies

At this chapter's beginning, I offered a rationale for our preferred intervention strategy. Every act of vandalism, I held, springs from *both* person and environment sources, a dualism that must similarly characterize efforts at its prevention and remediation.

The separate person-oriented and environment-oriented vandalism intervention strategies we have now explored—in addition to their several strengths and shortcomings—will be optimally implemented in diverse, prescriptively appropriate combinations. Casserly et al. (1980), Christensen et al. (1992), Cohen (1973), Geason and Wilson (1990), Kulka (1978), Vestermark and Blauvelt (1978) and Wilson (1979) are among the several vandalism theorists and researchers also championing a multilevel, multimodal person–environment intervention strategy. Several practitioners have already put in place such a joint strategy, and at least impressionistically, report having done so to good advantage (Hendrick & Murfin, 1974; Jamieson, 1987; Levy-Leboyer, 1984; Mason, 1979; Panko, 1978; Scrimger & Elder, 1981; Stover, 1990; Weeks, 1976; White & Fallis, 1980). In the chapter that follows, I will provide a comprehensive listing and cataloging of the many environment-oriented and person-oriented tactics which have been employed in an array of commonly vandalized settings as a means of enacting the strategies we have considered. Chapter 6 will then offer rationales by which such tactics may be meaningfully combined into effective, vandalism-reducing person–environment tactical combinations.

CHAPTER 5

INTERVENTION
IMPLEMENTATION TACTICS

This chapter consists primarily of a cataloging of vandalism intervention tactics that have been employed in school, business, mass transit, park, library, museum, and other settings. These several tactics, and their accompanying sources, are provided for the reader wishing to pursue any of these means further, whether for information, implementation, or evaluation purposes. In arranging this listing, I have incorporated and built upon Clarke's (1992) taxonomy for categorizing methods of situational crime prevention. I have employed his taxonomic system elsewhere to good advantage in an ecological analysis of aggression interventions targeted on a broader area than just vandalism (Goldstein, 1994), and I believe that, with the modified and additional categories I have placed in it, it will serve current purposes well. It should be noted that Clarke's (1992) Categories 1 through 11 list physical and social environment-oriented vandalism interventions, and (my own) Categories 12 through 17 are directly or indirectly targeted on changing the potential or actual vandal himself or herself.

1. TARGET HARDENING

This situational crime prevention approach involves the use of devices or materials designed to obstruct the vandal by physical barriers:

1. **Toughened glass (acrylic, polycarbon, etc.)** (Heller & Jones, 1990; Wenk & Harlow, 1978; Zeisel, 1976)
2. **Window-cover latticework or screens** (Boss, 1984; Sabo, 1993; Sharp, 1964; Weiss, 1974)

3. **Fire-retardant paint** (Neville, 1974)
4. **High-impact plastic or steel fixtures** (Robb, 1991)
5. **Hardened rubber or plastic swing seats** (Peuleche, 1976)
6. **Concrete or steel picnic tables, benches, bleachers** (Peuleche, 1976; Wilson, 1961)
7. **Bolting trash receptacles to concrete base** (Peuleche, 1976)
8. **Rough play-tolerant adventure playgrounds** (Peuleche, 1976)
9. **Original planting of large-caliper trees** (Peuleche, 1976)
10. **Slash-proof transit vehicle seats** (Carr & Spring, 1993; Wilson, 1988)
11. **Steel-framed bus seats** (Hawthorne & Henderson, 1992)
12. **Antigraffiti repellent spray on bus seats** (Hawthorne & Henderson, 1992)
13. **Tamper-proof sign hardware and fasteners** (Chadda & Carter, 1983)
14. **Door anchor hinges with nonremovable pins** (Spalding, 1971)
15. **Reinforced phone or meter coin boxes** (Wilson, 1988)

2. ACCESS CONTROL

These are architectural features, mechanical and electronic devices, and related means of maintaining control over the ability to gain entry:

16. **Key control systems** (Boss, 1987; Fey, 1986; Gamble, Sellers, & Bone 1987; Schumaker & Leitner, 1979)
17. **Locked gates, doors, windows** (Boss, 1987; Fey, 1986)
18. **Electromagnetic doors unopenable from outside** (Sabo, 1993)
19. **Deadbolt and vertical bolt locks** (Fey, 1986; Gamble et al., 1987; Schumaker & Lester, 1979)
20. **Metal door and window shutters** (Rourke, 1992; Zeisel, 1974)
21. **Protective grilles over roof access openings** (Fey, 1986; Zeisel, 1974)
22. **Fenced yards** (Brewer & Miller, 1990; Lyons, 1982; Neville, 1974; Wilson, 1988)
23. **Vertical metal or small-mesh (unclimbable) fencing** (Ward, 1973)
24. **Reduced number of building entrances** (Zeisel, 1974)
25. **Unclimbable trees and bushes next to building** (Zeisel, 1974)
26. **Prickly bushes next to site to be protected** (Higgins, 1992; Sabo, 1993)
27. **Sloped window sills** (Ward, 1973; Zeisel, 1974)
28. **Elimination of crank and gear window mechanisms** (Irwin, 1978)

29. **Steeply angled roofs with parapets and ridges** (Sabo, 1993)
30. **Use of guard dogs** (Zeisel, 1974)
31. **Use of student photo identification** (Abramson, 1977; Sabo, 1993)
32. **Partitioning off of selected areas from use during "downtime" hours** (Dust, 1984)
33. **Barriers (fence, bars, plexiglass) around archeological sites** (Higgins, 1992)
34. **High curbs along areas to be protected** (Peuleche, 1976)

3. DEFLECTING OFFENDERS

This is the channeling of potentially criminal or aggressive behavior in more prosocial directions by means of architectural, equipment, and related alterations:

35. **Street detours** (Brantingham & Brantingham, 1991)
36. **Graffiti boards and mural programs** (Allen & Greenberger, 1978; Brewer & Miller, 1990; O'Doherty, 1991)
37. **Schools and studios for graffiti-writer exposure and recognition** (Brewer & Miller, 1990)
38. **Interesting wallpaper, daily newspaper, or chalkboard on bathroom walls** (Anon, 1984)
39. **Litter bins** (Irwin, 1978)
40. **Placing of wash fountains and towel dispensers in school hall** (Anon., 1973)
41. **Steering of pathway circulation** (Hayes & Cone, 1977a; Ward, 1973; Zeisel, 1976)
    - **Paving of shortest walk between connecting points**
    - **Avoidance of sharp changes in direction**
    - **Paving of natural shortcuts after demonstrated use**
    - **Installation or landscaping of traffic barriers (e.g., with benches or bushes)**
42. **Next-step posters on broken equipment** (Moser & Levy-Leboyer, 1985)

4. CONTROLLING FACILITATORS

This is the alteration of the means of criminal or aggressive behavior by making such means less available, less accessible, or less potentially injurious:

43. **Sales control of spray paint and indelible marker** (Brewer & Miller, 1990; Haberstroh, 1989; Van D'Elden, 1992)
44. **Removal of debris from construction and demolition sites** (Irwin, 1978; Stefanko, 1989)
45. **Removal of waste paper, rubbish, and other combustibles** (Juillerat, 1972)
46. **Use of tamper-proof screws** (Spalding, 1971; Zeisel, 1976)
47. **Placement of permanent signs, building names, and decorative hardware out of reach from ground** (Chadda & Carter, 1983; Zeisel, 1976)
48. **Placement of school thermostats, fire alarms, and light switches far from "hangout" areas** (Zeisel, 1976)
49. **Placement of bus stops, public telephones, picnic tables, and other frequent targets at nonisolated locations** (Hawthorne & Henderson, 1992; Peuleche, 1976)

5. EXIT–ENTRY SCREENING

Rather than seeking to exclude potential perpetrators, as in access control, this set of tactics seeks to increase the likelihood of detecting persons not in conformity with entry requirements (entry screening) or detecting objects that should not be removed from protected areas (exit screening):

50. **Closed-circuit TV** (Batiste, 1991: Carr & Spring, 1993; Welsh & Cestare, 1993)
51. **Metal detectors** (Sabo, 1993)
52. **Vibration detectors** (Anon., 1978a)
53. **Motion detectors** (Anon. 1978a; Sabo, 1993)
54. **Perimeter alarm system** (Gamble et al., 1987)
55. **Library book tags** (Gouke & Murfin, 1980)
56. **Clearinghouse for archaeological-site raiding cases** (Waldbauer, 1992)

5. FORMAL SURVEILLANCE

This is surveillance by police, guards, monitors, citizen groups, or other paid or volunteer security personnel:

57. **Police, citizen, senior citizen, tenant, and parent patrols** (Amoroso, 1977; Anon., 1965, 1974a, 1978b; Bell, Bell, & Godefroy, 1992; Carr & Spring, 1993; Franchi, 1983; Nelken & Kline, 1971)

58. **Neighborhood Watch, School Watch, Block Watch, and Rail Watch** (Epstein, 1979; Meany, 1987; Schindler, 1983; Wilson & Healy, 1978; Worrell & Sparks, 1983)
59. **Provision of on-site living quarters for citizens or security personnel, for example, "school sitters," and "campground hosts"** (Anon., 1974a; Christensen & Clark, 1978; Harris, 1991; Irwin, 1978; Zeisel, 1976)
60. **Informant hotlines, for example, "rat-on-a-rat program" or "secret witness program"** (Christensen & Clark, 1978; Epstein, 1979; Whitt, 1980)
61. **Crime Solvers Anonymous reward program** (Schindler, 1983)
62. **Police antivandalism advice flyers placed on parked commuter vehicles** (Mancini & Jain, 1987)
63. **Mechanical, ultrasonic, infrared, and electronic intruder alarm systems** (Boss, 1984; Fey, 1986; Gamble, et al., 1987; Nelken & Kline, 1971; Siatt, 1981)
64. **Automatic fire-detection systems** (Anon., 1979a; Neville, 1974; Spalding, 1971)
65. **After-hours use of school public-address system for monitoring** (Neville, 1974)

7. NATURAL SURVEILLANCE

This is surveillance provided by employees, home owners, pedestrians, and others going about their daily activities:

66. **Community after-school use** (Anon., 1967; Gaudet & Doyle, 1979; Murphy, 1973; Smith, 1982; Steele, 1978; Weiss, 1974; Zeisel, 1974)
67. **Reduced teacher–student ratio** (Goldstein et al., 1994)
68. **Increased number of employees, for example, playground supervisors, bus conductors, and teachers** (Brantingham & Brantingham, 1991; Clarke, 1992)
69. **Twenty-four-hour custodial staffing** (Warren & Rubenow, 1984; Zeisel, 1976)
70. **Live-in custodian or caretaker** (Anon., 1974a; Hessling, 1992; Wilson, 1961; Zeisel, 1976)
71. **Distribution of faculty and staff offices throughout the school** (Dust, 1984)
72. **Assignment of additional faculty and staff to hall and cafeteria duty** (Massucci, 1984; Warren & Rubenow, 1984)

73. **Youth Vacation Vigil student surveillance program** (Anon., 1966)
74. **Use of bus or train employees as route vandalism-reporting system** (Hawthorne & Henderson, 1992; Klippert, 1992)
75. **Use of store aisle mirrors** (Hawthorne & Henderson, 1992)
76. **Improved exterior and interior lighting** (Anon., 1971; Carr & Spring, 1993; Daniels, 1982; Fey, 1986; Irwin, 1978; Sharp, 1964; Ward, 1973)
77. **Low trimming of shrubbery and plants** (Fey, 1986; Wilson, 1961)

8. TARGET REMOVAL

The physical removal or enhanced inaccessibility of potential vandalism targets:

78. **Use of graffiti dissuaders**
    - **Teflon, plastic laminate, fiberglass, or melamine covering** (Van D'Elden, 1992)
    - **Rock cement, slanted siding, or deeply grooved surfaces** (Wilson, 1988)
    - **Paint-outs or paint with contrasting colors in patterned surfaces** (Ward, 1973)
    - **Fast-growing wall vines or shrubbery, or built wall barriers** (Libby, 1980)
79. **Removal of archaeological art from site to museum** (Higgins, 1992)
80. **Nondisclosure of archaeological sites** (Higgins, 1992)
81. **Removal of pay phones from high loitering areas** (Hawthorne & Henderson, 1992)
82. **Removal of corner bus seats, hidden from (driver's) view** (Hawthorne & Henderson, 1992)
83. **Removal of outside plant bulbs** (Wilson, 1961)
84. **Windowless schools or other buildings** (Weiss, 1974; Zeisel, 1976)
85. **Omission of ground-level windows** (Zeisel, 1976)
86. **Concealed school door closers** (Spalding, 1971)
87. **Concealed pipework** (Ward, 1973)
88. **Moving of fittings out of reach, for example, from wall to ceiling** (Heller & Jones, 1990)
89. **Signs and fixtures flush with wall or ceiling** (Huntington, 1981; Irwin, 1978; Ward, 1973)
90. **Key-controlled light fixtures in public areas** (Irwin, 1978)
91. **Avoidance of planting easily damaged trees or bushes** (Zeisel, 1976)

9. IDENTIFYING PROPERTY

This is the physical identification marking of potential vandalism targets:

92. **Property marking with school district ID** (Gamble et al., 1987)
93. **Property marking with business logo** (Boss, 1984; Chadda & Carter, 1983)
94. **Property marking with identification seals** (Chadda & Carter, 1983)
95. **Property marking with organization stencil** (Wilson, 1961)
96. **Property marking with social security number** (Goldstein, 1994)

10. REMOVING INDUCEMENTS

This is the physical alteration of potential vandalism targets:

97. **Rapid repair of damaged property** (Allen & Greenberger, 1978; Stefanko, 1989; Wenk & Harlow, 1978; Wilson, 1961; Zeisel, 1976)
98. **Rapid removal of graffiti** (Brewer & Miller, 1990; Winter, 1992; Zeisel, 1976)
99. **Use of small windowpanes** (Allen & Greenberger, 1978; Ward, 1973; Zeisel, 1976)
100. **Use of plywood road signs** (Ward, 1973)
101. **Elimination of school washroom and toilet stall doors** (Anon., 1973)
102. **Elimination of bars over toilet stall doorways** (Anon., 1973)
103. **Keeping of school restroom thermostats at 62°F** (Irwin, 1978; Young & Soldatis, 1970)
104. **Removal of gates and fences** (Stefanko, 1989)
105. **Painting of playground equipment in bright colors** (Peuleche, 1976)
106. **Beautification programs, for example, landscaping, painting, and maintenance** (Pablant & Baxter, 1975)

11. RULE SETTING

This is the making of explicit prior statements of acceptable and unacceptable behavior, as well as penalties for noncompliance:

107. **Federal Antiquities Act of 1906** (Waldbauer, 1992)
108. **Federal Historical Sites Act of 1935** (Waldbauer, 1992)

109. **Federal Archaeological Resources Protection Act of 1979** (Waldbauer, 1992)
110. **Model Hate Crime Bill** (Sinenesky & Freeman, 1988)
111. **Antivandalism laws** (Chadda & Carter, 1983; Peuleche, 1976)
112. **Building design specifications** (Zeisel, 1976)
113. **Building security codes** (Anon., 1983a)
114. **Parental liability statutes** (Brenton, 1975; Severino, 1972; Warren & Rubenow, 1984)
115. **Prohibitions of spray-paint and indelible-marker sales** (Van D'Elden, 1992)
116. **Codes of rights and responsibilities** (Bayh, 1978)
117. **School rules of student conduct** (Griffin, 1982; Valentine, 1979)
118. **Rigorous, irregular, no-warning fire drills** (Juillerat, 1972)

12. EDUCATION

These are direct efforts to inform and persuade potential and actual vandals regarding vandalism costs, consequences, and alternatives:

119. **Vandalism education programs** (Chadda & Carter, 1983; Gaddy & Kelly, 1984; Huisman-Troost, Drenth, Lutterop, & deJong, 1991; Wilson, 1961; Winter, 1992)
120. **Arson education programs** (Epstein, 1979; Neville, 1974)
121. **Vandalism awareness walks** (Anon., 1980a)
122. **Vandalism case-study classroom discussions** (Diem, 1982)
123. **Classroom brainstorming on vandalism reduction** (Diem, 1982)
124. **Year-round education** (Ballinger, 1993)
125. **Student orientation handbook and meetings** (Anon., 1980c; Warren & Rubenow, 1984; Winter, 1992)
126. **Teacher multicultural sensitivity training** (Goldstein et al., 1994)
127. **Antivandalism lectures by older to younger students** (Olson, 1981)
128. **Antivandalism films** (Anon., 1972, 1976b)
129. **Antivandalism games** (Anon., 1979b)
130. **Antivandalism slide and tape program** (Anon., 1980c; Winter, 1992)
131. **Antivandalism, low-impact camping brochures** (Oliver, Roggenbuck, & Watson, 1985)
132. **Antivandalism trail-head signs** (Heberlein, 1971; Johnson & Swearingen, 1992; Martin, 1992)
133. **"Ride with Pride," antivandalism transit program** (Dews & Peters, 1986)

13. PUBLICITY

These are indirect efforts to inform and persuade potential and actual vandals, as well as the general public, regarding vandalism costs, consequences, and alternatives:

134. **Antivandalism advertising** (Conklin, 1994; Frith, 1985; Gramann, Christensen, & Vanderstoep, 1992; Riley, 1980)
135. **Antivandalism news releases** (Hawthorne & Henderson, 1992)
136. **Milk-carton and grocery-bag antivandalism messages** Klippert, 1992)
137. **Antivandalism decals on mass transit vehicles** (Hawthorne & Henderson, 1992)
138. **Antivandalism slogan contests** (Van D'Elden, 1992)
139. **Sign Amnesty Day** (Klippert, 1992)
140. **"Help the Ranger" and "Help the Playground" campaigns** (Christensen & Clark, 1978)
141. **Antivandalism buttons, T-shirts, rulers, bookmarks, and posters** (Van D'Elden, 1992; Winter, 1992)
142. **Posters and flyers on graffiti-removal procedures** (Bell et al., 1992)

14. PUNISHMENT

These are negative experiences directed to perpetrators consequent to their vandalistic behavior:

143. **Suspension from school** (Panko, 1978)
144. **Monetary fines** (Pedersen, 1990)
145. **Restitution** (Anon., 1979a, 1980b; Goldman, 1961; Gottesman, 1981; Graham, 1981; Kruissink, 1991; Panko, 1978)
146. **Student vandalism account** (McCord, 1973; Panko, 1978; Zeisel, 1976)
147. **Group billing for residence hall damage** (Richmond, 1989)

15. COUNSELING

These are remedial experiences directed to perpetrators consequent to their vandalistic behavior:

148. **Student counseling programs** (Bayh, 1978; Massucci, 1984)
149. **Conflict-negotiation skills training** (Goldstein et al., 1994)

150. **Moral-reasoning training** (Harvey, 1983; Olson, 1981, 1981)
151. **Interpersonal skills training** (Goldstein, 1988)
152. **Aggression replacement training** (Goldstein, Glick, Carthan, & Blancero, 1994)
153. **Behavior modification treatment for arson**
    - **Stimulus satiation** (Welsh, 1971)
    - **Contingency management** (Holland, 1969)
    - **Assertion training** (Mathie & Schmidt, 1977)

16. INVOLVEMENT

These are efforts to increase the sense of involvement with and ownership of potential vandalism targets:

154. **Encouragement of college students to personalize (paint and furnish) their dormitory rooms** (Anon., 1983b; Richmond, 1989)
155. **Permission for college students to retain same dormitory room several semesters** (Anon., 1983b)
156. **Student participation in school decision making** (Anon., 1979a; Stefanko, 1989; Warren & Rubenow, 1984)
157. **School administration collaboration with student organizations** (Warren & Rubenow, 1984)
158. **School–home collaboration** (Anon., 1979a, 1983c; Challinger, 1987; Fujimoto, 1987; Griffin, 1982)
159. **Hiring of unemployed youth as subway vandalism inspectors** (Andel, 1989; Batiste, 1991)
160. **Adopt-a-Station antivandalism program** (Corwin, 1978)

17. ORGANIZATIONAL CLIMATE

These are procedures for enhancing the quality of the potential or actual vandal's social, education, and daily living context:

161. **Teacher or staff approval or reward for student prosocial behavior** (Mayer et al., 1983)
162. **Teacher respect for students** (Flaherty, 1987; Herbert, 1990)
163. **Teacher and parent modeling of respect for others and for property** (Shalloo, 1954)
164. **Regular visible presence of school principal** (Anon., 1980c; Griffin, 1982; Ianni, 1979)
165. **School principal involvement in community activities** (Griffin, 1982)

166. **School curriculum revision** (Anon., 1979a; Bayh, 1978; Gaddy & Kelly, 1984)
167. **Improved student–custodian relationships** (Siden, 1978; Young & Soldatis, 1970)
168. **Improved school–community relationships** (Dust, 1984; Griffin, 1982; MacKenzie, 1979; Varady, 1986)
169. **Reorganization of large schools to schools-within-a-school or house plans** (Gaddy & Kelly, 1984; Garbarino, 1978)

The extended list of context-oriented and vandal-oriented interventions which constitutes this chapter forms a substantial pool of diverse means of seeking to prevent, control, and reduce vandalistic behavior. In the chapter that follows, I will propose and examine meaningful rationales for selecting wisely from this intervention pool in order to create synergistic sets or programs of vandalism interventions likely to have significant impacts on such behaviors. I will also explore useful means of rigorously evaluating the actual potency, depth, and durability of such intervention combinations.

CHAPTER 6

INTERVENTION
COMBINATIONS AND EVALUATIONS

One hundred and sixty-nine interventions with no doubt more on the way! Viewed collectively, the array of preventive and remedial tactics employed in the several venues frequently targeted for vandalism is diverse, creative, and evidence of the substantial energy that a wide variety of professionals continue to expend in their attempt to control and reduce such costly antisocial behavior. This array of *potentially* effective interventions is the good news. The bad news is that anything approaching hard evidence (or even "soft evidence" in most instances) that would aid potential users in sorting through and selecting among these several dozen interventions simply does not exist. In the second section of this chapter, I will examine a host of issues relevant to such (missing) research, issues designed to enhance both its quantity and quality.

One intervention issue that can be addressed with certainty at this point, however, concerns the need to identify potent *combinations* of interventions. Vandalism, like all instances of aggression, is a complexly determined behavior. Every act of vandalism derives from several causes and, therefore, will optimally be combated with equally complex interventions. The first section of this chapter seeks to examine and elaborate on these assertions regarding complexity of cause and the parallel need for complexity of intervention.

COMPLEXITY OF CAUSE

A teacher walking down a school corridor turns a corner and comes upon a student, one of her students, spray-painting his initials across the doors of several student lockers. Later that day, the teacher meets with the assistant principal to discuss the incident—both its causes and its consequences. It is in my experience quite common that, in discussions such as these, both teacher and administrator will focus their attention *exclusively* on the perpetrator. "Johnny is a chronically bad kid [or a good kid]. He is angry, or aggressive, or misunderstood, or abused, or sleepy, or whatever. We should caution him, deny him certain privileges, discipline him, detain him, suspend him." Is something missing here? Is the teacher's and the assistant principal's view of both causality and cure too limited. I do not want to belabor the central theme of earlier chapters of this book; I simply wish to reiterate that every act of aggression, including vandalistic acts, is a person–environment event. This perspective on complexity of cause is elaborated in Table 6.1.

If Table 6.1's assertion of complex person–environment causality for all acts of aggression is correct, then it logically follows that such complexity must also optimally characterize intervention attempts. Cure must follow cause. In a related context, I sought to concretize this perspective further:

> The call for complexity of solution has been heard before, from the community psychologist (Heller, Price, Reinharz, Riger, Wandersman, & D'Aunno, 1984), the ecological psychologist (Moos & Insel, 1974), the environmental designer (Krasner, 1980) and the systems analyst (Plas, 1986).... To have even a modest chance of enduring success, interventions designed to reduce aggression towards persons or property in school contexts must be oriented not only towards the aggressor himself, but also at the levels of the teacher, school administration and organization, and the larger community context. Furthermore ... an optimally complex intervention designed to reduce school violence ought to seek to do so via a variety of modes or channels. The first requisite, therefore, which we propose as necessary for the effective planning of a successful aggression reduction intervention is multilevel, multichannel complexity. (Goldstein, 1988, p. 294)

In the section which follows, I draw upon the vandalism intervention pool presented in Chapter 5 in order to illustratively reorganize the sample of intervention thus selected into just such multilevel, multichannel configurations. In the absence of efficacy evaluations, no particular interventions or intervention configurations can be singled out for recommended use at this time. However, I believe that the emphasis illustrated below on the selection and implementation of meaningful intervention *combinations* is likely to prove a major step forward vis-à-vis effective impact on vandalism prevention, control, and reduction.

TABLE 6.1. Multiple Causes of Aggressive Behavior

I. Person variables	
Physiological predisposition	Male gender and associated testosterone and temperament levels
Cognitive-affective patterns	Attribution of hostile intent, projection of blame, mislabeling, moral reasoning level
Interpersonal skills	Self-control, anger management, prosocial skill alternatives
II. Environment variables	
Cultural context	Societal traditions and mores which encourage or restrain aggression
Immediate interpersonal environment	Parental or peer criminality; peer pressure; video, film, and live models of aggression
Immediate physical environment	Temperature, crowding, surveillance probability, incivilities
Presence of disinhibitors	Alcohol, drugs, successful aggressive models
Presence of means	Weapons, tools, spray paint, markers, bricks
Presence of targets	Windows, walls, transit vehicles, fencing

COMPLEXITY OF INTERVENTION

Table 6.2 presents a level-by-channel intervention schema, in this instance targeted to the reduction of vandalism in school contexts. My intent here is clearly to urge both practitioners and evaluators of vandalism prevention and reduction efforts to include, in their packages or sets of interventions, interventions selected across both levels and channels.

A second, factorial schema seeking to reflect in its particulars the desirable complexity of vandalism intervention programming is that offered by Harootunian (1986). Instead of mode or channel of intervention, Harootunian's proposal crosses level of intervention with intended goal:

> Various actions taken against aggression are initiated to prevent or discourage hostile acts directed against persons or school property. Such measures as 24-hour custodial service and better lighting are designed to prevent aggression. The use of plexiglass windows may not prevent aggressive acts, but it will certainly reduce the incidence of broken windows. Compensatory inter-

TABLE 6.2. A Multilevel-Multichannel Schema for the Reduction of School Vandalism

Level of Intervention	Mode of Intervention				
	Psychological	Educational	Administrative	Legal	Physical
Community	Youth vacation vigil program	Arson education programs	Adopt-a-school programs	Monetary fines	Citizen, police, parent patrols
School	Conflict negotiation programs	Year-round education	Schools-within-a-school	Codes of rights responsibilities	Lighting, painting, paving programs
Teacher	School–home collaboration	Multicultural sensitivity training	Reduced teacher–student ratio	Property marking with school ID	Distribution of faculty offices throughout school
Student	Interpersonal skills training	Vandalism awareness walks	School detention, suspension	Restitution, student vandalism accounts	Graffiti boards, mural walls

ventions do not in themselves change aggressive or disruptive students, but they do offset the consequences of their actions. Remedial interventions, on the other hand, are aimed at changing students, not simply providing them with ways of circumventing their aggressive acts (Harootunian, 1994, p. 204)

Table 6.3 illustrates this levels-by-goals perspective.

Beyond the multilevel-multigoal vandalism intervention combinations derivable from Table 6.3, in the actual practice of planning and implementing vandalism prevention and reduction programs, the thrusts of Tables 6.2 and 6.3 may be combined. Such a three-dimensional schema, based simultaneously on intervention levels, channels, and goals, may be a bit complex to conceptualize but is no more complex than the multiply determined behavior it seeks to alter: vandalism. Further, as Harootunian (1994) noted:

> Any one strategy in isolation often has resulted in confusion, if not contradictory findings. A multiple perspective strategy makes it possible to determine where a suggested intervention or approach fits and how it may influence or be influenced by adjacent solutions. Also, a comprehensive view of school aggression may reveal gaps and overloads in the system. There is evidence, for example (Zwier & Vaughan, 1984), that almost one-half of the literature on school vandalism focuses on the physical dimensions of the school. (p. 206)

TABLE 6.3. A Multilevel-Multigoal Schema for the Reduction of School Vandalism

Level of intervention	Goal of intervention		
	Prevention	Compensatory	Remediation
Community	Adopt-a-school	Less restrictive child labor laws Short-term treatment centers	Family support services
School	24-hour custodial service	Use of plexiglass windows	Prescriptively tailored courses
Teacher	Programs to enhance knowledge of ethnic and minority milieu	Better teacher-pupil ratio	Acquisition of new training techniques in psychological skills, e.g., structured learning
Student	Identification cards	School transfers Part-time programs	Interpersonal training Behavior modification

Source: Harootunian (1986), p. 131. Copyright Allyn & Bacon. Reprinted by permission.

In quite the same factorial spirit as Tables 6.2 and 6.3, Zwier and Vaughan (1984) proposed a vandalism-intervention-combining schema which crosses level of intervention (defined differently from above) with ideological orientation. Educational practices in America's public schools have long been fair game for broad and often intense public concern and debate. This spotlight of attention most certainly includes disciplinary practices. Harootunian (1994) quite correctly noted that, in order for a specific intervention to be accepted and implemented and have a chance of succeeding, the values it elicits must, to an appreciable degree, overlap with the values or ideologies of those who are asked to accept and participate in its implementation. Table 6.4 details this level-by-ideology perspective.

As noted above, these ideological perspectives are the basis of considerable historical and current debate and contentiousness in the United States. My position is, at this point, appropriately an empirical one. Whether sets of vandalism interventions reflecting one or another ideological orientation (crossed with levels) will prove most efficacious, or mixing of ideological implementations, is a matter for yet-to-be conducted efficacy evaluations. Whichever ideological stance(s) guides the selection and implementation of interventions, and whichever levels, channels, or goals are also reflected therein, there are three qualities of such programming which I believe are essential to their success. Vandalism intervention, I would assert, must be comprehensive, prescriptive, and appreciative.

OPTIMAL INTERVENTION CHARACTERISTICS

Comprehensive Programming

As quite directly implied in the presentation and discussion of Tables 6.1 through 6.4, I view vandalism as a complexly determined phenomenon requiring equally complex intervention response. The notions of person–environment duet, levels of intervention, multiple channels or modes of responses, diverse intervention goals, and varied intervention ideologies are each in their respective ways calls for comprehensive intervention combinations.

Prescriptive Programming

This second, highly desirable quality of interventions offered was also examined earlier, in our look at the value of differential, tailored, individualized, or prescriptive interventions. *Vandalism* is a term identifying a very wide array of behaviors, expressing exceedingly diverse motivations, car-

TABLE 6.4. The Relationship between Ideological Orientation, Assumption Concerning the Cause of School Vandalism, and Type of Solution Offered[a]

Ideological orientation and assumption of cause	Type of solution: ← Specific — Physical environment	School system	Diffuse → Community at large
Conservative Vandals are deviant. They must be caught and punished.	Protection of school and school grounds, employment of security officers and caretakers[a]	Encouragement and enforcement of school rules, use of contingency contracts	Involvement of community in antivandalism patrols and (parent) restitution programs, dependence on judicial system
Liberal The school system is malfunctioning. Vandals capitalize on this.	(Superficial) improvement of the design, appearance, and layout of the school grounds	Modifications in school climate, curriculum, and use of special conflict management programs[a]	Extension of recreational activities, use of school after hours for health and social services
Radical The school system is debilitating. Vandalism is a response of normal individuals to abnormal conditions.	Promotion of radical changes in the structure and appearance of the school, approval of policy to decrease the size of large schools, and maintain small schools	Provision of student involvement in decision-making process, adoption of changes in assessment procedures, and exploration of alternative schooling methods	Involvement of the whole community in school affairs, installment of community education programs, improvement of social situation in society at large[a]

[a]The solution considered most favorably by the particular ideological orientation.
Source: Zwier and Vaughan (1984, p. 269). Copyright 1984 the American Education Research Association. Reprinted by permission.

ried out in a great variety of settings, and enacted by persons differing widely in age, experience, past antisocial behavior, peer-group affiliation, system support, and numerous other characteristics possibly relevant to intervention effectiveness. One size does not fit all.

Understandably, most discussions of differential or prescriptive intervention programming, whether directed toward vandalism or otherwise, have focused on examining which type(s) of interventions should be employed with which type(s) of perpetrators. There is, however, an important third aspect of optimal prescriptions.

> Optimal prescriptions should be tridifferential, specifying type of intervention by type of client by type of change agent. This last class of variable merits attention. Interventions as received by youths to whom they are directed are never identical to the [intervention] procedures as specified in a textbook or treatment manual. In actual practice, the intervention specified in a manual is interpreted and implemented by the change agent and perceived and experienced by the youths. The change agent looms large in this sequence.... Who administers the intervention does make a difference. (Goldstein, 1993b, pp. 479–480)

Appreciative Programming

Vandalism is committed by Caucasian, African-American, Latino, Asian, Native American and other children, adolescents, and adults. Such perpetrator diversity not only has implications for how a given intervention is best presented, and by whom, but also optimally impacts on the very structure and content of the intervention itself. One prime route to maximizing the impact of intervention structure and content is to involve persons representative of the ultimate target group(s) in the intervention's development. Effective interventions cannot be developed only from the outside looking in. The very meaning of vandalistic behavior; the perception and potency of its consequences; the role of peer pressure, neighborhood incivility, and other external influences; and the apparent appropriateness and utility of alternative interventions—all ought to be profitably viewed through the age-graded, gender-associated, and cultural lenses of the likely perpetrators and intervention targets. Whether by means of formal or informal "consumer consultants," focus groups, or in other ways, such "inside information" is likely to prove most useful in the effort to enhance intervention efficacy.

I have urged that rationally composed vandalism-intervention combinations be planned comprehensively, prescriptively, and appreciatively. I further urge that such interventions be implemented with adequate attention to intervention integrity, intensity, and coordination.

INTERVENTION INTEGRITY

Intervention integrity is the degree to which the intervention as actually implemented corresponds to the intervention as planned. Intervention integrity may be problematic for a number of reasons. An adequately detailed plan may never have been developed. Ideally, interventions to be carried out will first be described in full, sequential, user-friendly detail in "treatment manuals" that can both be widely distributed and serve as concrete, step-by-step intervenor systematic guides. Even when such a manual has been developed, distributed, and read, intervention monitoring will often reveal substantial discrepancies (i.e., low intervention integrity) between plan and reality. Other responsibilities, large teaching loads, extra bus routes to drive, and larger areas to surveil may all lead to overburdened, tired, or lazy intervenors. Distractions, emergencies, exigencies, or other "realities" may detour the practitioner from the intervention plan. Intervenor supervision or monitoring, intended to "keep interventions on track," may be inadequate or may fail to materialize altogether. Even if appropriately described, detailed, and exemplified in a vandalism intervention procedures manual, the plan may fail to anticipate an array of significant circumstances. For interventions to succeed in their intended purpose, integrity to plan is a crucial prerequisite.

INTERVENTION INTENSITY

Intensity concerns the amount, quantity, or dosage of the intervention provided. Vandalism, as but one expression of aggression, is often a chronic, overlearned, well-reinforced behavior. One-shot, short-term, or otherwise limited interventions will rarely, if ever, be potent enough to prevent or remediate such behavior on anything approaching a sustained basis. Consider a small sampling of the intervention tactics listed in the preceding chapter: locks, tamper-proof hardware, the steering of pathway circulation, spray paint sales control, the use of closed-circuit TV, the hiring of citizens for watch patrols, the collection of restitution, curricula revision, and antivandalism education and publicity. In each instance, the intervenor needs to ask: Is this enough, or strong enough, or numerous enough, or sustained enough? These are questions of intervention intensity.

INTERVENTION COORDINATION

Because I have placed so great an emphasis on intervention combinations or sets as a necessary requirement for successful vandalism prevention and reduction, and because person–environment targeting, levels of intervention, and multichannelness each mean that a variety of persons and agencies may be offering parts of the intervention combination, the coordination of effort becomes a significant concern. As I have observed elsewhere:

> Society's agents often work in splendid isolation from one another. Their efforts are sometimes conflicting or at cross purposes, often quite independent, and infrequently additive. Not unlike the far too specialized physician who has not a "whole patient" but "an interesting liver" on his ward, agency personnel often fail to see and respond to ... youth as a gestalt. Instead, they concern themselves exclusively with their own segmented, limited domain, or mandated agency focus. When this occurs, the potential for uncoordinated, nonadditive, and conflicting interventions is high. Major attention to intervention coordination is crucial, especially in the context of comprehensive intervention programming, in which a number of diversely targeted agencies may be simultaneously involved with the same youth. (Goldstein, 1993, p. 484)

Given that the intervenor has striven to incorporate in his or her intervention program the several desirable features described above, the remaining—and often ignored—crucial intervention task is competent evaluation of efficacy. The section which follows seeks to describe an array of considerations relevant to enhancing the quality of such efficacy evaluations.

INTERVENTION EVALUATION

With very few notable exceptions, the current state of the art regarding evaluations of vandalism interventions—whether singly or in combination—is rudimentary, inadequate, and, most often, nonexistent. Levy-Leboyer's (1984) observation of over a decade ago is equally accurate today:

> A large portion of the literature on vandalism is opinionative and characterizable by a lamentable lack of scientific rigor. The divergent conclusions and recommendations are, in large part, based on ad hoc interpretations and attributable to difference in (or the absence of) definitions of vandalism and the operationalization of contributing factors, the variety of data gathering techniques employed (if any), the lack of control for influences of extraneous variables, and the absence of systematic considerations concerning theory, research design, and sampling procedure. The evidence brought forward in support of a given viewpoint is more often than not informal in nature and based on casual observations and personal professional experiences. (p. 20)

Clearly, in the domain of vandalism research—be it about cause, cure, or otherwise—much investigative reform and reinvigoration is needed.

Such research must increasingly be *theory-driven*, its hypotheses derived from systematic theoretical positions, its findings feeding back to and refining such positions. At present, the pool of vandalism theories, and their stages of research-supported development, is meager. Enjoyment theory (Csikszentimihalyi & Larsen, 1978), aesthetic theory (Allen & Greenberger, 1978), and, especially, equity-control theory (Fisher & Baron, 1982) each seem to be positions pregnant with the promise of aiding our understanding of vandalism's cause, increasing our ability to predict its occurrence, and improving our success in intervening effectively. They, as well as several of the even-less-developed, nascent theories enumerated in Chapter 3, well deserve further investigative scrutiny.

In the planning and conduct of such research, the *experimental designs* employed must become more sophisticated, more able to rule out rival hypotheses regarding causation or intervention effectiveness. As Levy-Leboyer's (1984) observation above indicates, currently employed designs, for far too long, have remained those approaches typically employed in the beginning stages of a field of inquiry. In vandalism research, there has been near-exclusive reliance on case studies, mailed questionnaire surveys, interview series, and testimonials provided by professionals. Clearly, after decades of such necessary but preliminary inquiry, it is time to move on to more complex and informative designs. We urge the examination of vandalism intervention efficacy via both between-group and intrasubject designs.

Given the earlier stress on the value of implementing intervention combinations, the *evaluation strategies* suggested here each involve "intervention packages." Evaluators may compare full intervention combinations or packages with the full intervention minus one or more of its components in order to determine which components are active (the dismantling evaluation strategy). Or the evaluator, building incrementally, may begin with a single intervention or a circumscribed subset and proceed to add components, making stepwise comparisons with each addition (the constructive evaluation strategy). Alternatively, two or more full intervention combinations may be compared (the comparative evaluation strategy).

Measurement of effect in the more formal evaluation experiments I am urging will optimally possess certain desirable qualities. First, it will be multisource. No one concerned with the impact of an intervention—investigator, youth, teacher, peers, or family—perceives the "truth." Each reports her or his own, idiosyncratic, subjective perspectives. Truth can best be construed as information combined to reflect diverse subjective viewpoints, whether they converge or diverge. Second, measurement will also ideally be multimethod. It has been demonstrated that measuring-instrument responses are in part a function of the form of that measure. Use of diverse types of evaluation measures—self-report, other-report, archival, and behavioral—can potentially compensate in substantial part for this source of error variance. Both proximal and distal effectiveness criteria will optimally be included in the evaluation's dependent variable measurement. Proximal measures seek to reflect changes in the vandal's behavior and attitudes that were the direct target of the intervention provided. If, for example, interpersonal and conflict-management-skills training were the interventions implemented, the pre- to postchange in these very skill levels would be the proximal effectiveness measure. That is, did the youth learn what was taught? Distal measures seek to capture derivative changes, that is, changes that, in turn, are potentiated if direct changes first occur. If the youth's skill level (the proximal measure) has advanced, less actual vandalistic behavior (the distal measure) should occur.

Both proximal and distal measurement of intervention effectiveness will optimally be conducted on both an immediate postintervention and extended *follow-up* basis. Interventions rarely, if ever, serve as inoculations. Even when immediately effective, durability of gain quite frequently does not occur. Nor should we necessarily expect it to, both because existing interventions are often not that potent and because the real-life environment of many vandalistic persons (e.g., vandalistic peers and vandalized physical environments) often pushes such persons in a direction quite opposite from that targeted by the intervention. Thus, in order to discern whether and to what degree the intervention(s) being employed is powerful enough to reverse this common failure of generalization and yield proximal and/or distal effects that do endure, long-term follow-up measurements of the interventions outcome are crucial. Such long-term follow-up information, in addition to the central issue of discerning the degree of vandalism prevention and reduction, will also provide utilitarian cost–benefit information vis-à-vis the interventions being evaluated.

In selecting the investigation's experimental design, evaluation strategy, and battery of measures, it is important to strive for a balance of experimental rigor and real-world relevance in the research to be conducted. In speaking of this goal of *rigor-relevance balance*, Lindsley (1965) suggested there exist three orientations to intervention evaluation. The first is the "Rigorless Magician" orientation, a "shoot-from-the-hip," "impressions-count-for-everything" stance held by the individual who eschews objective measurement and relies totally on practitioner judgment. At the opposite extreme is the "Rigor Mortician," so fixated on objective measurement that he or she sacrifices the richness, uniqueness, and individuality of the phenomena being studied in the effort to obtain standardized measurement information. At an intermediate position, and to be recommended, is the Rigorous Clinician. Here, the balance of rigor of experimental design and measurement and relevance to the real world of those being studied is the goal. Rigor of the evaluation conducted is facilitated by use of the several design, strategic, and measurement recommendations I have offered above. Relevance of the evaluation to the real world of vandalistic behavior—that is, its external, ecological, or social validity—may be promoted in several ways, but most especially by assuming an appreciative intervention perspective calling at each stage of the research process for serious, in-depth consultation with, and open listening to, the several types of persons actually involved in the act of vandalism: vandal, victim, intervenor, and others. Vandalism research most certainly needs the efforts of the Rigorous Clinician.

CHAPTER 7

ECOVANDALISM AND PSYCHOLOGICAL INQUIRY

This book has sought, in both broad sweep and fine detail, to examine the nature of vandalism and vandalism intervention in contemporary society. We have considered its frequency and costs, definitions and demographics, typologies and theories of causation, strategies and tactics of intervention, means of combining tactics into effective intervention programs, and guidelines for rigorously evaluating the effectiveness of such programs. Collectively, those several topics combine to almost, but not quite, complete the psychology-of-vandalism picture we seek to present. What remains to be addressed is the topic of ecovandalism.

By all current definitions of the term, vandalism includes deliberately broken windows, initials carved in picnic tables, the building destroyed by arson, graffiti at the train station, and the numerous other individual and collective acts of damage, disfigurement, and destruction identified throughout this book. I would also assert, however, that an expanded, properly inclusive definition of vandalism is appropriate and desirable and ought to subsume such behaviors as environmentally damaging and disfiguring "illegal" (and much legal) waste disposal; the demolition of historically and socially irreplaceable structures in the name of "development"; air, water, and noise pollution; massive energy overconsumption; high levels of littering in a broad array of public venues; and many of the other environmental ills and degradation so prominently examined in recent years as part of what has come to be known as the *environmental movement* (Gore, 1993; Goudie, 1994; Hawken, 1993; Spirn, 1984; Stone, 1993). Such "official vandalism" (Ward, 1973), "corporate vandalism" (Hills, 1987), "political vandalism" (Cohen, 1984), institutional vandalism

(Perlgut, 1983), calculated and contrived vandalism (Ward, 1973), "pinstripe vandalism" (Downes, 1966), and "developer vandalism" (Cruickshank, 1973) very much belong as part of a comprehensive treatise on the psychological causes, prevention, and remediation of vandalistic behavior.

The contributions of psychology, actual and potential, to the domain of ecovandalism are numerous, but largely still in their initial stages. Many beginnings have been offered, and below I wish to both enumerate their topical concerns and encourage their continued development. Just as I indicated earlier was true of vandalism in school, transit, park, and other public settings, the overwhelming current emphasis of environmentally preventive and reparative efforts in contemporary society rests primarily on the alteration of technology, not human behavior. I believe the role of the human behavior expert vis-à-vis ecovandalism has been greatly underestimated and underused. As Cone and Hayes (1980) observed:

> The imbalance of physical and behavioral technology seems to be at the root of many of society's difficulties, and none more so than environmental problems. It is that without knowing how to control it we are in danger of its controlling us. Behavioral technology can help us put physical technology to appropriate use. (p. 5)

Thus, I wish to urge further commitment to—and hope for the blossoming of—such topics of inquiry as the study of environmental issues as they relate to human values (Clark, Hendee, & Campbell, 1971), personality (Borden, 1985a; Stokols, 1978), future orientation (McKnight, 1978; Randers & Meadows, 1973), political orientation (Arbuthnot, 1977; Dunlap, 1975), and authoritarianism (Barone, 1970; Schultz & Stone, 1994); environmental awareness (Hoover, & Schutz, 1963); environmental aesthetics (Cone & Hayes, 1980); environmental perception (Nasar, 1989; Zube, Sell, & Taylor, 1982); environmental concern (Borden & Schettino, 1979; Levinson, 1974); environmental beliefs (Bart, 1972; Borden, 1985b); environmental attitudes (Ramsey & Rickson, 1976; Weigel, 1985); the relation of such attitudes to environmentally relevant behavior (Dillehay, 1973; Fishbein & Ajzen, 1974); the measurement of environmental attitudes (Dunlap & Van Liere, 1978; Maloney, Ward, & Braucht, 1975); the diffusion of ecological responsibility (Peterson & Borden, 1978); the activation of prosocial environmental norms (Heberlein, 1972); the tragedy of the commons (Cass & Edney, 1978; Platt, 1973); the use of fear appeals (Baldassare & Katz, 1992; Hass & Bagley, 1975); and such additional, individual qualities as altruism (Bateson, 1991; Hopper & Nielsen, 1991), empathy (Goldstein & Michaels, 1985; Harter, 1992), ego development (Wood, 1983), moral reasoning level (Olson, 1981), and experience of personal environmental threat (Baldassare & Katz, 1992).

Psychology has also been active as a discipline regarding efforts to

The dimensions of toxic exposure are staggering, reflecting our dependence upon an increasingly synthetic world. Some 70,000 chemicals are in regular use in the United States and another 1,000 are added every year. This includes 1 billion pounds of pesticides, herbicides, and fungicides used in the United States every day. Beyond toxic exposure due to the manufacture, transportation, storage, and use of these materials, this country generates between 255 million and 275 million metric tons of hazardous waste annually, of which as much as 90 percent is improperly disposed of. Such figures routinely exclude the military, historically one of the worst polluters. In 1984 alone, more than 530,000 tons of hazardous waste were produced at 333 U.S. military installations.

The results of this societal chemical dependence are shocking if not surprising. The Office of Technology Assessment estimates that there are some 600,000 contaminated sites in the country, of which 888 sites have been designated or proposed by the Environmental Protection Agency for priority cleanup under the Superfund program, with another 19,000 sites under review. In addition, there are another 400,000 municipal landfills, more than 100,000 liquid waste impoundments, millions of septic tanks, hundreds of thousands of deep-well injection sites, and some 300,000 leaking underground gasoline storage tanks threatening groundwater. Hundreds of planned and operating garbage incinerators are generating new concerns about air pollution and highly toxic ash residues. And this list merely scratches the surface of causes for residential toxic exposure. A complete chronicle of residential toxic exposure would also include the countless sites where wastes have been illegally or inadvertently dumped; the existence of naturally occurring toxins such as radon gas; exposure to radioactive wastes; toxic substances in building materials, home heating sources, foods, and household items; and the widespread use of pesticides in agriculture, forestry, lawn care, termite control, utility right-of-way maintenance, and in routine home applications.

Source: M. R. Edelstein (1988). *Contaminated communities: The social and psychological impacts of residential toxic exposure*. Boulder, CO: Westview Press, p. 3.

> Modern industrial civilization, as presently organized, is colliding violently with our planet's ecological system. The ferocity of its assault on the earth is breathtaking, and the horrific consequences are occurring so quickly as to defy our capacity to recognize them, comprehend their global implications, and organize an appropriate and timely response. Isolated pockets of resistance fighters who have experienced this juggernaut at first hand have begun to fight back in inspiring but, in the final analysis, woefully inadequate ways. It is not that they lack courage, imagination, or skill; it is simply that what they are up against is nothing less than the current logic of world civilization. As long as civilization as a whole, with its vast technological power, continues to follow a pattern of thinking that encourages the domination and exploitation of the natural world for short-term gains, this juggernaut will continue to devastate the earth no matter what any of us does.
>
> I have come to believe that we must take bold and unequivocal action; we must make the rescue of the environment the central organizing principle for civilization. Whether we realize it or not we are now engaged in an epic battle to right the balance of our earth, and the tide of this battle will turn only when the majority of people in the world become sufficiently aroused by a shared sense of urgent danger to join an all-out effort.
>
> *Source*: A. Gore (1993). *Earth in the balance*. New York: Penguin, p. 269.

apply and evaluate interventions targeted to the prevention and reduction of ecovandalism. These several intervention targets have included waste management (Cone & Hayes, 1980; West, Lee, & Feiock, 1992); littering (Cope & Geller, 1981; Finnie, 1973); energy conservation (Doctors, Beck, & Hammond, 1980; Kohlenberg, Phillips, & Proctor, 1976); pollution (Hass, Bagley, & Rogers, 1975; Van Liere & Dunlap, 1978); recycling (Geller, Chaffee, & Ingram, 1975; Luyben & Bailey, 1979); transportation conservation (Foxx & Hake, 1977; Haywood & Everett, 1975); noise control (Glass & Singer, 1972; Meyers, Artz, & Craighead, 1976); and nuclear safeguards (Bowman & Fishbein, 1978). To date, by far the majority of such ecovandalism intervention efforts have employed primarily behavior modification procedures. These have included prior instructions (Dodge, 1972; Geller, Chaffee, & Ingram, 1973); environmental education (Reich & Robertson, 1979; Winett, 1980); feedback (Hayes & Cone, 1977a,b; Kohlenberg & Anschell, 1980); monitoring (Hayes, 1977; Winett, Neale, & Grier, 1979); modeling (Geller, Winett, & Everett, 1982; Jason, Zolik, & Matese, 1979); public commitment (Manzo & Weinstein, 1987; McCaul & Kopp, 1982); incentives of various types (Geller, 1992; Luyben & Bailey, 1979); and several combinations of the foregoing procedures (Baltes & Haywood, 1976; Clark, Burgess, & Hendee, 1972; McClelland & Belsten, 1979). Finally, as yet a further sign of the admirable degree of investigative rigor characteristic of so many of these beginning evaluations of ecovandalism interventions, a number of the reported studies have also given careful attention to the question of the generalization of ecological change (Cone & Hayes, 1980; Couch, Garber, & Karpis, 1978–1979; Kazdin, 1979).

I have provided above a substantial listing of ecological and ecovandalism topics, targets and interventions already receiving at least a beginning—and often more—of psychological investigative scrutiny. I am impressed by the range of these efforts and most strongly urge their continued and energetic pursuit.

REFERENCES

Abramson, P. (1977). How secure are your schools? *American School and University, 49,* 29–31.

Agnew, R. (1985). A revised strain theory of delinquency. *Social Forces, 64,* 151–167.

Akers, R. L. (1985). *Deviant behavior.* Belmont, CA: Wadsworth.

Akiyama, Y., & Pfeiffer, P. C. (1984). Arson: A statistical profile. *FBI Law Enforcement Bulletin, 53,* 9–13.

Allen, V. L., & Greenberger, D. B. (1978). An aesthetic theory of vandalism. *Crime and Delinquency, 24,* 309–321.

Altman, I., Brown, B. B., Staples, B., & Werner, C. M. (1992). A transactional approach to close relationships: Courtship, weddings and placemaking. In W. B. Walsh, K. H. Craik, & R. H. Price (Eds.), *Person-environment psychology: Models and perspectives.* Hillsdale, NJ: Erlbaum.

Amoroso, L. J. (1977). Public school property losses and vandalism. *Security World, 14,* 122.

Andel, H. V. (1989). Crime prevention that works: The care of public transport in the Netherlands. *British Journal of Criminology, 29,* 47–56.

Anderson, J. (1977). *Vandalism in the Unified School District of Los Angeles County.* Doctoral dissertation, University of Southern California, Los Angeles.

Angyal, A. (1959). *Foundations for a science of personality.* Cambridge: Harvard University Press.

Anon. (1965). How one district licked vandalism. *School Management, 9,* 93–94.

Anon. (1966). Vandalism: How one district fights it—and wins. *School Management, 10,* 101–105.

Anon. (1967). Putting an end to vandalism. *School Management, 11,* 25.

Anon. (1971). Vandals don't like the spotlight. *American School and University, 43,* 26–28.

Anon. (1972). Vandalism—Why? (Film) Los Angeles: Alfred Higgins Productions.

Anon. (1973). Vandalism: Take tempting targets out of washrooms. *The Nation's Schools, 92,* 44–45.

Anon. (1974a). Live-in "school sitters" are saving this district thousands of dollars. *The American School Board Journal, 161*, 36–39.

Anon. (1974b). Parent patrols are scaring would-be vandals. *American School Board Journal, 161*, 38–39.

Anon. (1976). Only you can stop it. (Film). Pasadena, CA: Barr Films.

Anon. (1978a). Protecting buildings from people. *Progressive Architecture, 59*, 88–95.

Anon. (1978c, March). Vandals. *Justice of the Peace*, pp. 169–172.

Anon. (1979a). *Vandalism: A study of school vandalism*. San Marcos: Center for Juvenile Delinquency, Southwest Texas State University.

Anon. (1979b). Vandalism game. Lincoln: Nebraska 4-H Activities.

Anon. (1980a). *Country crime: What you can do*. Washington, DC: American Association of Retired Persons.

Anon. (1980b). Vandalism—A police viewpoint. Winchester, England: Hampshire Constabulary Crime Prevention Department.

Anon. (1980c). *Violence and vandalism in the public schools of Hawaii*. Honolulu, HI: Hawaii Crime Commission.

Anon. (1983a). *Anti-vandalism guide for construction sites*. Baltimore: Baltimore Campaign Against Vandalism Business and Industry Subcommittee.

Anon. (1983b). *Dormitory vandalism on SUNY campuses*. Albany: New York Legislative Commission on Expenditure Review.

Anon. (1983c). *Reducing school crime: A guide to program interventions*. Berkeley, CA: Social Action Research Center.

Anon. (1984). *Wipe out vandalism*. Washington, DC: American Association of Retired Persons.

Anon. (1990). School crime in California for the 1988–1989 school year. Sacramento: California State Department of Education.

Anon. (1991). *School safety project: Product evaluation, 1990–1991*. Saginaw: Michigan Department of Evaluation Services.

Anon. (1992a). *Annual report and crime summary, 1992*. Overland Park, KS: Department of Safety and Security.

Anon. (1992b). Violence, vandalism, and substance abuse in New Jersey Schools, 1990–1991. Trenton: New Jersey Department of Education.

Arbuthnot, J. (1977). The roles of attitudinal and personality variables in the prediction of environmental behavior and knowledge. *Environment and Behavior, 9*, 217–232.

Baldassare, M., & Katz, C. (1992). The personal threat of environmental problems as predictors of environmental practices. *Environment and Behavior, 24*, 602–616.

Ballinger, C. (1993). *Annual report to the Association on the Status of Year-Round Education*. San Diego: National Association for Year-Round Education.

Baltes, M. M., & Haywood, S. C. (1976). Application and evaluation of strategies to reduce pollution: Behavioral control of littering in the football stadium. *Journal of Applied Psychology, 61*, 501–506.

Bandura, A. (1973). *Aggression: A social learning analysis*. Englewood Cliffs, NJ: Prentice Hall.

Bandura, A. (1986). *Social foundations of thought and action*. Englewood Cliffs, NJ: Prentice Hall.

Barker, R. G., & Gump, P. (1964). *Big school, small school*. Stanford, CA: Stanford University Press.

Barker, R. G., & Wright, H. F. (1954). *Midwest and its children*. New York: Harper & Row.

Barone, J. (Ed.). (1970). *An interdisciplinary study of some environmental, social, and economic factors affecting a section of the Cuyahoga River watershed*. Kent, OH: Kent State University Center for Urban Regionalism.

Bart, W. M. (1972). A hierarchy among attitudes toward the environment. *Journal of Environmental Education, 4*, 10–14.

Batiste, F. (1991). Invasion of the vandals. *Mass Transit, 18*, 50–51.

Bateson, C. D. (1991). *The altruism question: Toward a social-psychological answer*. Hillsdale, NJ: Erlbaum.

Baughman, P. (1971). *Vandalism and its prevention*. Los Angeles: Association of School Business Officials.

Bayh, B. (1978). School discipline, violence and vandalism: Implications for teacher preparation. *Action in Teacher Education, 1*, 3–10.

Bell, M. M., Bell, M. M., & Godefroy, K. (1992). The impact of graffiti on neighborhoods and one community's response. In H. H. Christensen, D. R. Johnson, & M. Brookes (Eds.), *Vandalism: Research, prevention, and social policy*. Portland, OR: U.S. Department of Agriculture Forest Service.

Bennett, D. W. (1977). *Statement of Donald W. Bennett, Federal Railroad Administration*. From Railroad Vandalism—Hearing before the House of Representatives, March 9, 1977.

Berlyne, D. E. (1960). *Conflict, arousal, and curiosity*. New York: McGraw-Hill.

Blauvelt, P. D. (1980). School security doesn't have to break the bank. *Independent School, 40*, 47–50.

Borden, R. J. (1985a). Personality and ecological concerns. In D. B. Gray (Ed.), *Ecological beliefs and behaviors: Assessment and Change*. Westport, CT: Greenwood Press.

Borden, R. J. (1985b). Psychology and ecology: Beliefs in technology and the diffusion of ecological responsibility. *Journal of Environmental Education, 7*, 14–19.

Borden, R. J., & Francis, J. L. (1978). Who cares about ecology? Personality and sex differences in environmental concern. *Journal of Personality, 46*, 190–203.

Borden, R. J., & Schettino, A. P. (1979). Determinants of environmentally responsible behavior: Fact or feelings? *Journal of Environmental Education, 10*, 35–39.

Boss, R. W. (1984). Collection Security. *Library Trends, 33*, 39–48.

Bowles, J. K. (1982). The residence hall vandalism problem: A model for examining destructive behavior. *The Journal of College and University Student Housing, 12*, 15–19.

Bowman, C. H., & Fishbein, M. (1978). Understanding public reaction to energy proposals: An application of the Fishbein model. *Journal of Applied Social Psychology, 8*, 319–340.

Bradshaw, W. G., & Huff, T. G. (1985). Arsonists in California and New York: A tentative look. *Pacific Southwest Forest Experiment Station Research, 372*, 1–5.

Brantingham, P. J., & Brantingham, P. L. (1991). *Environmental criminology*. Newbury Park, CA: Sage

Brenton, M. (1975). School vandalism. *Today's Education, 64*, 84–85.

Brewer, D. D., & Miller, M. L. (1990). Bombing and burning: The social organization and values of hip hop graffiti writers and implications for policy. *Deviant Behavior, 11*, 345–369.

Campbell, A. (1986). The streets and violence. In A. Campbell & J. J. Gibbs (Eds.), *Violent transactions: The limits of personality*. Oxford: Basil Blackwell.

Canter, D. (1980). *Fires and human behavior*. New York: Wiley.

Carr, K., & Spring, G. (1993). *Public transport safety*. Monsey, NY: Willow Tree Press.

Cass, R. C., & Edney, J. J. (1978). The commons dilemma: A simulation testing the effects of resource visibility and territorial division. *Human Ecology, 6*, 371–386.

Cassady, M. E. (1985). *An experimental test of the equity-control model of vandalism*. Master's thesis, University of Connecticut, Storrs.

Casserly, M. D., Bass, S. A., & Garrett, J. R. (1980). *School vandalism: Strategies for prevention*. Lexington, MA: Lexington Books.

Chadda, H. S., & Carter, E. C. (1983). Sign vandalism: Time for action—now. *Institute of Transportation Engineers Journal, 53*, 16–19.

Challinger, D. (1987, June). Principals and police—A pilot study. In D. Challinger (Ed.), *Crime at school*. Canberra, Australia: Seminar Proceedings.

Christensen, H. H., & Clark, R. N. (1978). Understanding and controlling vandalism and other rule violations in urban recreation areas. *National Urban Forestry Conference, 1*, 63–84.

Christensen, H. H., Johnson, D. R., & Brookes, M. (1992). *Vandalism: Research, prevention, and social policy*. Portland, OR: U.S. Department of Agriculture Forest Service.

Christensen, H. H., Mabery, K., McAllister, M. E., & McCormick, D. P. (1988). *Cultural resource protection*. Denver, CO: Rocky Mountain Forest & Range Experiment Station.

Clark, R. N. (1971). *Depreciative behavior in forest campgrounds: An exploratory study*. Portland, OR: Northwest Forest and Range Experiment Station.

Clark, R. N., Burgess, R. L., & Hendee, J. C. (1972). The development of anti-litter behavior in a forest campground. *Journal of Applied Behavior Analysis, 5*, 1–5.

Clark, R. N., Hendee, J. C., & Campbell, F. L. (1971). Values, behavior, and conflict in modern camping culture. *Journal of Leisure Research, 3*, 143–159.

Clarke, R. V. (Ed.). (1992). *Situational crime prevention: Successful case studies*. New York: Harrow & Heston.

Cleland, C. L. (1990). *Crime and vandalism on farms in Tennessee*. Knoxville: Agricultural Experiment Station, Tennessee University.

Cloward, R. A., & Ohlin, L. E. (1960). *Delinquency and opportunity: A theory of delinquent gangs*. New York: Free Press.

Coffield, F. (1991). *Vandalism and graffiti: The state of the art*. London: Calouste Gubbenkian Foundation.

Cohen, L., & Felson, M. (1979). Social change and crime rate trends. *American Sociological Review, 44*, 588–608.

Cohen, L. E., Kleugel, J., & Land, K. (1981). Social inequality and predatory crime victimization: An exposition and test of a formal theory. *American Sociological Review, 46*, 505–524.

Cohen, L. E., & Land, K. C. (1987). Sociological positivism and the explanation of criminality. In M. R. Gottfredson & T. Hirschi (Eds.), *Positive criminology*. Newbury Park, CA: Sage.

Cohen, S. (1971). Direction for research on adolescent school violence and vandalism. *British Journal of Criminology, 9*, 319–340.

Cohen, S. (1973). Campaigning against vandalism. In C. Ward (Ed.), *Vandalism*. London: Architectural Press.

Cohen, S. (1974). Breaking out, smashing up and the social context of aspiration. *Working Papers in Cultural Studies, 5*, 37–63.

Cohen, S. (1984). Sociological approaches to vandalism. In C. Levy-Leboyer (Ed.), *Vandalism: Behaviour and motivations*. North-Holland: Amsterdam.

Cone, J. D., & Hayes, S. C. (1980). *Environmental problems/Behavioral solutions*. Cambridge: University Press.

Conklin, J. E. (1994). *Art crime*. Westport, CT: Praeger.

Cope, J. G., & Geller, E. S. (1981). *Promoting the use of automobile litter bags in community settings*. Unpublished manuscript, Department of Psychology, Virginia Polytechnic Institute, Blacksburg.

Cordess, C., & Turgen, M. (1993). Art vandalism. *British Journal of Criminology, 33*, 95–102.

Cordilia, A. T. (1986). Robbery arising out of a group drinking context. In A. Campbell & J. J. Gibbs (Eds.), *Violent transactions: The limits of personality*. Oxford: Basil Blackwell.

Corwin, S. K. (1978). Adopt-a-station. *School Arts, 78*, 32–33.

Couch, J. V., Garber, T., & Karpis, L. (1978–1979). Response maintenance and paper recycling. *Journal of Environmental Systems, 8*, 127–137.

Cronbach, L. J., & Snow, R. E. (1977). *Aptitudes and instructional methods*. New York: Irvington.

Cross. A. (1979). Vandalism: An Anglo-American perspective. *Police Studies, 2*, 31–38.

Cruickshank, D. (1973). Developers as vandals. In C. Ward (Ed.), *Vandalism*. New York: Van Nostrand.

Csikszentmihalyi, M., & Larsen, R. (1978). *Intrinsic rewards in school crime*. Hackensack, NJ: National Council on Crime and Delinquency.

Csikszentmihalyi, M., Larsen, R., & Prescott, S. (1977). The ecology of adolescent activities and experience. *Journal of Youth and Adolescence, 6*, 281–294.

Dahlstrom, R. (1980). *Crime developments—A 1979 situation report*. Stockholm: Sweden National Council for Crime Prevention.

Daniels, R. (1982). *Controlling vandalism through design—Is it possible?* Rockville, MD: National Institute of Justice.

Davis, D. G. (1971). Security problems in college and university libraries: Student violence. *College and Research Libraries, 32*, 15–22.

DeBunza, C. (1974). *A study of school vandalism: Causes and prevention measures currently found in selected secondary schools throughout Alabama*. Doctoral dissertation, University of Alabama, Montgomery.

deCharms, R. (1968). *Personal causation*. New York: Academic Press.

deCharms, R. (1976). *Enhancing motivation: Change in the classroom*. New York: Irvington.

Deci, E. L. (1975). *Intrinsic motivation*. New York: Plenum.

DeMore, S. W., Fisher, J. D., & Baron, R. M. (1988). The equity-control model as a predictor of vandalism among college students. *Journal of Applied Social Psychology, 18*, 80–91.

Dews, P., & Peters L. (1986). *Ride with pride: Wipe out graffiti and vandalism on our trains and buses*. Brooklyn: New York City Board of Education.

Diem, R. A. (1982). Teaching strategies for dealing with violence and vandalism. *Social Studies, 73*, 172–174.

Dillehay, R. C. (1973). On the irrelevance of the classical negative evidence concerning the effects of attitudes on behavior. *American Psychologist, 28*, 887–891.

Doctors, S. I., Beck, P., & Hammond, D. Y. (1980). *Individual energy conservation behaviors*. Cambridge, MA: Oelgeshlager, Gunn & Hain.

Dodge, K. A. (1980). Social cognition and children's aggressive behavior. *Child Development, 51*, 162–170.

Dodge, K. A. (1993). Social cognitive mechanisms in the development of conduct disorder and depression. *Annual Review of Psychology, 44*, 559–584.

Dodge, M. C. (1972). *Modification of littering behavior: An exploratory study*. Master's thesis, Utah State University, Logan.

Doolittle, M. L., & Lightsey, M. L. (1979). *Southern woods-burners: A descriptive analysis*. Washington, DC: U.S. Department of Agriculture Forest Service.

Downes, D. (1966). *The delinquent solution*. London: Routledge & Kegan Paul.

Ducey, M. (1978). *Vandalism in high schools: An exploratory discussion*. Chicago: Institute for Juvenile Research.

Dukiet, K. (1973). Spotlight on school security. *School Management, 17*, 16–18.

Dunlap, R. E. (1975). The impact of political orientation on environmental attitudes and actions. *Environment and Behavior, 7*, 428–453.

Dunlap, R. E., & Van Liere, K. D. (1978). The "New Environmental Paradigm." *Journal of Environmental Education, 9*, 10–19.

Dust, F. A. (1984). Solution to vandalism lies in developing sense of community. *National Association of Secondary School Principals Bulletin, 68*, 23–26.

Endler, N. S., & Magnusson, D. (1976). Toward an interactional psychology of personality. *Psychological Bulletin, 83*, 956–974.

Epstein, S. (1979). LEAA and arson control. *International Fire Chief, 45*, 16–18.

Federal Bureau of Investigation. (1978). *Crime in the United States*. Washington, DC: U.S. Government Printing Office.

Federal Bureau of Investigation. (1993). *Crime in the United States*. Washington, DC: U.S. Government Printing Office.

Feldman, M. P. (1977). *Criminal behavior: A psychological analysis*. London: Wiley.

Feshbach, S. (1964). The function of aggression and the regulation of aggressive drive. *Psychological Review, 71,* 257–272.

Fey, T. M. (1986). Unholy war. *Security Management, 30,* 115–120.

Finnie, W. C. (1973). Field experiments in litter control. *Environment and Behavior, 5,* 123–144.

Fishbein, M., & Ajzen, I. (1974). Attitudes toward objects as predictors of single and multiple behavioral criteria. *Psychological Review, 81,* 59–74.

Fisher, J. D., & Baron, R. M. (1982). An equity-based model of vandalism. *Population and Environment, 5,* 182–200.

Flaherty, G. (1987). Reducing vandalism by changing the school community. *Thrust for Educational Leadership, 16,* 28–30.

Forgas, J. P. (1986). Cognitive representations of aggression. In A. Campbell & J. Gibbs (Eds.), *Violent transactions: The limits of personality.* Oxford: Basil Blackwell.

Foxx, R. M., & Hake, D. F. (1977). Gasoline conservation: A procedure for measuring and reducing the driving of college students. *Journal of Applied Behavior Analysis, 10,* 61–74.

Franchi, E. A. (1983). *Paraprofessional security aid in an educational setting: A long time needed, a long time coming.* Rockville, MD: National Institute of Justice.

Freedberg, D. (1985). *Iconoclasts and their motives.* Maarssen, The Netherlands: Uitgeverij Gary Schwartz.

Frith, K. (1985). Countering sign vandalism with public service advertising. *Transportation Research Record, 7,* 68–72.

Fujimoto, T. (1987). Problems of juveniles in schools in Japan. *Lay Panel Magazine, 18,* 16–18.

Gaddy, J. R., & Kelly, L. E. (1984). Down safe corridors: Eliminating school disruption. *National Association of Secondary Schools Principals Bulletin, 472,* 13–17.

Gamble, L. R., Sellers, C. P., & Bone, C. E. (1987). School building intrusions: Prevention strategies. *School Business Affairs, 53,* 18–21.

Garbarino, J. (1978). *The human ecology of school crime.* Hackensack, NJ: National Council on Crime and Delinquency.

Gaudet, M. L., & Doyle, P. (1979). *Vandalism—An overview.* Charlottetown, Canada: Prince Edward Island Department of Justice.

Geason, S., & Wilson, P. R. (1990). *Preventing graffiti and vandalism.* Canberra: Australian Institute of Criminology.

Geller, E. S. (1992). Solving environmental problems: A behavior change perspective. In I. Staub & P. Green (Eds.), *Psychology and social responsibility.* New York: New York University Press.

Geller, E. S., Chaffee, J. L., & Ingram, R. E. (1975). Promoting paper recycling on a university campus. *Journal of Environmental Systems, 5,* 39–57.

Geller, E. S., Winett, R. A., & Everett, P. B. (1982). *Preserving the environment.* New York: Pergamon Press.

Gibbs, J. J. (1986). Alcohol consumption, cognition and context: Examining tavern violence. In A. Campbell & J. J. Gibbs (Eds.), *Violent transactions: The limits of personality.* Oxford: Basil Blackwell.

Gladstone, F. J. (1978). Vandalism among adolescent boys. In R. V. G. Clarke (Ed.), *Tackling vandalism*. London: Her Majesty's Stationary Office.

Glass, D. C., & Singer, J. E. (1972). *Urban stress: Experiments on noise and social stressors*. New York: Academic Press.

Goldman, N. (1961). Socio-psychological study of school vandalism. *Crime and Delinquency, 7*, 221–230.

Goldmeir, H. (1974). Vandalism: The effects of unmanageable confrontations. *Adolescence, 9*, 49–56.

Goldstein, A. P. (1978). *Prescriptions for child mental health and education*. New York: Pergamon Press.

Goldstein, A. P. (1988). *The Prepare Curriculum*. Champaign, IL: Research Press.

Goldstein, A. P. (1990). *Delinquents on delinquency*. Champaign, IL: Research Press.

Goldstein, A. P. (1992). *School violence: Its community context and potential solutions*. Testimony presented to Subcommittee on Elementary, Secondary, and Vocational Education, Committee on Education and Labor, U.S. House of Representatives, May 4, 1992.

Goldstein, A. P. (1993a). *Delinquent gangs: A psychological perspective*. Champaign, IL: Research Press.

Goldstein, A. P. (1993b). Gang intervention: Issues and opportunities. In A. P. Goldstein & C. R. Huff (Eds.), *The gang intervention handbook*. Champaign, IL: Research Press.

Goldstein, A. P. (1994). *The ecology of aggression*. New York: Plenum.

Goldstein, A. P. Glick, B., Carthan, W., & Blancero, D. (1994). *The prosocial gang*. Thousand Oaks, CA: Sage.

Goldstein, A. P., Harootunian, B., & Conoley, J. C. (Eds.). (1994). *Student aggression: Prevention, control, replacement*. New York: Guilford.

Goldstein, A. P., & Michaels, G. (1985). *Empathy: Development, training and consequences*. Hillsdale, NJ: Erlbaum.

Goldstein, A. P., & Stein, N. (1976). *Prescriptive psychotherapies*. New York: Pergamon Press.

Gore, A. (1993). *Earth in the balance*. New York: Penguin.

Gottesman, R. (1981). Restitution and parent liability as alternatives to school discipline. *Education Digest, 47*, 25–28.

Goudie, A. (1994). *The human impact on the natural environment*. Cambridge: MIT Press.

Gouke, M. N., & Murfin, M. (1980). Periodical mutilation: The insidious disease. *Library Journal, 105*, 1795–1797.

Graham, F. (1981). Probability of detection and institutional vandalism. *British Journal of Criminology, 21*, 361–365.

Greenberg, B. (1969). *School vandalism: A national dilemma*. Menlo Park, CA: Stanford Research Institute.

Greenberg, M., & Speltz, M. (1988). Attachment and the ontogeny of conduct problems. In J. Belsky & T. Nezworski (Eds.), *Clinical implications of attachment*. Hillsdale, NJ: Erlbaum.

Griffin, P. A. (1982). *An analysis of the school principal's ability to recognize and resolve conflict and its effects on school violence and vandalism*. Doctoral dissertation. University of California, Berkeley.

Griffiths, R., & Shapland, J. M. (1979). The vandal's perspective: Meanings and motives. In P. Bural (Ed.), *Designing against vandalism*. New York: Van Nostrand Reinhold.

Grimditch, R. E. (1973). How to cut down school vandalism. *Education Digest, 38*, 31–33.

Harootunian, B. (1986). School violence and vandalism. In S. J. Apter & A. P. Goldstein (Eds.), *Youth violence: Programs and prospects*. New York: Pergamon Press.

Harootunian, B. (1994). The teacher. In A. P. Goldstein, B. Harootunian, & J. C. Conoley (Eds.), *Student aggression*. New York: Guilford.

Harris, G. D. (1991). "Destructive recreation" on our public forests. *American Forests, 97*, 37–44.

Harrison, A. (1976). Vandalism and depreciative behavior. In G. Sharpe (Ed.), *Interpreting the environment*. New York: Karger Press.

Harter, K. D. (1992). *Expansion of the psychological concept of empathy to include the human relationship to the natural environment*. Doctoral dissertation, California School of Professional Psychology, Los Angeles.

Harvey, P. L. (1983). *Moral development and residence hall vandalism*. Doctoral dissertation, University of Maryland, University Park.

Hass, J. W., Bagley, G., & Rogers, B. (1975). Coping with the energy crisis: Effects of fear appeals upon attitudes toward energy consumption. *Journal of Applied Psychology, 60*, 754–756.

Hauber, A. R. (1980). The social psychology of driving behaviour and the traffic environment: Research on aggressive behavior in traffic. *International Review of Applied Psychology, 29*, 461–474.

Hauber, A. R. (1989). Influencing juvenile offenders by way of alternative sanctions in community settings. In H. Wegener (Ed.), *Criminal behavior and the justice system*. New York: Springer-Verlag.

Hawken, P. (1993). *The ecology of commerce*. New York: Harper Collins

Hawkes, J. D., & Weiss, J. G. (1985). The social development model: An integrated approach to delinquency prevention. *Journal of Primary Prevention, 6*, 73–97.

Hawthorne, W., & Henderson, K. (1992). Combat vandalism program. In H. H. Christensen, D. R. Johnson & M. Brookes (Eds.), *Vandalism: Research, prevention, and social policy*. Portland, OR: U.S. Department of Agriculture Forest Service.

Hayes, S. C. (1977). *The effects of monthly feedback, rebate billing, and consumer directed feedback on the residential consumption of electricity*. Doctoral dissertation, West Virginia University, Morgantown.

Hayes, S. C., & Cone, J. D. (1977a). Decelerating environmentally destructive lawn-walking. *Environment and Behavior, 9*, 511–533.

Hayes, S. C., & Cone, J. D. (1977b). Reducing residential electrical energy use: Payments, information, and feedback. *Journal of Applied Behavioral Analysis, 10*, 425–435.

Haywood, S. C., & Everett, P. B. (1975, May). *A failure of response cost feedback to modify car driving behavior*. Presented at Midwest Association of Behavior Analysis, Chicago.

Hebb, D. O. (1965). Drive and the CNS. *Psychological Review, 62*, 243–252.

Heberlein, T. A. (1972). *Moral norms, threatened sanctions, and littering behavior*. Doctoral dissertation, University of Wisconsin, Madison.

Heller, K., Price, R. H., Reinharz, S., Riger, S., Wandersman, A., & D'Aunno, T. A. (1984). *Psychology and community change*. Homewood, IL: Dorsey Press.

Heller, M. C., & White, M. A. (1975). Rates of teacher verbal approval and disapproval to higher and lower ability classes. *Journal of Educational Psychology, 67*, 796–800.

Heller, N., & Jones, I. R. (1990, April). Highway in the city: Lighting historic Chester. *Highways and Transportation*, pp. 44–49.

Hendrick, C., & Murfin, M. (1974). Project library ripoff: A study of periodical mutilation in a university library. *College and Research Libraries, 35*, 402–411.

Herbert, R. L. (1990). Arson and vandalism in schools: What can the educational psychologist do? *Educational Psychology in Practice, 6*, 65–70.

Hessling, R. B. P. (1992). *Social caretakers and preventing crime on public housing estates*. The Hague: Netherlands Ministry of Justice Research and Documentation.

Higgins, H. C. (1992). Rock art vandalism: Causes and prevention. In H. H. Christensen, D. R. Johnson, & M. Brookes (Eds.), *Vandalism: Research, prevention, and social policy*. Portland, OR: U.S. Department of Agriculture Forest Service.

Hills, S. L. (1987). *Corporate violence: Injury and death for profit*. Savage, MD: Rowman and Littlefield.

Hirschi, T. (1969). *Causes of delinquency*. Berkeley: University of California Press.

Hogan, R., & Jones, W. H. (1985). A role-theoretical model of criminal conduct. In W. S. Laufer & J. M. Day (Eds.), *Personality theory, moral development, and criminal behavior*. Lexington, MA: Lexington Books.

Holland, C. J. (1969). Elimination by the parents of fire-setting behavior in a 7-year-old boy. *Behavior Research and Therapy, 7*, 137.

Hoover, K. H., & Schutz, R. E. (1963). Development of a measure of conservation attitudes. *Science Education, 47*, 63–68.

Hopper, J. R., & Nielsen, J. M. (1991). Recycling as altruistic behavior: Normative and behavioral strategies to expand participation in a community recycling program. *Environment and Behavior, 23*, 195–220.

Howard, E. R. (1978). *School discipline desk book*. West Nyack, NY: Parker.

Howard, J. (1978). Factors in school vandalism. *Journal of Research and Development in Education, 11*, 53–63.

Huisman-Troost, J. E., Drenth, R., Lutterop, E., & deJong, E. A. (1991, February). *Stop, don't destroy your own future: Vandalism prevention project*. Esbjerg, Denmark: Workshop for International Practitioners.

Hunt, D. E. (1972). Matching models for teacher training. In B. R. Joyce & M. Weil (Eds.), *Perspectives for reform in teacher education*. Englewood Cliffs, NJ: Prentice Hall.

Hunt, J. McV. (1965). Intrinsic motivation and its role in psychological development. In D. Levine (Ed.), *Nebraska Symposium on Motivation*. Lincoln: University of Nebraska Press.

Huntington, K. M. (1981). Defending elevators against vandalism. *American School and University, 53*, 46–47.

Ianni, F. A. J. (1979). The social organization of the high school: School-specific aspects of school crime. In E. Wenk & N. Harlow (Eds.), *School crime and disruption*. Davis, CA: Responsible Action.

Irwin, F. G. (1978). Planning vandalism resistant educational facilities. *Journal of Research and Development in Education, 11*, 42–52.

Irwin, J. R. (1976). Vandalism—Its prevention and control. *National Association of Secondary School Principals Bulletin, 60*, 55–59.

Jamieson, B. (1987). Public telephone vandalism. In D. Challinger (Ed.), *Preventing property crime*. Canberra: Australian Institute of Criminology.

Janowitz, M. (1975). Sociological theory and social control. *American Journal of Sociology, 81*, 82–108.

Jason, L. A., Zolik, E. S., & Matese, F. (1979). Prompting dog owners to pick up dog droppings. *American Journal of Community Psychology, 7*, 339–351.

Johnson, D. R., & Swearingen, T. C. (1992). The effectiveness of selected trailside sign texts in deterring off-trail hiking at Paradise Meadow, Mount Rainer National Park. In H. H. Christensen, D. R. Johnson, & M. Brookes (Eds.), *Vandalism: Research, prevention and social policy*. Portland, OR: U.S. Department of Agriculture Forest Service.

Juillerat, E. E., Jr. (1972). Fires and vandals: How to make them both unwelcome in your schools. *The American School Board Journal, 159*, 22–26.

Karchmer, C. (1982). Early intervention in arson epidemics: Developing a motive-based intervention strategy. In J. E. Chidester (Ed.), *Fire research and safety*. Washington, DC: National Bureau of Standards.

Keller, F. S. (1966). A personal course in psychology. In R. Ulrich, T. Stachnik, & J. Mabry (Eds.), *Control of human behavior*. Glenview, IL: Scott Foresman.

Kiesler, D. J. (1969). A grid model for theory and research. In L. D. Eron & R. Callahan (Eds.), *The relation of theory to practice in psychotherapy*. Chicago: Aldine.

Kingston, A. J., & Gentry, H. W. (1977). Discipline problems: Then and now. *National Association of Secondary School Principals Bulletin, 61*, 94–99.

Klippert, J. P. (1992). Reduction of vandalism to traffic control signs in King County, Washington. In H. H. Christensen, D. R. Johnson, & M. Brookes (Eds.), *Vandalism: Research, prevention, and social policy*. Portland, OR: U.S. Department of Agriculture Forest Service.

Kobetz, R. W. (1973). Juvenile vandali$m: The billion dollar prank. *The Police Chief, 40*, 32–34.

Koch, E. L. (1975). School vandalism and strategies of social control. *Urban Education, 10*, 54–72.

Kohlenberg, R. J., & Anschell, S. (1980). *Conclusions and recommendations for electrical energy conservation based on the Washington rate demonstrations project*. Seattle: University of Washington Institute of Governmental Research.

Kohlenberg, R. J., Phillips, T., & Proctor, W. (1976). A behavior analysis of peaking in residential electricity energy consumption. *Journal of Applied Behavior Analysis, 9*, 13–18.

Kornhauser, R. (1978). *Social sources of delinquency*. Chicago: University of Chicago Press.

Krasner, L. (1980). *Environmental design and human behavior*. New York: Pergamon Press.

Krause, D. (1985). Our school C.A.R.E.S. for good behavior. *Principal, 65*, 44–45.

Krause, R. M., Freedman, J. L., & Whitcup, M. (1978). Field and laboratory studies of littering. *Journal of Experimental Social Psychology, 14*, 109–122.

Kruissink, M. (1991). Halt program: Evaluation of a diversion program for juveniles. In J. Junger-Tas & L. Boendermaker (Eds.), *The future of the juvenile justice system*. Thousand Oaks, CA: Sage.

Krupat, E. (1985). *People in cities: The urban environment and its effects*. Cambridge, MA: Cambridge University Press.

Kulka, R. A. (1978). School crime as a function of person-environment fit. *Theoretical perspectives on school crime, 1*, 17–24.

LaGrange, R. L., Ferraro, K. R., & Supanic, M. (1992). Perceived risk and fear of crime: Role of social and physical incivilities. *Journal of Research in Crime and Delinquency, 29*, 311–334.

Lavrakas, P. J. (1982). Fear of crime and behavioral restrictions in urban and suburban neighborhoods. *Population and Environment, 5*, 242–264.

Leftwich, D. (1977). *A study of vandalism in selected public schools in Alabama*. Unpublished doctoral dissertation, University of Alabama, Birmingham.

Lemert, E. M. (1967). *Human deviance, social problems, and social control*. Englewood Cliffs, NJ: Prentice Hall.

Levinson, H. (1974). Involvement in antipollution activities and perceived negative consequences from pollution. *Perceptual and Motor Skills, 38*, 1105–1106.

Levy-Leboyer, C. (Ed.). (1984). *Vandalism: Behavior and motivations*. North Holland: Amsterdam.

Lewin, K. (1935). *A dynamic theory of personality*. New York: McGraw-Hill.

Lewin, K. (1936). *Principles of topological psychology*. New York: McGraw-Hill.

Lewis, D. A., & Salem, G. (1986). Community crime prevention: An analysis of a developing perspective. *Crime and Delinquency, 27*, 405–421.

Libby, T. J. (1980). Reclaiming our turf. *School Arts, 79*, 10–12.

Lindsley, O. (1965, June 6). Personal communication.

Little, B. R. (1987). Personality and the environment. In D. Stokols & I. Altman (Eds.), *Handbook of environmental psychology*. Malabar, FL: Krieger.

Luyben, P. D., & Bailey, J. S. (1979). Newspaper recycling: The effects of rewards and proximity of containers. *Environment and Behavior, 11*, 539–557.

Lyons, S. L. (1982). Lighting designed for defense. *Security Management, 26*, 83–88, 90–93.

MacKenzie, A. (1979). *Defensible space—A police officer's view*. Glasgow: Scottish Association for the Study of Delinquency.

Magaro, P. A. (1969). A prescriptive treatment model based upon social class and premorbid adjustment. *Psychotherapy: Theory, Research and Practice, 6*, 57–70.

Maloney, M. P., Ward, M. P., & Braucht, G. N. (1975). A revised scale for the measurement of ecological attitudes and knowledge. *American Psychologist, 30*, 787–790.

Mancini, A. N., & Jain, R. (1987). Commuter parking lots: Vandalism and deterrence. *Transportation Quarterly, 41*, 539–554.

Manzo, L. C., & Weinstein, N. D. (1987). Behavioral commitment to environmental protection: A study of active and nonactive members of the Sierra Club. *Environment and Behavior, 19*, 673–694.

Martin, D. C. (1992). The effect of three signs and a brochure on visitor's removal of pumice at Mount St. Helens. In H. H. Christensen, D. R. Johnson, & M. Brookes (Eds.), *Vandalism: Research, prevention and social policy*. Portland, OR: U.S. Department of Agriculture Forest Service.

Martin, J. M. (1959). *The vandals: A study of malicious mischief*. Doctoral dissertation, New York University, New York.

Martin, J. M. (1961). *Juvenile vandalism: A study of its nature and prevention*. Springfield, IL: Charles C Thomas.

Martin, R. G. (1972). Mutilation: A college and university survey concerning microfilm replacement for mutilated periodicals and circulation of microforms. *Nebraska Library Association Quarterly, 3*, 18–20.

Mason, D. L. (1979). *Fine art of art security—Protecting public and private collections against theft, fire, and vandalism*. New York: Van Nostrand Reinhold.

Massucci, J. (1984). School vandalism: A plan of action. *National Association of Secondary School Principals Bulletin, 68*, 18–20.

Mathie, J. P., & Schmidt, R. E. (1977). Rehabilitation and one type of arsonist. *Fire and Arson Investigator, 28*, 53–56.

Mayer, G. R., & Butterworth, T. W. (1979). A preventive approach to school violence and vandalism: An experimental study. *Personnel and Guidance Journal, 57*, 436–441.

Mayer, G. R., Butterworth, T., Nafpaktitis, M., & Sulzer-Azaroff, B. (1983). Preventing school vandalism and improving discipline: A three-year study. *Journal of Applied Behavior Analysis, 16*, 355–369.

Mayer, G. R., Nafpaktitis, M., Butterworth, T., & Hollingsworth, P. (1987). A search for the elusive setting events of school vandalism: A correlational study. *Education and Treatment of Children, 10*, 259–270.

Mayer, G. R., & Sulzer-Azaroff, B. (1991). Interventions for vandalism. In G. Stoner, M. R. Shinn, & H. M. Walker (Eds.), *Interventions for achievement and behavior problems*. Silver Spring, MD: National Association of School Psychologists.

Mayers, P. (1977). *The relation between structural elements and the experience of enjoyment in high school classes*. Unpublished manuscript, University of Chicago.

McCaul, K. D., & Kopp, J. T. (1982). Effects of goal setting and commitment on increasing metal recycling. *Journal of Applied Psychology, 67*, 377–379.

McClelland, L., & Belsten, L. (1979). Prompting energy conservation in university dormitories by physical, policy, and resident behavior changes. *Journal of Environmental Systems, 9*, 29–38.

McCord, J. (1973). Vandalism: A special report. *The Nation's Schools, 92*, 31–37.

McKnight, C. (1978). Is man interested in his future? *International Journal of Psychology, 13*, 159–162.

McPherson, M., & Carpenter, J. (1981). *Rural youth vandalism in four Minnesota counties*. Minneapolis: Minnesota Crime Prevention Center.

McQuoid, J., McKibben, L., & Heaney, P. (1989). *Verdict on vandalism: Young people's perceptions of vandalism in Brownlow, Craigavon*. Belfast, Ireland: Extern Centre for Independent Research and Analysis of Crime.

Meaney, F. (1987, June). Arson, vandalism and schools. In D. Challinger (Ed.), *Crime at school*. Canberra, Australia: Seminar Proceedings.

Meyers, A. W., Artz, L. M., & Craighead, W. E. (1976). The effects of instructions, incentive, and feedback on a community problem: Dormitory noise. *Journal of Applied Behavior Analysis, 9*, 445–457.

Miethe, T. D. (1994). Citizen-based crime control activity and victimization risks. An examination of displacement and free-rider effects. *Criminology, 29*, 419–440.

Miethe, T. D., & Meier, R. F. (1994). *Crime and its social context: Toward an integrated theory of offenders, victims, and situations*. Albany: State University of New York Press.

Mischel, W. (1968). *Personality and assessment*. New York: Wiley.

Moos, R. H., & Insel, P. M. (1974). *Issues in social ecology*. Palo Alto, CA: National Press Books.

Moser, G. (1992). What is vandalism? Toward a psycho-social definition and its implications. In H. H. Christensen, D. R. Johnson, & M. H. Brookes (Eds.), *Vandalism: Research, prevention, and social policy*. Portland, OR: U.S. Department of Agriculture Forest Service.

Moser, G., & Levy-Leboyer, C. (1985). Inadequate environment and situation control: Is a malfunctioning phone always an occasion for aggression. *Environment and Behavior, 17*, 520–533.

Murphy, G. (1947). *Personality: A biosocial approach to origins and structure*. New York: Harper.

Murphy, H. H. (1973, March). *Vandals, arsonists, bombs, dogs*. Presented at American Association of School Administrators, San Francisco.

Murray, H. (1938). *Explorations in personality*. New York: Oxford University Press.

Nasar, J. L. (1989). Perception, cognition, and evaluation of urban places. In I. Altman & E. H. Zube (Eds.), *Public places and spaces*. New York: Plenum Press.

National Education Association. (1973). *Danger-school ahead: Violence in the public schools*. Washington, DC: Author.

Nelken, I., & Kline, S. (1971). *Destruction or loss of school property: Analysis and suggestions for improvement of school security*. Chico, CA: California State University.

Neville, H. C. (1974). School arson: Is your protection adequate? *American School and University, 47*, 31–32.

Nicholson, D. H. (1975). Urban vandalism—Prevention or cure? *The Highway Engineer, 22,* 14–17.

Nowakowski, R. (1966). *Vandals and vandalism in the schools: An analysis of vandalism in large school systems and a description of 93 vandals in Dade County schools.* Doctoral dissertation, University of Miami, Miami.

O'Doherty, M. (1991, April). Positive responses to youthful graffiti: In J. Vernon & S. McKillop (Eds.), *Preventing juvenile crime.* Gosnells, Western Australia: Conference Proceedings.

Oliver, S. S., Roggenbuck, J. W., & Watson, A. E. (1985). Education to reduce impacts in forest campgrounds. *Journal of Forestry, 83,* 234–236.

Olson, J. R. (1981). Curbing vandalism and theft. *Educational Horizons, 59,* 195–197.

Pablant, P., & Baxter, J. C. (1975). Environmental correlates of school vandalism. *Journal of the American Institute of Planners, 41,* 270–279.

Page, R. A., & Moss, M. K. (1976). Environmental influences on aggression: The effects of darkness and proximity of victim. *Journal of Applied Social Psychology, 6,* 126–133.

Panko, W. L. (1978). *Taxonomy of school vandalism.* Doctoral dissertation, University of Pittsburgh, Pittsburgh.

Patterson, G. R. (1982). *Coercive family process.* Eugene, OR: Castalia.

Patterson, G. R., Reid, J. B., & Dishion, T. J. (1992). *Antisocial boys.* Eugene, OR: Castalia.

Pedersen, T. L. (1990). Theft and mutilation of library materials. *College and Research Libraries, 51,* 120–128.

Pepler, D. J., & Slaby, R. G. (1994). *Theoretical and developmental perspectives on youth and violence.* Unpublished manuscript, York University, Toronto.

Perlgut, D. (1983). Vandalism: The environmental crime. *Journal of Social Issues, 18,* 209–216.

Pervin, L. (1986). Persons, situations, interactions: Perspectives on a recurrent issue. In A. Campbell & J. J. Gibbs (Eds.), *Violent transactions: The limits of personality.* Oxford: Basil Blackwell.

Peterson, J. L., & Borden, R. J. (1978). *Environmental concern, beliefs in technology, and academic major: Paradise or parking lots for the future?* Presented at Midwestern Psychological Association, Chicago.

Peuleche, T. W. (1976). Vandalism as a design consideration in urban parks and plazas. Doctoral dissertation, University of Georgia, Athens.

Phillips, G. H. (1982). *Rural vandalism.* Washington, DC: National Institute of Justice Vandalism Prevention Workshop.

Phillips, G. H., & Donnermeyer, J. F. (1982, October). *Vandals and vandalism in the United States.* Presented at International Colloquium on Vandalism, Paris.

Pitt, D. G., & Zube, E. H. (1991). Management of natural environments. In D. Stokols & I. Altman (Eds.), *Handbook of environmental psychology.* Malabar, FL: Krieger.

Plas, J. M. (1986). *Systems psychology in the schools.* New York: Pergamon Press.

Platt, J. (1973). Social traps. *American Psychologist, 28,* 641–651.

Porter, G. V. (1980). *The control of vandalism in urban recreation facilities: A revision of the defensible space model.* Doctoral dissertation, Boston University, Boston.

Prewer, R. R. (1986). Some observations on window-smashing. *The British Journal of Delinquency, 10*, 104–113.

Rainwater, L. (1966). *Behind ghetto walls: Black families in a federal slum*. Chicago: Aldine.

Ramsey, C. E., & Rickson, R. E. (1976). Environmental knowledge and attitudes. *Journal of Environmental Education, 8*, 10–18.

Randers, J., & Meadows, D. (1973). The carrying capacity of our global environment: A look at ethical alternatives. In I. G. Barbour (Ed.), *Western man and environmental ethics*. Reading, MA: Addison-Wesley.

Rausch, H. L. (1967). Interaction sequence. *Journal of Personality and Social Psychology, 2*, 487–499.

Rausch, H. L. (1972). Process and change. *Family Processes, 11*, 275–298.

Rautaheimo, J. (1989). The making of an arsonist. *Fire Prevention, 223*, 30–35.

Reich, J. W., & Robertson, J. L. (1979). Reactance and norm appeal in antilittering messages. *Journal of Applied Social Psychology, 9*, 91–101.

Reilly, D. (1978). *Coping with vandalism in family, school, and community*. Hackensack, NJ: National Council on Crime and Delinquency.

Richards, P. (1976a). Middle-class vandalism and age-status conflict. *Social Problems, 27*, 482–497.

Richards, P. (1976b). *Patterns of middle class vandalism: A case study of suburban adolescence*. Doctoral dissertation, Northwestern University, Evanston, IL.

Richmond, D. R. (1989). Group billing for university residence hall damage: A common but questionable practice. *Journal of Law and Education, 18*, 375–409.

Rider, A. O. (1980, June). The firesetter: A psychological profile. *FBI Law Enforcement Bulletin*, pp. 2–23.

Riley, D. (1980). Evaluation of a campaign to reduce vandalism. In S. Geason & P. Wilson (Eds.), *Designing out crime*. Canberra: Australian Institute of Criminology.

Riopelle, P. J. (1978). *Wisconsin: The growing problem of arson*. Madison, WI: Council on Criminal Justice.

Robb, S. (1991). How to vandal-proof your restrooms. *Parks and Recreation, 26*, 56–57.

Rothstein, R. (1963). Explorations of ego structures of firesetting children. *Archives of General Psychiatry, 77*, 247–250.

Rotter, J. B. (1954). *Social learning and clinical psychology*. Englewood Cliffs, NJ: Prentice Hall.

Rourke, A. (1992). Street furniture. *Landscape Design Extra, 22*, 7–10.

Rubel, R. J. (1977). *Unruly schools: Disorders, disruptions, and crimes*. Lexington, MA: D.C. Heath.

Rubel, R. J. (1980). Vandalism in public schools: Combining new theories provides new insights. *National Association of Secondary School Principals Bulletin, 64*, 67–75.

Sabo, S. R. (1993). Security by design. *American School Board Journal, 180*, 37–39.

Sadler, W. L. (1988). Vandalism in our schools: A study concerning children who destroy property and what to do about it. *Education, 108*, 556–560.

Schindler, R. A. (1983). *Block watch and crime solvers anonymous*. Sandusky, OH: Sandusky County Crime Prevention Association.

School violence prevention manual. (1980). New York: Oelgeschlager, Gunn, & Hain, Publishers.

Schultz, P. W., & Stone, W. F. (1994). Authoritarianism and attitudes toward the environment. *Environment and Behavior, 26,* 25–37.

Schumaker, R. E., & Leitner, D. W. (1979). A survey of principals' perceptions towards vandalism, record keeping and prevention measures in southern Illinois. *Illinois School Research and Development, 16,* 27–37.

Scott, C. (1954). Vandalism and our present day pattern of living. *Federal Probation, 18,* 10–12.

Scrimger, G. C., & Elder, R. (1981). *Alternative to vandalism—"Cooperation or wreckreation."* Sacramento: California Office of the Attorney General School Safety Center.

Severino, M. (1972). Who pays—or should pay when young vandals smash things up in your schools? *American School Board Journal, 159,* 33–34.

Shalloo, J. P. (1954). Vandalism: Whose responsibility? *Federal Probation, 18,* 6–8.

Sharp, J. S. (1964). Proper design limits vandalism. *American School Board Journal, 149,* 22–23.

Shaw, W. (1973). Vandalism is not senseless. *Law and Order, 12,* 14–19.

Shields, M. A. (1975). Social impact studies: An expository analysis. *Environment and Behavior, 7,* 265–284.

Siatt, W. (1981). School security with a solid track record. *Security World, 18,* 50–54.

Siden, D. M. (1978). Vandalism: How classified personnel might be able to help in shaping student attitudes toward school property. *The School Security Journal, 5,* 101–102.

Simmons, C. R. (1979). Vandalism is robbing us all. *Our Public Lands, 29,* 3–5.

Sinenesky, J. P., & Freeman, S. M. (1988). *Hate crime statutes: Response to Anti-Semitism, vandalism, and violent bigotry.* New York: Anti-Defamation League of B'nai B'rith.

Skogan, W. G. (1990). *Disorder and decline.* Berkeley: University of California Press.

Smith, C. (1982). Use these strategies for stronger school security. *The Executive Educator, 4,* 21–22.

Spalding, T. L. (1971). Door hardware to check vandalism. *School Management, 15,* 30–31.

Spirn, A. W. (1984). *The granite garden: Urban nature and human design.* New York: Basic Books.

Steele, M. (1978). enrolling community support. *Journal of Research and Development in Education, 11,* 84–94.

Stefanko, M. S. (1989). *Rates of secondary school vandalism and violence: Trends, demographic differences, and the effects of the attitudes and behaviors of principals.* Doctoral dissertation, Claremont College, Claremont, CA.

Stokols, D. (1978). Environmental psychology. In M. R. Rozenzweig & L. W. Porter (Eds.), *Annual Review of Psychology, 29,* 253–295.

Stokols, D., & Altman, I. (1987). *Handbook of environmental psychology.* New York: Wiley.

Stone, C. D. (1993). *The gnat is older than man.* Princeton: Princeton University Press.

Stoner, G., Shinn, M. R., & Walker, H. M. (Eds.). (1991). *Interventions for achievement and behavior problems*. Silver Spring, MD: National Association of School Psychologists.

Stover, D. (1990, November). How to be safe and secure against school vandalism. *The Executive Educator*, pp. 20–30.

Sturman, A. (1980). Damage on buses—The effects of supervision. In R. V. G. Clarke & P. Mayhew (Eds.), *Designing out crime*. Campbell, CA: Pendragon House.

Sutherland, E. H., & Cressey, D. R. (1974). *Criminology*. New York: Lippincott.

Taylor, R. B., & Gottfredson, S. (1986). Environmental design, crime, and prevention: An examination of community dynamics. In A. J. Reiss & M. Tonry (Eds.), *Communities and crime*. Chicago: University of Chicago Press.

Thaw, R. F. (1976). *Acts against property model—A case study, an extension of the traditional vandalism model*. Doctoral dissertation, United States International University, San Diego.

Tygart, C. (1980). Student social structures and/or subcultures as factors in school crime. *Adolescence*, *15*, 13–22.

Tygart, C. (1988). Public school vandalism: Toward a synthesis of theories and transition to paradigm analysis. *Adolescence*, *23*, 187–199.

Valentine, C. F. (1979, February). *Program to reduce vandalism and to improve student behavior at Vineland High School North*. Presented at National Association of Secondary School Principals, Houston.

Van D'Elden, K. H. (1992). Gangs and graffiti: A Minneapolis perspective. In H. H. Christensen, D. R. Johnson, & M. Brookes (Eds.), *Vandalism: Research, prevention, and social policy*. Portland, OR: U.S. Department of Agriculture Forest Service.

Van Liere, K. D., & Dunlap, R. E. (1978). Moral norms and environmental behavior: An application of Schwartz's norm-activation model to yard burning. *Journal of Applied Social Psychology*, *8*, 174–188.

Varady, D. P. (1986). Neighborhood confidence: A critical factor in neighborhood revitalization? *Environment and Behavior*, *18*, 480–501.

Vernon, R. F. (1979). *Dimensions of juvenile arson and false fire alarms for the urban areas of San Diego*. Washington, DC: U.S. Department of Housing and Urban Development.

Vestermark, S. D., & Blauvelt, P. D. (1978). *Controlling crime in the school: A complete security handbook for administrators*. West Nyack, NY: Parker.

Wade, A. (1967). Social processes in the act of juvenile vandalism. In M. Clinard & R. Quinney (Eds.), *Criminal behavior systems*. New York: Holt, Rinehart & Winston.

Waldbauer, R. C. (1992). National goals for protecting archeological sites. In H. H. Christensen, D. R. Johnson, & M. Brookes (Eds.), *Vandalism: Research, prevention, and social policy*. Portland, OR: U.S. Department of Agriculture Forest Service.

Walden, J. (1980). Property damage and acts of vandalism by different groups of perpetrators in big cities—Prevention, repression, additional measures. *Schriftenreihe der Polizei Führungsakademie*, *3*, 267–282.

Ward, C. (1973). *Vandalism*. New York: Van Nostrand.

Ward, C. (1991). Notes of a vandal-watcher. *Town and Country Planning*, *1*, 232–234.

Warren, J. H., & Rubenow, R. C. (1984). Combatting school vandalism—A blueprint for action. *National Association of Secondary School Principals Bulletin, 68*, 8–12.

Warzecha, S., Fisher, J. D., & Baron, R. M. (1984, April). *An equity-control model as a predictor of vandalism among college students*. Presented at Eastern Psychological Association, Baltimore.

Webster's Ninth New Collegiate Dictionary. (1984). Springfield, MA: Merriam-Webster.

Weeks, S. (1976). Security against vandalism: It takes facts, feelings and facilities. *American School and University, 48*, 36–46.

Weigel, R. H. (1985). Ecological attitudes and actions. In D. B. Gray (Ed.), *Ecological beliefs and behaviors: Assessment and change*. Westport, CT: Greenwood Press.

Weinmayr, V. M. (1969). Vandalism by design: A critique. *Landscape Architecture, 59*, 286.

Weiss, D. (1981). Book theft and mutilation in a large urban university library. *College and Research Libraries, 47*, 341–347.

Weiss, J. N. (1974). Vandalism: An environmental concern. *National Association of Secondary School Principals Bulletin, 58*, 6–9.

Wells, E. (1971). *Vandalism and violence: Innovative strategies reduce in schools*. Arlington, VA: National School Public Relations Association.

Welsh, R., & Cestare, P. (1993). Elevator vandalism squad. *FBI Law Enforcement Bulletin, 62*, 10–13.

Welsh, R. S. (1971). The use of stimulus satiation in the elimination of juvenile fire-setting behavior. In A. M. Graziano (Ed.), *Behavior therapy with children*. Chicago: Aldine.

Wenk, E., & Harlow, N. (1978). *School crime and disruption*. Davis, CA: Responsible Action.

West, J. P., Lee, S. J., & Feiock, R. C. (1992). Managing municipal waste: Attitudes and opinions of administrators and environmentalists. *Environment and Behavior, 24*, 111–133.

White, J., & Fallis, A. (1980). *Vandalism prevention programs used in Ontario schools*. Toronto, Canada: Ontario Ministry of Education.

Whitt, L. A. (1980). *The effect of posters, feedback, and incentives on vandalism in a residential setting*. Doctoral dissertation, University of Maryland, College Park.

Wiesenthal, D. L. (1990). Psychological aspects of vandalism. In P. J. D. Drenth, J. A. Sergeant, & R. J. Takens (Eds.), *European perspectives in psychology* (Vol. 3). New York: Wiley.

Wilson, G. T. (1961). *An analysis of effective practices employed to reduce vandalism in park, recreation, and combined departments in American cities of over 50 thousand population*. Doctoral dissertation, Indiana University, Bloomington.

Wilson, J. Q., & Kellog, G. L. (1982). Broken windows: The police and neighborhood safety. *Atlantic, 249*, 29–38.

Wilson, P., & Healy, P. (1978). *Vandalism and graffiti on State Rail*. Canberra: Australian Institute of Criminology.

Wilson, P. R. (1988). Preventing vandalism and graffiti. *Journal of Security Administration, 11*, 28–35.

Wilson, S. (1977). Vandalism and design. *The Architect's Journal, 166*, 795–798.

Wilson, S. (1979). Observations on the nature of vandalism. In P. Bural (Ed.), *Designing against vandalism*. New York: Van Nostrand Reinhold.

Winett, R. A. (1980). An emerging approach to energy conservation. In D. Glenwick & L. Jason (Eds.), *Behavioral community psychology*. New York: Praeger.

Winett, R. A., Neale, M. S., & Grier, H. C. (1979). Effects of self-monitoring and feedback on residential electricity consumption. *Journal of Applied Behavior Analysis, 12*, 173–184.

Winter, R. A. (1992). Metro Awareness Program: Education, enforcement, and elimination. In H. H. Christensen, D. R. Johnson, & M. Brookes (Eds.), *Vandalism: Research, prevention, and social policy*. Portland, OR: U.S. Department of Agriculture Forest Service.

Wise, J. (1982, September). A gentle deterrent to vandalism. *Psychology Today*, pp. 28–31.

Wood, D. (1991). In defense of indefensible space. In P. J. Brantingham & P. L. Brantingham (Eds.), *Environmental criminology*. Prospect Heights, IL: Waveland Press.

Wood, S. H. (1983). *Attitudes toward the environment and vandalism in relation to ego development during late adolescence*. Doctoral dissertation, Boston University, Boston.

Worrell, P. B., & Sparks, A. T. (1983). *Study of residential property crime in Thunder Bay*. Thunder Bay, Ontario: Thunder Bay Police Force.

Yambert, P. A., & Donow, C. F. (1984). Are we ready for ecological commandments? *Journal of Environmental Education, 3*, 13–16.

Yankelovich, D. (1975). How students control their drug crisis. *Psychology Today, 9*, 39–42.

Young, G. P., & Soldatis, S. (1970). School vandalism can be stopped. *American School and University, 42*, 22–23.

Zeisel, J. (1974, February). *Planning facilities to discourage vandalism*. Presented at American Association of School Administrators. Atlantic City, NJ.

Zeisel, J. (1976). *Stopping school property damage: Design and administrative guidelines to reduce school vandalism*. Boston: American Association of School Administrators.

Zeisel, J. (1977). Stopping school property damage. *CEFP Journal, 15*, 6–11, 18–21.

Zimbardo, P. G. (1973). A field experiment in auto-stripping. In C. Ward (Ed.), *Vandalism*. London: Architectural Press.

Zimbardo, P. G. (1969). The human choice: Individuation, reason, and order versus deindividuation, impulse and chaos. In W. J. Arnold & D. Devine (Eds.), *Nebraska Symposium on Education*. Lincoln: University of Nebraska Press.

Zube, E. H., Sell, J. L., & Taylor, J. (1982). Landscape perception: Research, application and theory. *Landscape Planning, 9*, 1–33.

Zweig, A., & Ducey, M. H. (1978). *A paradigmatic field: A review of research on school vandalism*. Hackensack, NJ: National Council on Crime and Delinquency.

Zwier, G., & Vaughn, G. M. (1984). Three ideological orientations in school vandalism research. *Review of Educational Research, 54*, 263–292.

RESEARCH APPENDIX

As noted a number of times throughout this book, both the quality and sheer quantity of research on the antecedents of vandalism and on the means of its effective reduction are sorely deficient. What is known about such behavior and its modification rests primarily on a tenuous base of anecdote, impression, and advice from those who have been its target. But some noteworthy exceptions to this rudimentary literature base do exist. These few investigations are worthy of our special attention and hence constitute this appendix as exemplars of precisely the types of efforts most needed toward the dual goals of better understanding of and more skilled intervention for vandalistic behavior.

The first two articles begin where all interventions optimally should begin, with a focus on prevention. Christensen et al. (1988) offer a comprehensive research plan for cultural resource protection. Theirs is an article I have placed first in this array of readings for its cogent position regarding the complexity of vandalism prevention. Far too much of the vandalism literature consists of overly simple, single-focus interventions. Complexly determined behaviors, most certainly including vandalism, require for their prevention or reduction equally complex interventions. Christensen et al.'s urging that preventive efforts jointly reflect site characteristics, value differences in cultural resource management, perpetrator motivations for theft and defacement of such resources, and diverse site protection strategies amply captures such appropriate complexity.

Moving from a preventive plan to an actual vandalism prevention program, Mayer et al. (1983) demonstrate that rigorous research designed to evaluate an ambitious behavior-analytic program in real-world school settings can be carried out and can yield valuable applied information regarding vandalism prevention. Theirs is a multiyear study, sited in both elementary and secondary schools, showing the decidedly positive effects on such negative behavior of an enhanced school climate.

One may learn valuable information from research at all levels of complexity. Even straightforward, rather uncomplicated survey studies have much to teach us—both by their own findings and by leads they may provide to more experimental inquiry. The next two articles are of this survey type. Frith's (1985) study evaluating the effectiveness of public service advertising to reduce sign vandalism and Pedersen's (1990) effort to determine the motivations underlying the mutilation and theft of library materials each provide this combination of utilitarian findings as well as valuable direction for further research inquiry.

It is quite understandable that efforts to reduce antisocial behavior are primarily directed to those persons directly responsible for such behavior. As I commented elsewhere:

> Most efforts to better understand, and reduce, human aggressive behavior focus upon the perpetrator. Whether specialist or general public; psychologist, sociologist, or criminologist, theoretician, researcher, or practitioner; or concerned with prediction, prevention, rehabilitation, or public policy—the person or persons actually committing the aggressive act are almost always the primary target of attention. Who he or she is, the person's relevant background experiences, history of similar behaviors, mood and rationality at the time the act occurred, and related intraindividual matters are the typical questions addressed. The abuser's parenting; the delinquent's early temperament; the offender's personality traits; hormonal levels; television viewing habits; and other in-the-person markers are posited, examined, and held responsible. For most of those concerned, aggression is in the perpetrator, by the perpetrator, and from the perpetrator. (Goldstein, 1994, p. VII).

The articles by DeMore et al. (1988) and Grasmick et al. (1991) capture this in-the-perpetrator perspective. The vandal's perceived equity and sense of control in the first study and his or her shame and embarrassment in the second are the specific person qualities evaluated. To be sure, these are but a few of many, many dozens of postulated and examined person qualities suggested in the literature as possible antecedents to or concomitants of vandalistic behavior. I have chosen the DeMore et al. and Grasmick et al. reports for inclusion in this compilation of exemplary studies partly because they are good-quality examples of this common focus on the perpetrators of vandalism, but more because both articles share one other very desirable but frequently lacking characteristic. Each explicitly derives its particular predictions from relevant theory and tests them in a manner designed to help further clarify the stance from which the theory originated. Equity-control theory in the first instance and deterrence theory in the second are both the sources and the targets of inquiry here. The vandalism literature, with the few pregnant exceptions examined earlier in this text, rests on a remarkably sparse theoretical base. More, much more, of what these two theory-based articles attempt to accomplish is clearly needed.

The perpetrator is indeed due his or her fair share of research attention. What has not received its fair share, however, is the ecology of the vandalistic event.

> Our perspective is responsive to one of the most significant developments in the study of human behavior—the ascendance of interactionism. Broadly defined, interactionism is a philosophical stance toward understanding and predicting human behavior which holds that such efforts will be optimized when they reflect both intraindividual (e.g., trait) qualities and relevant characteristics of the individual's environment. These latter ecological features may be other people (e.g., victims, fellow gang members) or qualities of the immediate or larger physical location in which the perpetration occurs. (Goldstein, 1994, p. II)

Mayer et al.'s (1987) investigation, conducted in a school context, as is much of the vandalism literature, places its emphasis on the implications of the school's *social* ecology as the "setting events" covarying with student vandalism. A combination of school rule clarity, administration consistency, and curricular allowance for individual differences substantially correlated with a lowered number of incidents of vandalism. Many other administrator, teacher, and fellow student qualities have been pointed to in the vandalism literature as probable covariates of defacing and destructive behavior; very few have been carefully investigated.

The *physical* ecology of the vandalistic act has been even more ignored, though three excellent and very diverse examples of such inquiry are the next articles in this compilation. Pablant and Baxter's (1975) admirable study involved the careful matching of 16 sets of schools on a host of relevant attributes, one school within each pair showing high vandalism rates, one low. By means of such comparisons, these authors were able to identify a series of physical ecological differences between the high- and low-vandalism schools: aesthetic quality, property maintenance, area population density, illumination, and others. Ley and Cybriwsky's (1974) examination of "the spatial ecology of stripped cars" achieved a directly analogous purpose with regard to a very different type of vandalism. This creative study of "the geography of crime" highlights emphatically that vandalism is both a person and a place event—an event which must be both conceptualized and studied in this ecologically interactionist manner. Underscoring this conclusion yet further is Samdahl and Christensen's (1985) clever investigation of picnic table carvings as possible "releasor cues" for more of the same—but one of a great many suggestions in the literature that existing evidence of vandalism encourages, permits, and actually yields more of the same. These authors' findings were in fact just this: New carvings occurred more on previously carved tables, especially in "low-authority" campground areas.

I wish to end this commentary with reference to two final, high-quality research reports—by Christensen and Clark (1983) and Krauss et al. (1978). These studies permit us to elaborate further on a key investigative-strategy matter mentioned briefly earlier, namely, the need for complex research designs to match the complexity of the phenomenon under study. Christensen and Clark sought to evaluate a program designed to reduce depreciative behavior in public recreation settings. In doing so, they experimentally manipulated the type of appeal delivered, the type of message delivered, and the recipient response format as these variables individually and in combination impacted upon littering behavior. Studying the same behavior in very different venues, Krauss et al. (1978) focused on the influence of prior litter as a releasor cue, the gender of the subjects, the stress levels to which they were subjected, and the effects of having earlier signed an antilitter petition. These programmatic, multivariate examinations of one form of vandalism accurately reflect the complex, multiply determined nature of such behavior and thus are very much the types of real-world, veridical investigative inquiry needed so badly in this domain.

CULTURAL RESOURCE PROTECTION

A PREDICTIVE FRAMEWORK FOR IDENTIFYING SITE VULNERABILITY, PROTECTION PRIORITIES, AND EFFECTIVE PROTECTION STRATEGIES

HARRIET H. CHRISTENSEN, KEN MABERY, MARTIN E. MCALLISTER, AND DALE P. MCCORMICK

INTRODUCTION

Federal land managers have limited personnel and funds to accomplish many programs mandated by Congress, one of which is cultural resource protection. Thousands of cultural resource sites have been recorded on Federal lands in the Southwestern United States, and more are discovered daily. It has been estimated, for example, that only seven percent of the sites on Federal lands in the Four Corners area have been found and recorded (General Accounting Office 1987). Many of the recorded and unrecorded sites are targets for unauthorized disturbance, including the looting and theft of artifacts and other types of defacement, but only a few known sites have been protected through law enforcement activities or other measures

---

Source: *Rocky Mountain Forest and Range Experiment Station General Technical Reports*, RM No. 164, pp. 62–67, 1988.

(Downer in press; McAllister in press; Nickens et al. 1981; Waldbauer in press). The majority are unprotected.

The recent General Accounting Office (GAO) report (1987) was highly critical of all aspects of the Federal cultural resource protection program in the Four Corners region. The GAO found that approximately 43,848 cultural resource sites, or nearly one-third of those recorded on Federal lands in the area, have been damaged by theft or defacement to some degree. However, between 1980 and 1986, only 1,222 incidents of cultural resource theft or defacement were documented by the region's Federal land management agencies, and only 27 cases produced convictions under the Archaeological Resources Protection Act. These figures indicate that current protection strategies are not effective in combating cultural resource theft and defacement.

If cultural resource preservation was the only concern in Federal land management, it would be desirable to apply some form of protection against theft and defacement to all known sites. However, it is clear that available funding and other management goals will not permit full protection of all cultural resource sites on Federal lands. Agency land managers are increasingly faced with hard questions. What sites do we protect and how do we protect them effectively? It is critical that managers have some documented and supportable means by which they can assess relative protection priorities for known sites and reassess priorities as new sites are recorded.

PROPOSED RESEARCH

Frameworks have been developed to determine relative natural resource and ecological protection needs on public lands (Hoose 1981; United States Department of the Interior 1982). These frameworks have been modified by some Federal land managers to meet local cultural resource protection needs, but the thoroughness and effectiveness of the resulting criteria have not been formally evaluated, and remain in question for application beyond the level at which they were developed.

The goal here is to propose research to develop and test a framework specifically designed as a tool managers can apply to assess cultural resource vulnerability, prioritize sites for protection, and select effective protection strategies. The resulting evaluative criteria must be designed to rank site vulnerability on an ongoing basis and to assign higher protection priorities and the most effective protection strategies to the most vulnerable sites.

Overall management rankings of cultural resource sites will depend on a variety of factors such as importance to Native Americans, prehistoric and historic research values, and susceptibility to natural or management impacts.... In order to develop a predictive framework for site protection, information is needed in four critical areas: site characteristics which affect vulnerability, value differences toward cultural resource management, motivations for theft and defacement, and evaluation of effective site-protection strategies.

The initial focus of the proposed research will be cultural resource sites managed by the USDA [U.S. Department of Agriculture] Forest Service in the agency's Southwestern Region (Arizona and New Mexico). At the same time, it will be desirable to develop a framework which is flexible enough in scope to allow future utilization by other Federal land management agencies in the Southwest.

Site Characteristics

Certain physical characteristics of cultural resource sites and their environmental settings have been found to be important attributes in overall vulnerability to theft and defacement in the southwestern United States (Downer in press; Nickens et al. 1981). Examples of variables of this type which have been utilized to analyze vulnerability are the following:

1. Site density, usually quantified as the number of sites per square mile or square kilometer.
2. Site visibility, in terms of the obviousness of physical features.
3. Site type, such as a village site with remains of houses versus a quarry and tool manufacturing site where only stone artifacts are present.
4. Types of artifacts present, for example, sites with decorated and undecorated pottery as opposed to those with only undecorated ceramics.
5. Types of features present, including items such as houses, storage facilities, ceremonial structures, and graves or burials.
6. Site accessibility, for example, distance to trails, roads, private property, and towns.

An analysis of vulnerability in relation to site characteristics such as these will be based on information on the condition of known sites in terms of the extent and nature of theft and defacement. Relevant categories of baseline information include the following:

1. Sites recorded as being disturbed by theft, defacement, or both.
2. Sites recorded as being undisturbed by these activities.
3. Sites which are in an unknown condition because information on theft and defacement was not recorded or is unclear or problematic.

4. The extent of theft, defacement, or both at disturbed sites, if quantified.
5. The type of theft or defacement activities evident, if specified.

The analysis must measure the degree of association between potentially significant site characteristics and site condition variables for those sites for which usable information is available. Site characteristics which are found to be strongly associated, either positively or negatively, with disturbance from theft or defacement will become important criteria in the framework for site protection. Continuing analysis of newly obtained site information can be used to further evaluate known associations and to measure relationships to variables not previously identified as significant.

The site data base for an analysis of this type may be derived from several sources. The computerized inventory for sites recorded on National Forest lands in the Southwestern Region is probably capable of providing much usable information. In addition, each Forest's physical inventory of site forms may contain additional relevant data not entered in the computerized system. All newly recorded sites in the Region also can be included in the data base as information on them becomes available. Finally, as the opportunity arises, previously recorded sites will need to be periodically reinspected to document disturbance from theft or defacement not properly recorded initially, as well as any new damage from these activities. Eventually, sites recorded on other Federal lands in the Southwest also may become part of the data base.

Value Differences toward Cultural Resources Management

Knowledge is needed that identifies agreements and disagreements in perceptions, values, and behaviors between users, nonusers, and managers toward cultural resources. The problem of value conflicts and lack of consensus is an important one and must involve the Forest user, nonuser, and Southwest cultural groups such as Native Americans.... The nonuser is identified as a Southwest resident who does not use the Forests, but who may nonetheless value the preservation of cultural resources. Also, it is important to note that Southwest cultural resources have national significance and a sample of nonusers nationally may be necessary.

Protection issues are important, and the management and protection of cultural resources requires knowledge and understanding of behaviors, values, and perceptions. Most management and research have focused on single components such as discussions about archeological laws, the criminal justice system, or the network of commercial collecting. These evaluations and discussions are needed, but most of the problems in resource management are found in the areas of conflict—or overlap (Clark et al. 1985). We know least about where the conflicts interact.

The rationale for this research is to develop new information that identifies areas of conflict in perceptions, values, and behaviors. The protection framework is based on an understanding of these conflicts and resolutions. The relative value of cultural resources emerges from the contexts of the various managers and cultural groups contacted. This information is analyzed for interrelationships and emerging factors are weighed for the predictive framework. For instance, the Federal land manager's responsibility in many agencies is to manage for multiple use; these mangers are the designated stewards of our cultural heritage. The archeologist looks at cultural resources as a professional relationship. Law enforcement officers look at the enforcement of archeological laws as a professional duty but frequently have real conflicts with other enforcement priorities. The commercial collectors see looting as their legitimate right, while other types of collectors have similar rationales. The Native American looks at cultural resources with religious and spiritual values while wildlife organizations see cultural resources as secondary to wildlife values. Moreover, economic values of energy, industry, and land development often take precedence over preservation values. Congruence and lack of congruence between values are to be identified in order to develop guidelines for protection.

Information needed from managers (across Districts, Forests, and Regions), users, and nonusers includes:

1. The relative importance of cultural resource values versus other resource values (for instance, timber, range, recreation, wildlife, and water).
2. The perceived seriousness of the extent of theft and defacement.
3. Attitudes about selected management practices. For instance, an assessment needs to be made of the relative acceptability of selected practices or treatments in known cultural resource areas. These practices include:
   a. timber cutting
   b. fuelwood cutting
   c. grazing
   d. recreation uses
   e. chaining treatments
   f. water control devices
   g. range improvement
   h. stock tanks
   i. road construction

j. oil and gas operation
k. controlled burns
l. wildland fire

4. The perceived effectiveness of protection strategies such as retrieving artifacts, offender sentencing by the courts, law enforcement efforts, and interpretation and education efforts to instill values about cultural resources.

One data collection approach is self-administered questionnaires given to randomly selected managers, users, and nonusers. Preliminary to this, it is suggested that exploratory, informal conversations be made with users and managers; this effort will identify key issues.

Motivations for Theft and Defacement

Causal factors need to be identified that explain why people conform or commit theft and defacement behaviors. The benefit of knowing why an individual or group comes to act illegally allows researchers and managers to develop and test prevention and control strategies for targeted groups. Motivation research also allows for the development of a profile of people (in conjunction with research on site vulnerability). Types of people potentially profiled include: (1) the commercial collector; (2) the intentional collector who loots for personal interest and possible material reward; (3) the recreational collector; and (4) the complier or person who is committed to the law and preservation values (Christensen in press). Theories from several disciplines have been offered to explain illegal behavior (Christensen 1978; Wilson and Herrnstein 1985), as have typologies of such behavior (Cohen 1973; Gramann et al. in press; Wade 1967). None of these perspectives has been tested with regard to theft and defacement of cultural resources. Some typologies are based on acts (behaviors), actors (people), or motivations or reasons for action. A suggested approach to this research issue is to provide a rationale for the acceptance or rejection of previous typologies and develop revised or new paradigms relative to cultural resources. Possible respondents include violators, where participation is on a volunteer basis and information is treated confidentially. Oftentimes, violators are willing to respond to personal interviews or self-administered questionnaires and provide researchers and managers with valuable information. New information about perceptions of users and nonusers regarding the types of people who commit destructive behavior is also valuable. New knowledge about cause will be integrated with other factors in the development of a protection framework.

SITE PROTECTION STRATEGIES

There are a number of protection strategies in use or potentially utilizable to prevent and control theft and defacement at cultural resource sites both on National Forest lands in the Southwestern Region and on other Federal lands in the Southwest. General categories of techniques now in use with some specific examples of each are listed:

1. Site Intervention
   a. Signing (Dustin 1985; Johnson and Swearingen, in press)
   b. Fencing
   c. Access control
   d. Anti-intrusion devices (including remote cameras)
   e. Less obvious project-related marking of sites
   f. Restoration or complete excavation of damaged sites
2. Public Involvement
   a. Prosocial behavior such as reporting violations by the public (Christensen and Clark 1983)
   b. Volunteer programs such as adopt-a-site and site stewardship (Pilles in press)
   c. Community programs (Pilles in press)
3. Public Education and Interpretation (Alderson et al. 1976; Sharpe 1976; Tilden 1957)
   a. On-site programs
   b. Outreach programs
   c. Volunteer excavations
   d. Media relations (including press coverage of successful law enforcement cases and undercover operations)
   e. Behavior modification programs (Gramann and Vander Stoep 1986)
4. Regulatory Controls
   a. Written orders and closures
   b. Action plan implementation
   c. Directing use through trail and road location
   d. Policy and regulation development
   e. Permittee compliance
5. Law Enforcement
   a. Investigations, citations, and arrests
   b. Informants
   c. Rewards
   d. Patrol techniques
   e. Specialized training
6. Legal Controls

a. Alternative sentencing
b. Selective acceptance of cases
c. Court-imposed penalties
d. Administrative settlements
e. Forfeiture

7. Other Management Strategies
a. Inter-agency communication and cooperation
b. Action planning
c. Modification of existing laws and regulations.

At present, there is no general evaluation of the conditions under which each of these protection strategies will prevent or control theft and defacement at cultural resource sites in the Southwest. Analysis of their relative effectiveness will produce criteria which Federal land managers can apply to select the appropriate strategy or strategies to protect a site once its vulnerability and priority for protection are known.

SUMMARY AND CONCLUSIONS

The protection of cultural resource sites is a serious problem on National Forests and other Federal lands in the Southwest. Sites are being disturbed by theft and defacement at an alarming rate, and the majority are totally unprotected. Unfortunately, it is not possible to protect all currently known sites and the problem will increase in magnitude in the future as more sites are discovered. Faced with this situation, Federal land managers are asking which sites should receive priority for protection, and how most effectively to prevent or control theft and defacement at those sites. The research proposed here focuses on four factors in cultural resource protection: site characteristics, value differences toward cultural resource management, motivations for theft and defacement, and effective site-protection strategies. All of these must be analyzed to answer the questions managers are asking. The goal of this research is [to] provide managers with a protection framework to assess site vulnerability, prioritize sites for protection, and select effective protection strategies. There is a critical need for this research in order to provide a sound basis for making difficult cultural resource protection decisions now and in the future.

LITERATURE CITED

Alderson, William T. and Shirley Payne Low. 1976. *Interpretation of historic sites.* American Association for State and Local History, Nashville, Tenn.

Christensen, Harriet H. 1978. Understanding and controlling vandalism and other rule violations in urban recreation areas. In *Proceedings of the National Urban Forestry Conference* (Washington, D.C., November 13–16, 1978), Vol. 1, pp. 63–84. USDA Forest Service, Washington, D.C.

Christensen, Harriet H. in press. Cultural resources: National treasure or personal trophy? An eco-structural model of looting. In Christensen, Harriet H., and Darryll Johnson (eds.), *Vandalism State of the Art: Research, Prevention, and Social Policy*. USDA Forest Service, Pacific Northwest Research Station, Seattle, Wash.

Christensen, Harriet H. and Roger N. Clark. 1983. Increasing public involvement to reduce depreciative behavior in recreation settings. *Leisure Sciences* 5(4): 359–379.

Clark, Roger N., Dave R. Gibbons, and Gilbert B. Pauley. 1985. Influences of recreation. In Meehan, W. R. (tech. ed.), *Influence of forest and rangeland management on anadromous fish habitat in western North America*. USDA Forest Service General Technical Report PNW-178. Pacific Northwest Research Station, Portland, Ore.

Cohen, Stanley. 1973. Property destruction: Motives and meanings. In Ward, Colin (ed.), *Vandalism*. Van Nostrand Reinhold, New York.

Downer, Alan, in press. Vandalization and looting of archeological sites on Indian lands: A case study from the Southwestern United States. In Christensen, Harriet H., and Darryll Johnson (eds.), *Vandalism State of the Art: Research, Prevention, and Social Policy*. USDA Forest Service, Pacific Northwest Research Station, Seattle, Wash.

Dustin, Daniel L. 1985. To feed or not to feed the bears: The moral choices we make. *Parks and Recreation* (October): 54–57/72.

General Accounting Office. 1987. *Report to congressional requesters: Cultural resources: Problems protecting and preserving federal archeological resources*. U.S. General Accounting Office RCED-88-3. Washington, D.C.

Gramann, James H. and Gail A. Vander Stoep. 1986. *Reducing depreciative behavior at Shiloh National Military Park*. Technical Report No. 2. National Park Science Cooperative Park Studies Unit, Texas A&M University, College Station, Tex.

Gramann, James H., Harriett H. Christensen, and Gail A. Vander Stoep. in press. Protecting cultural and natural resources. In Christensen, Harriet H., and Darryll Johnson (eds.), *Vandalism State of the Art: Research, Prevention, and Social Policy*. USDA Forest Service, Pacific Northwest Research Station, Seattle, Wash.

Hoose, Phillip M. 1981. *Building an ark: Tools for the preservation of natural diversity through land protection*. Island Press, Covelo, Calif.

Johnson, Darryll and Thomas C. Swearingen. in press. Dayhiker noncompliance to selected trailhead signs. In Christensen, Harriet H., and Darryll Johnson (eds.), *Vandalism State of the Art: Research, Prevention, and Social Policy*. USDA Forest Service, Pacific Northwest Research Station, Seattle, Wash.

McAllister, Martin E. in press. The archeological vandalism problem and a cost analysis of damage assessments in vandalism cases. In Christensen, Harriet H., and Darryll Johnson (eds.), *Vandalism State of the Art: Research, Prevention, and Social Policy*. USDA Forest Service, Pacific Northwest Research Station, Seattle, Wash.

Nickens, Paul R., Signa L. Larralde and Gordon C. Tucker, Jr. 1981. *A survey of vandalism to archeological resources in southwestern Colorado*. Cultural Resources

Series No. 11. Bureau of Land Management, Colorado State Office, Denver, Colo.

Pilles, Peter J., Jr. in press. Archeological site vandalism and the Arizona response. In Christensen, Harriet H., and Darryll Johnson (eds.), *Vandalism State of the Art: Research Prevention, and Social Policy*. USDA Forest Service, Pacific Northwest Research Station, Seattle, Wash.

Sharpe, Grant W. 1976. *Interpreting the environment*. John Wiley & Sons, New York.

Tilden, Freeman. 1957. *Interpreting our heritage*. University of North Carolina Press, Chapel Hill, N.C.

United States Department of the Interior. 1982. *New tools for land protection: An introductory handbook*. U.S. Department of the Interior, Washington, D.C.

Wade, Andrew L. 1967. Social processes in the act of juvenile vandalism. In Clinard, Marshall B. and Richard Quinney (eds.), *Criminal behavior systems: A typology*. Holt, Rinehart, and Winston, New York.

Waldbauer, Richard C. in press. National goals for protecting archeological sites. In Christensen, Harriet H., and Darryll Johnson (eds.), *Vandalism State of the Art: Research, Prevention, and Social Policy*, USDA Forest Service, Pacific Northwest Research Station, Seattle, Wash.

Wilson, J. Q. and R. J. Herrnstein. 1985. *Crime and human nature*. Simon and Schuster, New York.

to a subgroup of students within the class. In all cases, however, teacher responses were scored as praise only if directed to students when they were attending.

After allowing for adaptation, baseline data were collected each year during the last 2 weeks in November and the first week in December. Three observations, one per week, were made in each of the four classrooms (two project and two barometer) in each school during that period. An interim assessment consisting of three observations in all schools was made during February, and the final assessment, again consisting of three observations, was completed during the last 3 weeks of May 1978, 1979, and 1980 following the same procedures used for baseline.

Interobserver Agreement

Observer reliability assessments initially occurred during observer training with a videotape of a fifth-grade classroom. The observers had to obtain an agreement coefficient of at least .85 with a scoring key before observing a live classroom. More than 20 reliability assessments for student and teacher behavior were also completed during the adaptation, baseline, interim, and final observation periods. Each school consultant and a trained individual unfamiliar with the project simultaneously observed a classroom and independently recorded student and teacher behavior. Each reliability session lasted 20 min. The interobserver agreement was calculated by dividing the number of agreements by the number of disagreements for scored intervals (occurrences only) and ranged from .86 to 1.0 with a mean of .93.

Procedure

The schedule of implementation of staff development activities is summarized in Table 1. The table shows that the frequency of workshops and consultation contacts was gradually reduced over the 3-year-period.

The consultants followed a standard procedure in that they assisted teachers in implementing programs that were either introduced in the inservice workshops or described by Butterworth (Note 5). In addition, consultants followed the consulting format outlined in Table 2 and elaborated in *Behavioral Consulting* (Mayer & McGookin, Note 4).

First Project Year (1977–1978)

After baseline data collection, the project consultants began visiting and consulting with each project classroom teacher in the experimental schools on an average of twice a week. They arranged and conducted

TABLE 1. Summary of Schedule of Staff Development Activities

	Number of workshops	Workshop participants/school	Frequency of consultation
Year 1			
Group I	10	principal psychologist 2 project teachers	twice a week
Group II	0	none	none
Year 2			
Group I	3	principal psychologist	once a week
Group II	10	principal psychologist 2 project teachers	twice a week
Year 3			
Group I and Group II	5	principals and psychologists	every other week

approximately two team meetings per month at each school. These were attended by the project consultant, the principal, the two project teachers, and usually two or three other interested staff members. Each team attempted to identify and eliminate the conditions that foster vandalism and that hinder academic and personal-social development. This process involved working with the social staff in developing classroom and schoolwide programs that would teach students alternative behavior to vandalism and disruption. For example, lunchroom and playground management programs and classroom management programs were planned that stressed the use of specific positive reinforcement (Bernhart & Forehand, 1975), with students being informed as to which of their behaviors were being reinforced or recognized. The teams also planned community activities, such as neighborhood walks, to inform citizens of the school's concern with stopping vandalism and to solicit their cooperation. Involvement by youth clubs was sought in some schools to help keep the campus clean and to decide how to use money saved from reduced vandalism costs. These programs are described in detail elsewhere by Butterworth (Note 5).

Ten workshops were presented between the middle of October and the end of May. The three introductory workshops scheduled prior to the onset of treatment did not include programs and strategies for dealing with discipline and vandalism problems. Rather, these workshops introduced consultation skills that participants used to assist teachers in implementing the treatment strategies which were not presented until after baseline.

TABLE 2. Elements of Effective Consulting

1. Establish a professional working relationship and develop rapport (communication skills).
   - Reflection of content and affect
   - Pace of speech
   - Summarizing
   - "I" message
   - Posture, eye contact, facial expression, and other nonverbal behaviors
   - How to take notes
   - Clarifying
   - Confrontation
2. Identify behaviors of concern and goals.
   - Role of clarification
   - Begin to operationalize
3. Start contingency analysis during interview.
4. Observe behaviors in classroom situation.
   - Contingency analysis of student behavior
   - Contingency analysis of teacher behavior
   - Measuring rate of target behavior (optional)
5. Confer with teacher; discuss what has been tried and to what degree.
6. Jointly develop treatment strategy (goal for teacher).
7. Develop and apply strategies to facilitate treatment.
   - Reinforcing consultees
   - Utilizing a variety of reinforcing sources from the natural environment
   - Shaping
   - Cues, prompts, and modeling
   - Providing feedback
   - Uses of data
8. (Optional) Observe and record frequency of target behaviors.
9. Develop and apply strategies to facilitate treatment maintenance.
   - Fading
   - Generalization
   - Scheduling
10. Share results!

Because of the holidays during December and planning necessary for program implementation and enlisting student involvement, teachers and school teams were unable to start implementing programs until January. For this reason, vandalism costs prior to January 1 were attributed to pretreatment effects.

Funds were provided to the districts to be used to hire substitutes for the 18 teachers attending the training sessions. Only the school psychologists and counselors were requested to attend all 10 workshops. Activities at four of their meetings included learning and practicing behavioral consultation skills and analyzing school and classroom environments

(Mayer & McGookin, Note 4), and sharing alternative strategies and materials used by teachers to improve classroom environments (Kaplan, Kohfeldt, & Sturla, 1974; Sulzer-Azaroff & Mayer, 1977). These meetings were also attended by one or two of the school principals, although principals were not required to attend. Four of the 10 meetings were designed for the entire school team (principal, psychologist, or counselor, or both, and two project teachers) to deal with classroom and schoolwide discipline and vandalism problems encountered by different schools. Attendance at these meetings was close to 100%. The first team workshop began immediately after the collection of baseline data. A presentation of preliminary results was given at the last meeting for the principals, psychologists, and counselors.

The content of all 10 workshops is described elsewhere (Butterworth, Note 5; Nafpaktitis, Mayer, Butterworth, & Jones, Note 6) and was presented through lecture, audiovisual materials, and simulation activities. Tables 2 and 3 list the topics included.

None of the other teachers in the school, including the barometer teachers, attended the off-campus workshops. However, any teacher was welcome to receive consultation services on request. Typically three to five teachers in a school requested and received such services each year with usually one of these being a barometer teacher.

Second Project Year (1978–1979)

The treatment that was given to the 1977–1978 experimental schools during the first year was provided for the control, or Group II schools, during the second year of the project. Group I schools were provided three off-campus workshops which only the psychologist and principal were requested to attend. These workshops were intended to provide a follow-up to the work begun the previous year and to invite the participants to share programs and projects going on at their sites.

Consulting with school site personnel began during October 1978 in the Group I schools, because treatment had already started the previous year. Through on-campus team meetings, assessment of present school needs was made, and the previous year's schoolwide programs (i.e., cafeteria or playground improvement, reduction in tardiness, community improvement) were reevaluated. Consultants visited each project classroom on the average of once a week to assist the teacher in implementing programs or to collect observational data.

While consulting in the experimental schools, some of the project staff collaborated with the team that had been involved in the country workshops in conducting several workshops directly in the schools. These were attended by an interested staff and covered material similar to that of the

TABLE 3. Topics and Activities Included in Team Training Workshops

Behavioral Concepts
Conditions that engender school vandalism and disruption
Antivandalism programs
Positive reinforcement
Methods of identifying reinforcers
Negative reinforcement
Extinction
Reinforcing alternative responses
Modeling
Differential reinforcement of low rates
Differential reinforcement of other responses
Response cost
Time-out
Overcorrection
Punishment and its side effects
Practical Applications
Using certificates and awards
Improving staff morale
Teaching students to get positive recognition
Teaching students to reinforce teachers
Readability assessment procedures
Adapting material to student reading level
Positive reinforcement bombardment
Secret Pal Game
I Spy Game
Good Behavior Game
Slot Machine Game
Other group contingency games and programs
Token systems
Daily report cards
School discipline plans

original workshops. An average of two such workshops was held in almost every school.

Third Project Year (1979–1980)

Consulting began in early October 1979, and continued through May 1980 in the remaining 11 schools at a reduced rate. Each consultant was required to spend one-half day every other week at each school as services continued to be phased out. Team meetings were organized and scheduled every 2 to 4 weeks. At these meetings, possible additions to and changes in existing schoolwide behavior improvement groups were discussed and planned. Consultants endeavored to work closely with the school psychologist, when available, and with the principal, while modeling consulting behavior and providing feedback and reinforcement to all who were involved in behavior change programs. Efforts were continued, as in prior years, to include as many site personnel as were willing to participate, including student groups.

A series of five workshops was presented, and involved interested principals and psychologists. Four of these workshops offered instruction in improving consultation skills (see Table 2 and Mayer & McGookin, Note 4) to enable the principals and psychologists to enhance their ability to continue the project at its termination. The material was presented through lecture, simulation activities by project staff, and role playing by participants. The fifth workshop was set aside as a sharing period, and project participants were invited to discuss programs and projects going on at their sites.

Feedback to Teachers

During the first year of the project, behavioral data on teachers' types and amount of praise and students' behavior were graphed and shared with the project teachers in the experimental schools. During years two and three, this feedback was given to all project teachers. A minimum of three informal meetings between the consultant and each individual project teacher (except in control schools the first year) were held each year to discuss the behavioral data. Feedback was accompanied by social praise to maximize its usefulness (Cossairt, Hall, & Hopkins, 1973). During the third year only, barometer teachers were informed by the consultant that these data ware available from the consultant if they were interested in receiving them.

Experimental Design

The intervention program consisted of a "package" including inservice training of selected staff members, on-site consultation with selected teachers, consultation with other teachers who requested service, and establishing a team at each school to develop schoolwide programs. The experimental design was applied to the total intervention "package" without an analysis of the relative contributions by individual components to outcomes. A delayed treatment control (multiple baseline) design was used with schools randomly assigned to control and experimental conditions. The pre-post gain score variables were also compared between the control and experimental groups. In the case of vandalism cost, the number of schools that increased or decreased was compared. Thus, a number of different analyses were permitted due to the large sample sizes.

RESULTS

VANDALISM

First Year

For each school the average monthly vandalism cost per 100 students during January through May 1978 (the time span that the full complement of personnel were involved in program implementation) was subtracted from the average monthly vandalism cost per 100 students during September through December 1977 (the "baseline" period for schools receiving treatment for the first year). Each school was identified as having increased or decreased in cost of vandalism. According to this analysis during the first year of the experiment, vandalism decreased in six of nine schools receiving treatment but in only one of nine schools not receiving treatment. Application of the Fisher Exact Probability Test (Seigel, 1956), selected for its suitability with discrete ordinal data of small sample size, determined that significantly more treated than untreated schools experienced a decrease in the cost of repairing or replacing vandalized property ($p < .05$).

Second Year

For the schools that began receiving treatment in January 1979 (Group II), the average monthly vandalism cost per 100 students during January through May 1979 was subtracted from the average monthly vandalism cost per 100 students during September through December 1978. On this basis, each of these schools was identified as having increased or decreased in costs of vandalism during the second year of the experiment. It was previously determined that one of nine of these schools improved without treatment during their first year as controls in the study. This compared with five of seven of the same schools that improved after treatment during the second year. Application of the Fisher Exact Probability Test indicated that significantly more schools experienced a decrease in the cost of vandalism after treatment (i.e., the second year) than before treatment (i.e., the first year) ($p < .05$).

All Three Years

Ten out of 13 schools (schools A, B, C, E, G, H, I, J, L, and M) receiving treatment experienced decreases in the cost of vandalism or maintained their very low levels during intensive staff training. These included all the schools with vandalism greater than $200/100 students in any month of baseline. Two schools (schools D and K) showed increases, and one school (school F) showed little change during intensive staff training. During the entire follow-up period, six of the 10 schools remaining in the study maintained vandalism cost reductions (schools A, B, G, H, I—except one month—and J), one increased (school F), and three showed little change (C, E, and M) from baseline. However, with inflation, costs would be expected to increase over the 3-year period, not remain about the same. Thus, the treatment package appears to have been effective in nine of the 10 schools.

Generally there is less vandalism from September through December than from January through May. This finding has been consistently borne out by data collected by the office of the Los Angeles County Superintendent of Schools. For example, the average for all Los Angeles County Schools was $766,917/mo in vandalism costs during September through December 1980, and $1,004,667/mo during January through May 1981. Thus, when interpreting the graphed data, it is best to compare treatment months back to the same nontreatment months.

Comparing the baseline period September through December with the same months during treatment years shows the effect of treatment in reducing vandalism in Group I Schools. A similar comparison can be made between the January through May period for Group II schools. Thus, maximal reduction in vandalism costs occurred following the onset of treatment in both experimental groups.

Table 4 depicts [an] analysis of the cost data. The initial average mean cost during the 1977 baseline period of September through December for Group I schools was compared to the same time periods during treatment for 1978 and 1979. A similar comparison was done for Group II schools. However, these schools had a much longer baseline and received treatment only from January through May in 1979. Thus the 1978 January through May baseline for Group II schools was selected to compare to the same time periods during treatment for 1979 and 1980. An average reduction in vandalism cost for all schools of 78.5% was obtained without adjusting for inflation.

TABLE 4. Mean Monthly Vandalism Costs/100 Students

	Group I schools		Group II schools	
	September to December	Decrease from baseline	January to May	Decrease from baseline
Baseline (1977–1978)	$121.35	—	$77.12	—
Treatment (1978–1979)	$ 10.10	91.7%	$14.29	81.5%
Follow-up (I) or Treatment (II) (1979–80)	$ 30.85	74.6%	$26.00	66.3%

Teacher Behavior

Due to the large number of teachers involved in the study, behavior observations of a teacher's delivery of praise were averaged. The mean of baseline observations was subtracted from the mean of posttreatment delivery of praise for each teacher for each year of the study.

A 2 × 2 factorial analysis of variance (i.e., elementary and junior high grade level by treatment and control groups) was used to analyze changes in teacher praise between baseline and treatment observations. The following is a brief summary of the results that were found when teachers from Group I schools receiving treatment were compared to teachers in Group II control schools during 1977–1978.

1977–1978

Project teachers in schools receiving treatment significantly increased rates of praise by the interim assessment while improvement by barometer teachers in the same schools was not significant until the posttreatment assessment ($p < .05$). Junior high school project and barometer teachers showed a significantly greater mean increase in their delivery of praise than that shown by elementary project teachers ($p < .05$). (The junior high school teachers started at a lower level than the elementary teachers.) Elementary barometer teachers in control schools not receiving treatment decreased their rate of delivering praise during the school year significantly more than elementary teachers in schools receiving treatment ($p < .05$).

The following results were found when teachers from Groups I and II schools were compared to their control year (1977–1978):

1978–1979

Teachers from project and barometer classrooms showed a significantly greater increase in their delivery of praise ($p < .01$). Project and barometer teachers attained significant increases in delivery of praise by the interim assessment ($p < .05$) and rates continued to increase by the posttreatment assessment ($p < .01$).

1979–1980

There was no significant effect of follow-up treatment on the amount of praise delivered by teachers.

Student Behavior

Students were dropped from the analysis if they were not present at least once during the baseline and once during posttreatment data collection periods. Disruptive behavior and nontask behavior were combined and designated as off-task behavior—the reciprocal of attending behavior. Baseline observations of off-task behavior were averaged for each student. The mean of baseline observations was subtracted from the mean posttreatment off-task behavior for each student for each year of the study. (No significant interim changes were noted.) The student was selected as the unit of analysis because analysis of variance results are identical "irrespective of whether group means or individual observations are employed. The use of individual observations also allows the exploration of other interesting questions pertaining to interaction and generalizability" (Hopkins 1982, p. 5).

A 2×2 factorial analysis of variance (school level by treatment) was used to evaluate changes in student off-task behavior between baseline and posttreatment observations. (A multiple baseline comparison, though preferable, was deemed impractical due to the limited number of observations and resources.)

The following results were found when students from schools receiving treatment were compared to students in control schools during 1977–1978: Students from project classrooms in schools receiving treatment showed a significantly greater ($p < .05$) mean decrease in off-task behavior during all 3 years of the study. There was a significantly greater mean decrease in student off-task behavior for the elementary than the junior high grades during 1977–1978 ($p < .05$). Students from barometer classrooms in schools receiving treatment showed a significantly greater ($p < .05$) mean decrease in off-task behavior during all 3 years of the study.

DISCUSSIONS AND CONCLUSIONS

Statistically significant reductions in vandalism were obtained for two consecutive years. A multiple baseline design also compared the vandalism costs of both treatment groups throughout the 3-year duration of the study. Because vandalism costs tend to be higher during certain months than others, it is best to compare treatment months back to nontreatment months in interpreting the graphed data. Recognizing this, it can be seen that maximum vandalism cost reductions occurred only following implementation of treatment in both groups. Further, decreases from baseline, though somewhat smaller, were obtained during the third year, as shown in Table 4. These smaller decreases were probably due to the double digit inflation that was occurring at the time.

Off-task behavior (e.g., hitting, yelling, throwing objects, not doing assigned work) of target students in both experimental project and barometer classrooms decreased from baseline significantly more than did the behavior of similar students in control project classrooms, throughout each of the 3 years of the study. Similarly, the average rate of positive teacher–student contacts improved significantly more in both the experimental project and barometer classrooms than in similar controls during the first 2 years of the study.

These findings are substantiated by a 1979 survey of the teachers and principals who participated in the project. All team members were given a questionnaire and a structured interview was conducted with team members. Fewer discipline problems, greater cooperation, and more positive feelings among students and staff were reported to be a result of the project programs. The survey was developed and completed by outside evaluators for the project and reported elsewhere (Jones, Mayer, & Butterworth, Note 7).

The present study indicates that the total school climate might be affected by initially working with the strong, influential members of a school staff, while making some additional consultation contacts with other staff members on request. Barometer teachers, a sample of other teachers in the school who did not attend off-campus workshops, changed positively in the way they interacted with their students, giving strong support to a schoolwide generalization of these results. Unfortunately, records were not kept of how many barometer or other teachers requested consultation. However, several reported events indicated that numerous teachers were influenced by the project teachers and other team members. Project teachers shared materials with other teachers and involved them in departmental or grade-level programs to provide students positive reinforcement for pro-social behaviors. Some principals suggested to groups of staff members and individuals that they try activities introduced by the project staff. Principals also praised project teachers at faculty meetings for their participation in the project. During the second year, consultants and school team members gave inservice training to all interested staff members. Thus, the staff development model used in this study appears to be both feasible and economical. It is difficult and often economically impossible to provide workshops and frequent ongoing consultation services to all members of a staff.

The intervention was also cost-effective in another respect. When average vandalism costs during treatment were compared with baseline, reductions of 66–92% (mean = 78.5%) were obtained without adjusting for inflation. These reductions occurred while schools throughout Los Angeles County were experiencing *increases* of 56% during 1978–79 and 35% during 1979–1980 (compared to the baseline year 1977–1978). When the data from Table 4 for the 1978–1979 school year were averaged with the pilot study data from 1976–1977 (Mayer & Butterworth, 1979), a mean vandalism cost reduction of 73.5% for 23 elementary and junior high schools was obtained. Thus, vandalism costs within project schools were reduced by at least two-thirds. A junior high school containing 1,500 students with an average monthly vandalism cost of $121.35/100 students could potentially save from $10,861 to $24,197 over a 9-month period. (The $10,861 figure is based on the two-thirds decrease only, whereas the $24,197 figure is the estimated savings if the vandalism cost had increased 56% rather than decreased 91.7%.)

Some bias could have entered into reports of vandalism by school principals. Principals might appear to be doing a better job if reported rates of vandalism were kept to a minimum. In actuality, it is quite unlikely that such biasing occurred. On the contrary, it is far more probable that data on vandalism costs from the "treated" schools were biased in the other direction, because the project staff visited those school sites weekly and reported any occurrences of damage that they noted. These were added to those of the principals. Naturally, because staff were not visiting the "control" schools at the same rate, supplementary reports could not have been added to the total figures. Thus, reported differences would reflect an underestimate rather than an overestimate.

Student and teacher behaviors were assessed both in target and in barometer classrooms to provide assurance that changes were implemented and to probe for possible spread of effects within the schools. Financial and other practical considerations (e.g., training, supervision, familiarity with contingencies in the classroom) limited the number of observations made and required that some of the observers also participate in the consultation during the first 2 years of the study. Thus, it is quite possible that their presence served to cue the teachers to practice their skills. However, only two of the six observers consulted extensively with teachers. These two did not collect data in the classroom. The other four only consulted sporadically. The three people who observed during the third year had no history as consultants to any of the teachers. Further, the experimental data showing improved student behavior also indicates that the teachers' performance probably did change. Thus, any reactivity during that period of time was probably no greater than that which is integral to any applied situation in which the behavior of the participants is under direct observation.

No one study, of course, provides a definitive answer. The area of vandalism involves more complex and temporally distant behavior than the immediate antecedents and consequences to behavior emphasized in current applied behavior analysis research (Wahler & Fox, 1981). Further, any investigation that uses a treatment package, or as broad an intervention program as was used in this study, will have a number of problems. Thus, this study should be viewed as a beginning, "an inspection of global categories ... a reasonable first step in methodology" (Wahler & Fox, 1981, p. 332) pointing to a possible direction of future research.

For future research, many modifications could be made in systematically replicating the present study. For example, even though it is almost impossible to measure directly the acts of vandalism, future investigation might attempt to assess the reliability of vandalism cost and frequency data by using two independent observers or reporters. Also, some investigators may wish to exclude verified *accidental* property damage from their data. In the present study, it was not possible to separate out those data because the figures were obtained from totals reported to the state. More frequent classroom observations could also supply more valid means of measuring teacher and pupil behavior, and permit independent observers to verify the extent to which consultants followed any standard procedure.

Because the treatment consisted of a "package" of procedures, it was impossible to determine to what degree classroom changes, planned community activities, involvement of youth clubs, or other aspects of the project were responsible for the obtained changes. Thus, further research should also attempt to tease out these differential contributors to the effectiveness of the program. In particular, we would like to see investigations on the refinement and relative contribution of various setting events.

The present study attempted to assess the environment, to determine whether it was becoming less punitive and more positive, by measuring rates of praise delivered by teachers. Behavior of other staff members (i.e., administrators) and interactions among peers could also be measured. Degree of match between students' reading levels and the difficulty of assigned materials could be assessed and compared or correlated to frequency of vandalism and differential costs. Similar investigations could be made with other potential setting events.

The present study and a previous one by Mayer and Butterworth (1979) focused on just a few factors that might provoke school disruption and vandalism. Because of the limited number of variables examined and the global measure of vandalism that was used, the magnitude of the results is impressive. The data solidly support the conclusion that educators can act successfully to reduce vandalism and inappropriate student behavior. However, much more work needs to be done to isolate effective treatment programs. We may find that certain treatment programs are best suited to preventing specific categories of vandalism such as theft or property damage. Currently, we are attempting to see if aspects of this approach can be shown reliably to bring about similarly marked changes at the secondary school level. It is hoped that the conditions that contribute to vandalism within the school can ultimately be identified and managed, permitting us then to direct our efforts to some of the factors that influence vandalism from the outside.

REFERENCE NOTES

1. *Attendance and Welfare 1979–80*. Bulletin, No. 35. Downey, Calif.: Office of the Los Angeles County Superintendent of Schools.
2. *Project PRIDE Progress*, I (1) (whole number). Burlingame, Calif.: 1976.
3. Azrin, N. H. *Aggressive responses of paired animals*. Paper presented at the symposium on Medical Aspects of Stress, Walter Reed Institute of Research, Washington, D.C., April 1964.
4. Mayer, G. R., & McGookin, R. B. *Behavioral consulting*. Downey, Calif.: Office of the Los Angeles County Superintendent of Schools, 1977.
5. Butterworth, T. *Strategies for reducing violence and vandalism. Project REVIVE*. Office of the Los Angeles County Superintendent of Schools. An ESEA, Title IV-C Innovative-Developmental Grant, September 1979.
6. Nafpaktitis, M., Mayer, G. R., Butterworth, T., & Jones, J. *Implementing project REVIVE: Workshops and guidelines*. Downey, Calif.: Office of the Los Angeles County Superintendent of Schools, 1980.
7. Jones, J., Mayer, G. R., & Butterworth, T. *REVIVE: Reducing violence and vandalism in education*. (ESEA Title IV C #3969), Downey, Calif.: Office of the Los Angeles County Superintendent of Schools, 1978.

REFERENCES

Azrin, N. H., & Holz, W. C. Punishment. In W. A. Honig (Ed.), *Operant behavior: Areas of research and application*. New York: Appleton-Century-Crofts, 1966.

Azrin, N. H., Hutchinson, R. R., & Hake, F. F. Pain-induced fighting in the squirrel monkey. *Journal of the Experimental Analysis of Behavior*, 1963, **6**, 620.

Bernhardt, A. H., & Forehand, R. The effects of labeled and unlabeled praise upon lower and middle class children. *Journal of Experimental Child Psychology*, 1975, **19**, 536–543.

Cossairt, A., Hall, R. V., & Hopkins, B. L. The effects of experimenter's instructions, feedback, and praise on teacher praise and student attending behavior. *Journal of Applied Behavior Analysis*, 1973, **6**, 89–100.

Gee, J. S. Community schools: Sunnyvale action against delinquency. *Crime Prevention Review*, 1974, **1**, 25–32.

Greenberg, B. School vandalism. Its effects and paradoxical solutions. *Crime Prevention Review*, 1974, **1**, 1–5.
Hopkins, K. D. The unit of analysis: Group means versus individual observations. *American Educational Research Journal*, 1982, **19**, 5–18.
Horton, L. E. Generalization of aggressive behavior in adolescent delinquent boys. *Journal of Applied Behavior Analysis*, 1970, **3**, 205–211.
Kaplan, P., Kohfeldt, J., & Sturla, K. *It's positively fun*. Denver, Colo: Love Publishing Co., 1974.
Mayer, G. R., & Butterworth, T. A preventive approach to school violence and vandalism: An experimental study. *The Personnel and Guidance Journal*, 1979, **57**, 436–441.
National Institute of Education. *The safe school study*. Washington, D.C.: U.S. Department of Health, Education, and Welfare, Office of Education, 1978.
Siegel, S. *Nonparametric statistics for behavioral sciences*. New York: McGraw-Hill, 1956.
Sulzer-Azaroff, B., & Mayer, G. R. *Applying behavior analysis procedures with children and youth*. New York: Holt, Rinehart, and Winston, 1977.
Thomas, J. D., Presland, I. E., Grant, M. D., & Glynn, T. Natural rates of teacher approval in grade 7 classrooms. *Journal of Applied Behavior Analysis*, 1978, **11**, 95–109.
Wahler, R. G., & Fox, J. J. Setting events in applied behavior analysis: Toward a conceptual and methodological expansion. *Journal of Applied Behavior Analysis*, 1981, **14**, 327–338.
Ziesel, J. *Stopping school property damage*. Boston: American Association of School Administrators and Educational Facilities Laboratories in collaboration with City of Boston Public Facilities Department, 1976.

COUNTERING SIGN VANDALISM WITH PUBLIC SERVICE ADVERTISING

KATHERINE FRITH

In a study compiled for the Transportation Research Board in 1983 by Chadda and Carter (1), it was noted that about $50 million is being spent annually in the United States by state departments of transportation to replace stolen and vandalized highway signs. In addition, the indirect costs incurred by state governments for injury and tort liability in accidents that result from missing and vandalized highway signs are estimated to be of about the same magnitude.

Highway signs have become a symbol of modern culture to today's teenagers. They often hang stolen highway signs on the walls of their university dormitories and fraternity or sorority houses (1). So common is the practice of using highway signs as room decorations that stop signs can even be seen on current television shows (The Whiz Kids, CBS, 1984) hanging on the kids' bedroom walls. In current catalogs of home furnishings (J.C. Penney's, Fall 1985) signs are displayed as the typical wall hanging in a teenager's room.

Vandalism has been described in the literature as an activity that is most common among teenage boys (2–4). Studies show that vandalism is seldom committed alone. Around 90 percent of all vandalism is committed by groups of teenagers (5).

Source: *Transportation Research Record 1069* (1985): 68–72. Reprinted by permission of the Transportation Research Board, National Research Council, Washington, D.C., and the author.

THE SITUATION IN IOWA

Stealing or vandalizing a highway sign is a crime under Iowa law. However, few vandals are caught or prosecuted because most acts of vandalism toward signs occur at night and in areas where there is little surveillance.

With regard to accidents that occur because of sign vandalism, exact statistics are not known. However, several people have been injured in Iowa, and at least one person was killed in an accident that occurred where a sign was missing. A 1982 legal case involving an accident directly attributable to a stolen sign cost the state $250,000.

PUBLIC SERVICE ADVERTISING

Recent research on the persuasive effects of media campaigns has produced some striking data on their effectiveness (6–8). Several theoretical models have been suggested to explain the persuasive effects of mass media messages on public attitudes, perceptions, and behaviors (9). With varying degrees of sophistication, these authors suggest that attitude and behavior change take place in a linear fashion, beginning with the building of awareness or knowledge and culminating in behavior change (9,10).

Chadda and Carter (1) note that media campaigns have been used in certain states to reduce the incidence of sign vandalism. The purpose of their study was to develop public service messages that could be effective in raising teenagers' awareness of the problem and the consequences of sign vandalism.

RESEARCH QUESTIONS

In order to develop advertising messages that would have salience for the target audience, data were first needed on the attitudes, perceptions, and knowledge levels of teenagers regarding sign vandalism. A survey was designed to gather information on the following research questions:

1. How widespread is the incidence of sign vandalism?
2. Do teenagers perceive of sign vandalism as a serious crime?
3. Is public service advertising an effective way to raise awareness among teenagers of the problem and the consequences of sign vandalism?

METHODOLOGY

A questionnaire was distributed to 506 Iowa teenagers (207 males and 299 females). The sample represented a broad range of Iowa's teenage population.

In addition to the survey, formative research was gathered in an attempt to identify leads for the development of mass media messages. Focus group interviews were conducted with teenagers who admitted to having first-hand knowledge of sign vandalism. Although the survey enabled the identification of attitudes, perceptions, and behaviors, the formative research provided a way to probe deeper into the motivations for sign vandalism.

Based on the survey data and interviews, four print advertisements were prepared and tested. These ads were run over a period of 6 weeks in *The Iowa State Daily*. A random sample of college students was surveyed before and after the campaign appeared in the newspaper to determine the effectiveness of the advertisements.

SURVEY RESULTS

In order to determine how widespread the incidence of sign vandalism was, respondents were asked whether they had ever been part of a group that had stolen or vandalized a sign. They were also asked whether they had ever individually stolen or vandalized a sign. Table 1 presents the data gathered on these questions.

Approximately 20 percent of the total sample said that they had been part of a group that had stolen a sign. Sign theft appeared to be the most prevalent type of sign vandalism and it appeared to be a group, rather than an individual, activity.

In order to determine how widespread sign vandalism was, teenagers were asked if they knew anyone who had a sign as a room decoration. Approximately 71 percent of the sample admitted knowing someone who had a stolen sign in his or her room.

It was hypothesized that teenagers might not be aware of the traffic danger that results when signs are stolen or vandalized. However, when asked whether they thought stealing stop signs would create dangers to drivers, approximately 97 percent of the sample said that the removal of a stop sign would very likely result in a traffic accident. Ironically, although they appeared to be aware of the dangers of removing a sign, few appeared concerned about taking action to stop sign vandals. When asked what they

TABLE 1. Incidence of Sign Vandalism

Question	Percent answering "Yes"		
	Males (N = 207)	Females (N = 299)	Total (N = 506)
Have you ever been part of a group that has taken a sign?	27	14	20
Have you ever been part of a group that has painted on a sign?	5	5	5
Have you ever been part of a group that has shot at a sign?	26	4	14
Have you ever personally taken a sign?	17	7	11
Have you ever personally painted on a sign?	3	3	3
Have you ever shot at a sign?	22	3	10
Have you ever run down a highway sign?	8	4	6

would do if they saw a sign being stolen or vandalized, 63 percent said that they would ignore the act. The total responses to this question were as follows ($\chi^2 = 35.82$, $p < .0001$):

Response choice	Total percent
Tell them to stop	11
Report them to the authorities	26
Ignore them	63

FORMATIVE RESEARCH

The qualitative data gathered in focus groups with sign vandals provided useful insights into the sign vandalism problem. Generally, students perceived of sign theft and vandalism as a prank rather than a serious crime. These kinds of comments were recorded in the focus groups:

> It's not really stealing, I just took a sign.
>
> Within a few days they usually have the signs replaced. They have more than enough signs to replace the one I take. If they can replace them in a few days, then what's the big deal? No one gets hurt because the sign is missing.
>
> It isn't stealing. My taxes paid for them.

Ironically, two students added that although they had stolen a sign, they would never deface signs because that was "silly and unnecessary and could lead to serious traffic accidents."

When students were asked to explain why they had taken the signs, the answers varied. These are a few comments that were recorded:

> They really make neat room decorations, especially stop signs. I stole a cow crossing sign once because my friend in Illinois lives on a ranch and Illinois doesn't have as creative cow crossing signs as Iowa does.
>
> I guess the sign is some sort of a status symbol because it proves you had to go through something to get it.
>
> I mean, if you see a stop sign in someone's room, you can imagine what they've gone through. You could just buy a poster or something like that in a store.

THE PUBLIC SERVICE ADVERTISEMENTS

The survey data and formative research provided valuable insights for the development of the public service advertising campaign. The objectives for the advertising campaign were

- To increase awareness among the primary target audience of the fact that $1 million is spent annually to replace stolen and vandalized signs,
- To increase awareness among the target audience of the serious traffic accidents that can result from a missing or defaced sign, and
- To increase awareness among the primary target audience that sign vandalism is a crime with serious consequences by stressing the severe fine ($1,000) and the maximum jail sentence (1 year in jail) in the advertising campaign.

The slogan that was chosen as the campaign theme was "Sign vandalism. It's no joke. It's a crime." It was hoped that the slogan would reinforce the perception that sign vandalism was a serious crime.

Each of the advertisements had a headline that identified a specific sign vandalism problem, followed by the slogan line. The copy explained the problem in greater detail. A grid that graphically showed the fines and penalties attached to sign vandalism appeared in each ad.

TESTING THE ADVERTISEMENTS

The aim of pretesting advertising messages is to determine whether the advertisements are capable of producing a trend in the desired direction of attitude and behavior change in the target audience. The Iowa State University campus was selected as the site for the pretest and posttest because of the availability of the campus newspaper, *The Iowa State Daily*, which offered a greater degree of control in disseminating the messages than did the commercial mass media.

A random sample of 250 undergraduates was contacted by telephone before and after the advertisement appeared in *The Iowa State Daily*. Different students were selected for the pretest and posttest. The advertisements ran a total of eight times over a 6-week period. The results of the tests are presented in Table 2.

CONCLUSIONS

Sign vandalism is a costly problem that creates hazards. It requires a concerted effort at the national, state, and local levels. Yearly national cost for replacing stolen and vandalized signs has been estimated to be in excess of $50 million.

This study suggests that public service advertising can be an effective

TABLE 2. Pretest and Posttest Comparison of Students' Knowledge About Sign Vandalism

	Percent Correct responses	Percent incorrect responses
Fine for Stealing Signs[a] ($\chi^2 = 65.37$, $df = 1$, $p < .05$)		
Pretest	16	84
Posttest	51	49
Fine for Possession of Stolen Sign[b] ($\chi^2 = 4.38$, $df = 1$, $p < .05$)		
Pretest	48	52
Posttest	57	43
Jail Term for Sign Vandalism[c] ($\chi^2 = 35.96$, $df = 1$, $p < .05$)		
Pretest	39	61
Posttest	66	34
Yearly Cost to Iowa of Sign Vandalism[d] ($\chi^2 = .697$, $df = 1$, $p = < .05$)		
Pretest	19	81
Posttest	22	78

[a]Correct response: $1,000; incorrect responses: $25, $100, other.
[b]Correct response: $100; incorrect responses: $25, $1,000, other.
[c]Correct response: 30 days; incorrect responses: none, 1 year, other.
[d]Correct response: $1 million; incorrect responses: $1,000; $500,000; other.

method for increasing awareness among teenagers of the serious consequences of vandalizing highway signs. In three out of four cases, the knowledge levels of teenagers significantly increased with exposure to the print advertisements. Whether or not the increased knowledge of the fines and penalties for sign vandalism will ultimately effect behavior change is beyond the scope of this study. However, behavior change is the long-term goal of any social change public service advertising campaign.

Chadda and Carter (1) noted that the state of Wisconsin was able to reduce the incidence of sign vandalism by 57 percent with the use of brochures, media announcements, and educational materials developed for driver's education classes. It is the author's contention that public service advertising combined with other educational materials can be an effective method for reducing sign vandalism throughout the United States.

ACKNOWLEDGMENTS

Much of the work described in this paper was performed under a grant from the Iowa Department of Transportation. The opinions and conclusions expressed in this paper are those of the author and are not an official statement of the department. Publication of this paper sponsored by Committee on Traffic Control Devices.

REFERENCES

1. H. S. Chadda and E. C. Carter. *Sign Vandalism: A Costly and Dangerous National Problem*. Presented at the 62nd Annual Meeting of the Transportation Research Board, Washington, D.C., 1983.
2. R. Griffiths. The Vandal's Perspective: Meanings and Motives. In *Designing against Vandalism* (J. Sykes, ed.), London, 1979.
3. S. Stainforth and T. Twyman. *Researching a Complex Social Problem: Vandalism in the U.K.* European Research, May 1980.
4. C. Castleman. *Getting Up: Subway Graffiti in New York*. MIT Press, Cambridge, Mass., 1982.
5. Home Office Standing Committee on Crime Prevention. *Studies in the Causes of Delinquency and the Treatment of Offenders*. Her Majesty's Stationery Office, London, 1975.
6. R. K. Manoff. *Social Marketing: Imperatives for Public Health*. Praeger, New York, 1985.
7. A. McAlister. Anti-Smoking Campaigns: Progress in Developing Effective Communications. In *Public Communication Campaigns* (R. Rice and W. Paisley, eds.). Sage, Beverly Hills, Calif., 1981.

8. G. J. O'Keefe and H. Mendelsohn. *Taking a Bite Out of Crime: The Impact of a Mass Media Crime Prevention Campaign*. U.S. Department of Justice, 1984.
9. W. J. McGuire. Theoretical Foundations of Campaigns. In *Public Communication Campaigns* (R. Rice and W. Paisley, eds.). Sage, Beverly Hills, Calif., 1981.
10. R. Cialdini, R. Petty, and J. Cacioppo. Attitude and Attitude Change. *Annual Review of Psychology*, Vol. 32, 1981.

THEFT AND MUTILATION OF LIBRARY MATERIALS

TERRI L. PEDERSEN

According to research, the problem of periodical and book theft and mutilation is laying waste to vital and expensive library collections throughout the country. Too often the damage is done quietly and is not discovered until long after the act has taken place. Damage ranges from a few pages to entire books and journals. Information is scarce on why theft and mutilation occur and on how much they cost libraries. From 1972 to 1987, less than fifteen articles and papers have been written on the subject. Very few studies have been undertaken.

REVIEW OF RELATED RESEARCH

In the early 1970s Ron G. Martin, a librarian at Kearney State College in Nebraska, surveyed libraries. He received responses from ninety-two of them regarding instances of periodical mutilation. Eighty percent reported considerable damage to periodicals. Forty-seven percent said that they replaced mutilated periodicals with microforms.[1]

Around the same time, another study was conducted by Mary Noel Gouke and Marjorie Murfin. It was undertaken three years after the conclusion of a widespread publicity campaign. Their purpose was to determine the extent and cost of periodical mutilation at the library in which they worked and to locate possible solutions. They discovered that the rate of

Source: *College and Research Libraries*, 1990, *51*(2): 120–128.

mutilation of periodicals was 15 percent. This amounted to 1,295 issues annually with $7,700 to $12,950 spent on repair. The authors also estimated that in the previous ten years $13,860 to $23,100 was spent for 2,310 issues. They also found that the public relations campaign was a viable method of reducing periodical mutilation and that the presence of damaged periodicals led to more mutilation. Among the preventive methods used were signs stating that there would be no replacement of lost articles, offers of better copiers, and the beginning of a copy of machine loan fund.[2]

A study was also undertaken at Kent State University in 1973 by Clyde Hendrick and Marjorie Murfin in which 168 students were issued questionnaires assessing their knowledge of and opinions about periodical mutilation. The respondents were enrolled in introductory psychology and social psychology classes at the institution. The first portion of the questionnaire dealt with personal information; familiarity with the library; and attitudes toward mutilation, copier use, penalties, and replacement. The closing section asked for opinions about possible solutions. The students were also given the option of signing their questionnaire so that Hendrick and Murfin could identify and interview professed mutilators.[3]

In 1978 Dana Weiss attempted to replicate the Murfin–Hendrick study. She surveyed 201 students and found that mutilation involved good students who were motivated by academic pressure. However, no connection was discovered between a student's attitude toward the library and the acts of theft and mutilation. Also, her theory that more photocopy machines might alleviate the problem was not supported.[4]

In 1981 the University of Nebraska at Omaha reported a rise in mutilation and theft. During the year, 1,000 magazine pages and 672 complete issues had to be replaced. To combat the problem, the library launched a public relations campaign alerting students to the fact that mutilation is a crime.[5]

Collectively these studies demonstrate that all libraries encounter the problem of mutilation and theft. The damage is especially troublesome for academic libraries and leads to costly damage that causes frustration for both patrons and library staff members. The present study was conducted because a need exists for research into the causes and prevention of mutilation and theft in libraries.

There were four major goals of the study. The desired result of the project was to discover the answers to inquiries related to these stated goals:

1. Through the examination of the attitudes and characteristics of students who mutilate and steal as compared with those who do not, to uncover the reasons why theft and mutilation occur.

2. In discovering the reasons for an circumstances surrounding the theft and mutilation of library materials, to find out how it is accomplished.
3. By looking at the proportion of students involved in theft and mutilation of periodicals or books, to discover who is responsible.
4. Finally, to locate preventive methods that students feel would be good deterrents to the problem of mutilation and theft.

METHODOLOGY OF DATA COLLECTION

The study was conducted during the 1988 spring semester at Emporia State University. At that time the school had an enrollment of 5,134 students. As in the Hendrick–Murfin and Weiss studies, it was determined that an anonymous questionnaire would yield the greatest results. It was in the selection of the sample that this study deviates from the previous two. In those studies, the methods of obtaining students were limited, thus biasing their results. The test group and final data were thrown off by a young population that was mainly female. In this project, an attempt was made to choose a sample that was more representative of the entire student population. Courses were randomly selected from each subject division making up the university structure.

The questionnaires were administered to the students during class time, with the permission of the instructor. This method was chosen to help ensure a high survey return. Sixteen classes were visited with the questionnaire during a two-week period. It was administered to 235 students. Data analysis is based upon the results from those respondents.

RESULTS

The first section describes the makeup of the sample. The next section presents the results of the questionnaire and compares those who admitted to being involved and theft and mutilation (violators) and those not involved (nonviolators).

CHARACTERISTICS OF THE SAMPLE

The 235 students surveyed represented approximately 5 percent of the total population of the university. Of the 235 students, 54%, or 122, were female and 46%, or 104, were male. This came fairly close to the university's ratio of 60/40.... The sample population was also very close to the university's totals in regard to student grade classification. The breakdown was as follows: freshmen, 65, or 28%; sophomores, 41, or 17%; juniors, 61, or 26%; seniors, 54, or 23%, and graduate students, 14, or 6%. The university class breakdown was 18%, 13%, 16%, 18%, and 32%, respectively. The obvious downfall in the sampling was the low questioning of graduate students, which could have been avoided by visiting more graduate courses. The students involved in the survey were fairly evenly spread between the ages of 18 and 23, with only 13% of the sample over the age of 25. The students were also from the various colleges, with the highest percentages in either the school of business or the teachers college, which was not overly surprising.

Two of the most significant questions asked if the students had ever stolen books or magazines from the library or if they had ripped out pages. Twenty-four students admitted ripping out pages and 11 confessed to stealing library materials. Only 6 students circled yes to both questions, for a total of 29 violators, 12% of the sample surveyed. Of this group of violators, most were involved in fewer than five instances.

One goal was to determine whether a violator differed drastically from a nonviolator and to devise a composite sketch of a violator. The belief was that those involved would be younger students with poor to average grades, lacking responsibility and looking for an easy way out. What emerged as the typical violator was a male or female student, aged 20–22, junior or senior, with a G.P.A. in the 2.0–2.9 range.

One important fact was that students do not spend much time in the library. The study indicated that those spending more time in the library were less likely to damage and steal library materials. Most students also admitted to writing very few papers in their college career. Seventy-five percent completed less than ten. Students writing fewer papers were more inclined to damage periodicals, but this was not as true for the theft of books. Another interesting fact is that paying for one's own college education does not seem to make a student more responsible or less likely to mutilate and steal.

Replacement

Several questions asked students what they knew about the replacement time and cost involved when pages, books, and periodicals have been stolen or mutilated. Students believe that things are replaced fairly easily. This usually only holds true for magazine articles and books pages that are missing and not entire books and periodicals. Students made a good guess at the replacement cost and time when only the pages were missing. Most missing pages at Emporia State are ordered through the interlibrary loan department. These replacement pages may be received in a month, and 66% of the students answered this question accurately. The cost usually involves only staff time in locating and ordering replacement pages. This probably averages $5 to $10, which was the response of 48% of the students. In terms of replacing entire books and whole periodicals, the sample perceived it as being easier than it actually is. Only 16% of the students answered that replacements may never be found and bought. Most students (62%) felt that materials could be replaced within a three-month period. When it comes to changing the perceptions of students regarding periodical and book theft and mutilation, information concerning replacement costs and time should probably be used in a campaign. Perhaps if more patrons realized that items may not be replaced, they might think before acting rashly. In terms of cost, 84% of the students felt that stolen items could be replaced for under ten dollars. Once again, this is an area where the students' beliefs need to be changed (see Table 1).

Perceptions of the Problem and Penalties

A major group of questions involved students' perceptions of the problem of mutilation and theft and the penalties assessed. One of the most important conclusions is that students felt that the library would be or is a very easy place from which to steal. This belief could be altered. Most students recognized that the theft and mutilation of library materials are crimes. Eighty-two percent felt that the penalty for getting caught should be a fine. Very few (under 4%) felt that no penalty should exist. When asked what they would do if they saw someone ripping out pages or stealing a magazine or book, 61% said they would do nothing. Thirty percent indicated they would report it, and the remaining 9% would either tell the offender what they were doing was wrong or ask them to stop.

When asked if they had ever considered tearing out articles or pages from a book, most of the students (56%) said that they had never thought about it. Thirty-eight percent admitted to considering the act once or twice, with only 6% thinking about it more than a few times. Twenty-five percent admitted considering stealing a magazine or book, while 75% never considered it. When admitted violators were asked about their concerns for getting caught in the act, 50% were not concerned at all, 34% were mildly to moderately concerned, and only 16% were very worried about someone catching them.

Of the 235 students questioned, only 33% said that they had never been inconvenienced by missing or torn-out pages. Fifty-five percent had been bothered once in a while, and 12% were either inconvenienced quite often or all of the time. Of the violators, only 58% had ever been inconvenienced through stolen or damaged periodicals or books.

In the sampling of the student population, only 10% admitted to

TABLE 1. Results on Library Use and Perceptions of the Problem

Question		Nonripoffs (%)	Thieves (%)	Page rippers (%)
Library use				
A. Number of term papers done so far in college	0–9	74	36	80
	10–19	20	46	16
	20+	6	18	4
B. Amount of times one goes to the library	Almost never	41	82	33
	1–5 times weekly	55	9	63
	Daily	4	9	4
C. Hours a week spent in the library	0	30	36	17
	1–5	55	55	75
	6–15	12	0	4
	16+	3	9	4
Perceptions on theft and mutilation of library materials				
A. How easy would it be to tear out an article or to steal library materials?	Very easy	61	90	63
	Somewhat difficult	28	10	29
	Moderately difficult	8	0	8
	Very difficult	3	0	0
B. What is the penalty for theft and mutilation of library items?	None	20	36	35
	Misdemeanor	72	46	57
	Higher than misdemeanor	8	18	8
C. What should the penalty be?	None	2	18	17
	Fine	83	82	75
	More severe	15	0	8
D. If you saw someone violating library materials, what would you do?	Nothing	59	91	88
	Tell them it's wrong and ask to stop	8	9	4
	Report it	33	0	8
E. Time to replace a torn-out article	Less than 1 month	48	54	59
	1–6 months	39	28	29
	Over 6 months	13	18	12
F. Time to replace a stolen magazine	Less than 1 month	30	46	46
	1–6 months	43	18	30
	Over 6 months	10	9	11
	Never Replaced	17	27	13
G. Cost to the library to replace torn pages	$1 and under	27	55	54
	$5–10	51	27	21
	Over $15	22	18	25
H. Cost to replace a stolen book or magazine	Under $10	84	91	96
	$15–20	11	9	0
	Over $20	5	0	4

(*Continued*)

TABLE 1. (*Continued*)

Question		Nonripoffs (%)	Thieves (%)	Page rippers (%)
I. Have you ever been inconvenienced by missing pages, magazines or books?	Never	32	63	42
	Once in a while	56	27	50
	Quite often	10	10	4
	All the time	2	0	4
J. Have you ever considered tearing out an article or book pages?	Never	60	18	17
	Once or twice	36	37	63
	Occasionally	3	27	12
	All the time	1	18	8
K. Have you ever considered stealing a magazine or book?	Never	76	9	54
	Once or twice	22	64	33
	Occasionally	2	9	4
	All the time	0	18	9
L. What percentage of the student body is involved in theft and mutilation?	0–15%	51	18	20
	15–30%	29	27	42
	30–50%	15	18	17
	Over 50%	5	37	21

periodical and book theft or mutilation. When students were asked to estimate what percentage of the student body might rip out articles or steal books or magazines: 18% answered under 5%; 30% responded with 5–15%; 30% also marked 15–30%; and 28% felt that over 30% of the student body might be involved in the theft and damage. Students who admitted to being violators were more inclined to believe that a large percentage of the students were involved in theft and mutilation.

Opinions on the Reasons for Theft and Mutilation

Another section asked students why they thought books and periodicals were mutilated and stolen (see Table 2). They were to circle as many responses as they felt correct. Seventy-eight percent of the nonviolators felt that students did not consider the needs of others, as compared with 83% of the violators. Few respondees believed that students were unable to afford the copy machine or the price of the book, with only 36% of the nonviolators and 50% of the violators answering yes to that question. Because more violators felt this was true, it may explain why some were involved in the damage. When asked if students were aware of the cost of the theft and mutilation to the library, 55 percent of both the violators and nonviolators felt that this was a problem. Again, both groups were in agreement when

TABLE 2. Question: Books and Periodicals Are Stolen and Mutilated Because Students ...

		Responses		
		Thieves (%)	Page rippers (%)	Nonviolators (%)
A. Do not consider the needs of others	(T)	72	83	79
	(F)	28	17	21
B. Cannot afford the copy machine or the price of the book, but want to own a copy	(T)	45	54	36
	(F)	54	45	64
C. Are not aware of the cost of theft and mutilation to the library	(T)	36	55	56
	(F)	64	45	44
D. Need the photographs or charts and cannot photocopy them	(T)	19	50	70
	(F)	81	50	30
E. Do not think about the act or the library, but steal and mutilate casually and thoughtlessly	(T)	27	45	53
	(F)	73	55	47
F. Steal and mutilate items as an expression of hostility toward the library and university	(T)	18	9	13
	(F)	82	91	87

asked if students need the photographs or charts that could not be copied. Only 30% in each group answered yes to this question, indicating a problem. When asked if mutilation and theft were done casually and thoughtlessly, 52% of the nonviolators felt this was true. A big difference was shown in the responses of the violators. Fifty-five percent of the article and page rippers felt that it was done thoughtlessly, but only 27% of the book or magazine stealers indicated this was true. Very few students viewed theft and mutilation as an expression of hostility towards the library.

Effective Preventive Methods

Opinions were asked on which measures would be effective in eliminating the problem (see Table 3). The only option that received an overwhelming response was the availability of free copying. Sixty-three percent of both the violators and nonviolators felt that this would help prevent the problem. Other options included the following: (1) periodicals kept on reserve for checkout—30% for and 70% against; (2) periodicals on limited access or not able to be removed from the area—35% for and 65% against; (3) sign warning of the penalty, $500 fine or 30 days in jail—45% felt this would work, while 55% said it would not; (4) signs indicating the cost and time of replacement—32% felt this would be effective, while 68% felt it

TABLE 3. Results for Effective Preventive Measures

Measure	Thieves, rippers, nonviolators	Effective (%)	Not effective (%)
A. Periodicals kept on reserve and have to be checked out	T	36	64
	R	33	67
	NV	29	71
B. Limited access—Periodicals not taken from area	T	36	64
	R	33	67
	NV	35	65
C. Sign warning of penalty: $500 or 30 days in jail	T	64	36
	R	46	54
	NV	44	56
D. Signs indicating cost and time of replacement	T	18	82
	R	38	62
	NV	31	69
E. Periodicals could be checked out like books	T	27	73
	R	54	46
	NV	45	55
F. Publicity campaign showing the extent of problem and urging concern for others	T	0	100
	R	25	75
	NV	22	78
G. Free copying available	T	45	55
	R	63	37
	NV	63	37
H. Copying loan service or copy cards bought in advance	T	27	73
	R	42	58
	NV	24	76

would not be; (5) a publicity campaign showing the extent of the problem and urging concern for others—23% in favor and 77% opposed; and (6) a copying loan service or copy card bought in advance—25% for and 75% against. Forty-five percent of the nonviolators favored checking out periodicals like books as compared with 54% of the violators.

General Attitudes Concerning the Library and Its Services

The final section of the questionnaire dealt with the library, its services, and copy machines (see Table 4). Generally, students were positive toward the library (87%). Most usually found what they needed in the library, with only 20% disagreeing. A majority felt they were treated fairly by the library, with only 18% feeling unfairly treated. When asked if the library discriminates against undergraduate students by having more lenient policies for graduate students and faculty, most of the students either disagreed or had

TABLE 4. General Attitudes Concerning the Library and Services

Question	Thieves, rippers, nonviolators	Agree (%)	Somewhat agree (%)	No opinion (%)	Disagree (%)
A. In general, I feel very positive toward the library	T	36	55	0	9
	R	67	25	4	4
	NV	64	23	10	3
B. The library is a cold and anonymous place	T	36	18	27	18
	R	13	25	12	50
	NV	5	23	27	45
C. I find the library staff to be quite friendly and helpful	T	64	27	9	0
	R	63	29	8	0
	NV	39	38	15	8
D. I always find what I need in the library	T	18	45	27	9
	R	39	52	4	4
	NV	16	57	5	21
E. I have been treated unfairly by the library at least once	T	9	27	27	36
	R	8	13	25	54
	NV	10	8	25	57

F. The library discriminates against undergraduates because it has more lenient policies for grads and faculty	T	18	9	36	36
	R	0	17	50	33
	NV	6	12	52	30
G. Copy machines are too expensive	T	46	18	18	18
	R	50	29	0	21
	NV	44	23	17	16
H. Copy machines take too long to use	T	9	18	18	55
	R	8	25	17	50
	NV	9	13	23	55
I. The copy machines are usually out of order	T	18	46	27	9
	R	17	54	8	21
	NV	17	34	28	21
J. The library can easily replace stolen or mutilated books and periodicals	T	27	9	18	46
	R	8	25	25	42
	NV	1	9	24	56
K. No harm is done since no one else will need that particular item	T	9	18	9	64
	R	4	13	17	66
	NV	1	1	10	88

no opinion. When asked if the library was a cold and anonymous place, 71% answered either no opinion or disagreed. If was interesting to find out that 54 percent of those admitting to stealing items agreed that the library was cold and anonymous. Most of those students also found the library staff to be friendly and helpful and felt positive toward the library. Basically, these questions helped library employees to know that they are viewed positively but need to work on helping patrons more in finding what they need.

Three questions were asked about the copy machines. As expected, a large majority felt that the copy machines were too expensive and usually out of order. Neither can be changed when the cost of operation and high level of use are considered. When a machine breaks down, the repairmen are contacted immediately. When asked if copy machines take too long to use, most students disagreed, so this does not seem to be a problem.

The final two questions dealt with the perceptions on mutilation and theft. It was surprising to find that 80% of the nonviolators disagreed with the statement that the library could easily replace stolen items and over 30% of the violators felt that stolen and damaged materials could be easily replaced. It was encouraging to note that 85% agreed that theft and mutilation are harmful because someone may need an item.

SUMMARY

Based on the data, the violators did not seem to differ greatly from the nonviolators. Basically, it was discovered that students cannot be identified as potential violators of library materials. It appears that situational circumstances lead a student to mutilation and theft. A number of the nonviolators expressed the temptation to steal pages, articles, books, or journals, thus indicating a potential group for more damage to library materials. Dana Weiss noted in her research:

> Because this study was done in an urban university library, it could be said that the "toughness" of city life causes the theft. However, I believe a case could be made for "danger" on a rural college campus.[6]

Because Emporia is in a rural area, the "toughness of city life" is not a cause of mutilation and theft. The fault does not appear to lie with the library being unfriendly, cold, and anonymous. Students did not view the theft and mutilation problem as an expression of hostility toward the institution but instead felt that their fellow students were selfish and did not consider the needs of others. In the 1980s, the emphasis has been on the success of the individual striving for personal gain no matter what cost is involved. With the thought of academic achievement leading to professional success for the individual, there is the pressure to do well and to earn high grades. Thus, as Weiss remarked, "Good grades may serve to reinforce for ... students that it is more important what happens in their individual careers than sensitivity to the needs of fellow students."[7]

The present study points to certain steps that the library can take to reduce instances of theft and mutilation. Staff should watch carefully for and be aware of those students having trouble using the library and possibly looking for help, thus reducing the frustration level that may ultimately lead to desperate measures. As in previous studies, the survey indicates that patrons are not really aware of the difficulty and expense involved in replacing damaged and stolen library materials. A publicity campaign could inform students of the cost associated with lost, stolen, or mutilated books and magazines. Informed students should be less likely to steal and mutilate.

Other measures are the setting of equitable penalties for violation, with signs that cite the law and list penalties. Those surveyed, however, felt that the theft and mutilation of library materials were easy to do with limited consequences and little chance of being apprehended. If students found that the theft and mutilation of library materials were more difficult to accomplish and that the penalties were stiffer and enforced, the problem would decrease. A library's lowering the cost of photocopying should diminish the problem as well.

This study has uncovered possibilities for further work, such as initiating some preventive measures and evaluating their usefulness. If preventive measures are effective, libraries will be able to overcome the costly damage that causes frustration for both patrons and library staff members. Further means to deter possible violators of library materials still need to be developed.

REFERENCES

1. Ron Martin, "Microforms and Periodical Mutilation," *Microform Review* 2:6–8 (Jan. 1973).
2. Mary Noel Gouke and Marjorie Murfin, "Periodical Mutilation: The Insidious Disease," *Library Journal* 105:1795–97 (Sept. 15, 1980).
3. Clyde Hendrick and Marjorie Murfin, "Project Library Ripoff: A Study of Periodical Mutilation in a University Library," *College & Research Libraries* 35:402–4 (Nov. 1974).
4. Dana Weiss, "Book Theft and Mutilation in a Large Urban University Library," *College & Research Libraries* 42:341–47 (July 1981).
5. "University of Nebraska Reports Sharp Rise in Mutilation," *Library Journal* 107:2212 (Dec. 1, 1982).
6. Weiss, "Book Theft and Mutilation," p. 345.
7. Ibid.

THE EQUITY CONTROL MODEL AS A PREDICTOR OF VANDALISM AMONG COLLEGE STUDENTS[1]

Sylvia Warzecha DeMore, Jeffrey D. Fisher, and Reuben M. Baron

Investigations into the problem of vandalism have been limited in scope and quantity. Vandalism constitutes a rather common form of aggression, and its roots need to be more thoroughly understood. Basic research on this phenomenon could be an important adjunct to extant work on human aggression. From a practical standpoint, the societal costs of vandalism are simply enormous. Vandalism in American schools, parks, recreation areas, public housing, and transit systems is estimated to cost from \$1 to \$4 billion per year, and the figure is increasing rapidly (Einolander, 1976; U.S. Senate Judiciary Subcommittee, 1975).

Cohen (1973) formulated a useful taxonomy to differentiate among the various types of vandalism. He identified five categories: *acquisitive* van-

[1]The authors gratefully acknowledge the assistance of David A. Kenny and Laurin Hafner in the data analysis, David A. Wicklund for comments on an earlier draft of this manuscript, and Lisa Cassady for comments on the manuscript as well as for providing additional data analyses found in the discussion section. An earlier version of this paper was presented at the Annual Meeting of the Eastern Psychological Association in April, 1984.

Source: *Journal of Applied Social Psychology* 1988, *18*(1):80–91.

dalism (damage that results in the process of looting or petty theft), *tactical/ideological* vandalism (to draw attention to an issue or to oneself), *vindictive* vandalism (a form of revenge), *play* vandalism (accidentally breaking something as part of a game), and *malicious* vandalism (a directed and responsive act to express malice, aggression or anger, often occurring in public settings wherein the target is depersonalized).

Characterizations of the vandal and his or her act have varied in the literature. Ward (1973) describes the stereotype of the vandal as a working-class male adolescent engaging in a "wanton" act—the "senseless" or motiveless destruction of property, usually public property of some kind. However, others assert that vandalism *is* meaningful (Allen & Greenberger, 1980; Baron & Fisher, 1984; Fisher & Baron, 1982; Zimbardo, 1972). It is an act that has meaning both to the vandal and to society at large (Baron & Fisher, 1984; Cohen, 1973; Fisher & Baron, 1982), and society's refusal to recognize the basis of the vandal's problem may be the reason that much vandalism is directed at public property, a symbol of the "unfair system" (Clinard & Quinney, 1973).

Theories attempting to explain vandalism have been narrow in range, focusing on two aspects of the problem—identifying the causes and studying the consequences. The former have investigated certain conditions that promote vandalism, such as specific aspects of the physical and social environment, or the motives of the vandal. Newman (1972) has theorized that vandalism becomes more likely when the design of a setting does not allow occupants to exert territorial control. Greenberger and Allen (1980) studied the possibility that aesthetic variables associated with an object's physical appearance (e.g., whether it breaks in an aesthetically interesting way) determine whether vandalism will occur, or at least which objects will be chosen for destruction. In addition, Allen and Greenberger (1980) suggested that, under certain conditions, a lowered level of perceived control will lead individuals to engage in acts of destruction in an attempt to modify aspects of the physical environment.

Other approaches have considered the consequences of vandalism for both the vandal and society. Allen and Greenberger (1980) proposed that committing vandalism may lead to heightened feelings of control in individuals experiencing a state of lowered perceived control. From the perspective of the larger society, merely viewing the acts of vandals may lead to the perception that the social order has broken down, and may elicit fear of victimization (Lavrakas, 1982).

The lack of a general theory of the roots of vandalism and a comprehensive societal program of prevention or remediation led Fisher and Baron (1982) to propose a social psychological model of vandalism with broad applicability. The model predicts that the underlying motive behind much vandalism is *perceived inequity*. The goal of vandalism is equity restoration. The vandal attempts to restore equity by responding to one type of perceived rule-breaking (i.e., perceived violations of norms of fairness in social or environmental arrangements) by breaking another set of rules regarding the sanctity of property rights.

Fisher and Baron (1982) propose that *perceived control* is the primary factor which moderates how inequity will be dealt with. Under inequitable conditions certain levels of perceived control are associated with vandalism, while others are not. Perceived control can be defined as the strength of a person's belief that he or she can effectively modify existing outcomes and arrangements (Fisher & Baron, 1982). It is determined by the following factors, among others: actual opportunities available within the system for achieving control and one's ability to use these, whether an individual can identify the source of the inequity, and a person's learned expectations for control in similar situations.

One's level of perceived control can affect the assumed functionality of options for coping with inequity which differ in selectivity, utilitarianism, intensity, and so forth. Vandalism is most likely to emerge as a coping option when there are low perceived equity and a low to moderate level of perceived control. Since the individual with low equity and low to moderate control is less apt to believe he or she can restore equity through socially acceptable means, he or she will look for a solution that is immediate, low cost, and difficult to thwart (e.g., vandalism or personal assault). Those with high perceived control are more likely to use socially acceptable means for restoring equity, which may also take more time and effort (e.g., becoming active in a social action committee or a political party). Extremely low levels of perceived control result in helplessness.

Fisher and Baron (1982) further assume that the types of vandalism can be ordered along an instrumental-expressive continuum. Under conditions of relatively lower control, more expressive-cathartic forms of vandalism will be chosen (i.e., malicious or vindictive vandalism), which tend to restore *psychological* equity. These involve more spontaneous and violent reactions regulated by intense emotional states such as rage and are likely to be misinterpreted by society. With higher degrees of control (yet still insufficient for a socially acceptable response within the system), more instrumental forms of vandalism will be chosen (i.e., acquisitive or tactical/ideological vandalism). These are more apt to restore *actual* equity, are less intense, and more accurately interpreted by society.

The model also identifies secondary moderators of vandalism. These are sufficient but not necessary for its occurrence and affect the likelihood and intensity of certain types of vandalism. Aspects of the physical environment (e.g., whether targets are "hardened," the degree of surveillance possible, etc.) constitute one secondary moderating variable. Other secondary moderators include *group variables*. Two types are discussed: those associated with the *target* group (e.g., a strong, cohesive target group may be less likely to be vandalized), and those of the *vandal* group. Concerning the latter, peers may contribute to vandalism if they provide models of antisocial behavior and diffuse responsibility for it (cf. Darley & Latané, 1968). On the other hand, a peer group which does not vandalize or which suggests disapproval of vandalism may inhibit such acts.

Baron and Fisher (1984) propose that vandalism is likely to recur if the sources of instigation stay the same, and if vandalism does not become too risky or effortful. For example, malicious vandalism may lead to short- but not long-term reductions in inequity, because society will miss the message. Since the source of instigation remains the same, the impetus for subsequent vandalism will be high. On the other hand, tactical/ideological vandalism may at times result in long-term reductions in inequity which reduce the impetus for subsequent vandalistic acts.

The present study comprises an initial test of Fisher and Baron's (1982) equity-control model of vandalism. The major assumptions of the model regarding equity and control are evaluated in the context of predicting vandalism among students at a large northeastern university. In line with the equity-control model, it is predicted that students who perceive low equity and low control vis-à-vis the university (i.e., those who perceive they are being treated unfairly but have little potential to modify this situation) are more apt to vandalize than those who perceive any other combination of equity and control.

METHOD

Subjects

Subjects were students in introductory psychology at a large northeastern university who participated in the research to receive extra course credit. Fifty-eight students participated—30 males and 28 females. They were all dormitory residents.

Procedure

When subjects arrived at the study site they were given a questionnaire to fill out. It was explained that the experimenter was a psychology major conducting a study on dormitory living. Subjects were guaranteed anonymity and instructed not to write their names on the questionnaire or computer response sheets.

Part one of the questionnaire tapped subjects' perceived equity and control vis-à-vis the university. Part two ascertained whether subjects had engaged in vandalism and was not handed out until everyone had completed part one. This was done so that subjects would not receive the items about vandalism until after they had answered those measuring perceived equity and control. Upon completion of part two, both sections were collected together.

INSTRUMENTATION

An instrument was developed to measure perceived equity and control as these constructs are reflected in aspects of university and dormitory life, as well as whether subjects had actually engaged in vandalism.

Part one of the instrument consisted of 39 equity/control items to be answered on 5-point Likert-type scales ranging from *definitely* agree (1) to *definitely* disagree (5). Of these, 20 items were designed to measure subjects' *perceived inequity* in the context of the university and dormitory life. According to Fisher and Baron (1982), perceived inequity that may lead to vandalism can result from ordinary economic exchange, discriminatory practices, inequitable rules and regulations, and aspects of the physical environment itself. The items measuring perceived inequity referred to these potential sources and assessed subjects' reactions to statements such as "I always get the grade that I deserve," and "The university makes up rules arbitrarily and unfairly." Items were counterbalanced in both a "positive" and a "negative" direction.

Integrated with these statements in part one were 19 items designed to measure *perceived control*. These referred to the same potential sources of inequity (e.g., inequity accruing from economic exchange, inequitable rules and regulations, etc.) but were worded so as to measure how much control subjects felt over the rules of the university, the physical environment, and so forth (e.g., "No matter how hard I study, it won't affect my grades," and "Student committees could be helpful in making and modifying the university's rules"). Again, items were counterbalanced in both a "positive" and a "negative" direction.

A reliability analysis of part one was performed using the data from this study. The questionnaire was split into two scales—an equity scale and a control scale. The reliability of the equity scale (Cronbach's alpha) was estimated to be .72, and the reliability of the control scale was estimated to be .76.

The second part of the questionnaire included 21 items pertaining to whether the subject had engaged in vandalistic acts, and, if so, the conditions under which vandalism occurred. These were also arranged in a

5-point Likert-type format. The first item was used to assign subjects to either a campus "vandal" or "nonvandal" group. The item used for this purpose was: "I vandalize dorms and/or university facilities ..." (vandalism was not defined for subjects). Responses were scored from 1 to 5—1 indicating that the subject had never vandalized, 5 indicating that the subject had engaged in a great deal of vandalism. A subject who answered "Never" to this item was classified as a nonvandal. Any other response constituted a vandal. The remaining 20 items were employed for ancillary analyses to further explore the motivations for and the targets of vandalism. Only individuals classified as "vandals" responded to these items.

RESULTS

To determine whether perceived equity and control were related to campus vandalism, a multiple regression analysis was performed for the item "I vandalized dorms and/or university facilities ..." The interaction of perceived equity and control was predictive of vandalism ($p < .02$) when controlling for the main effects of perceived equity, perceived control, and sex.[2] Using the regression coefficients to predict vandalism, persons who perceived low equity and low control vandalized more often than those who perceived any other combination of equity and control.

The main effect of control was also a significant predictor of vandalizing dorms and/or university facilities ($p < .03$). Using the regression equation and controlling for perceived equity and sex, people with low perceived control are more likely to vandalize than those with high perceived control. Taken together, the main and interaction effect variables accounted for approximately 34% of the variance (R^2 adjusted) (see Table 1).

Sex was found to be highly significant as a predictor of vandalism ($p < .002$). Of the 23 persons who vandalized on campus 19 were male and 4 female; of the 35 nonvandals 11 were male and 24 female. Furthermore, males and females differed in mean perceived equity (Ms = 58.8 and 52.6, respectively, $t(56) = -2.32$, $p < .03$) and control scores (Ms = 43.8 and 39.0, respectively, $t(56) = -2.88$, $p < .01$). A high equity or control score indicates low perceived equity or control. In effect, males perceived significantly lower levels of equity and control than females *and* were also more likely to engage in vandalistic acts, providing support for the equity-control model.

Since in the present context vandalism seemed to be predominately a male phenomenon, separate multiple regression analyses were performed

[2]We employed essentially the procedure outlined by Appelbaum and Cramer (1974) for estimating the effects of interactions and main effects.

TABLE 1. *F* Values and Significance Values as Predicted by Multiple Regression for Campus Vandalism, Males and Females Combined

	F value	*p* value
Interaction	5.910	.02
Control main effect	5.189	.03
Equity main effect	0.242	.62
Sex main effect	10.976	.002

Note. F values were calculated when controlling for all other variables in the equation.

for each sex. When looking only at the response of males, the interaction of perceived equity and control was marginally significant ($p < .07$), controlling for the main effects of perceived equity and control. Table 2 shows the relationship of perceived equity and control to mean campus vandalism scores. The data support the hypothesis that males who perceived low equity and low control vandalized more often than those who perceived any other combination of equity and control. The difference between the highest and lowest mean vandalism scores (i.e., low equity, low control and low equity, high control) is significant [$t(26) = 1.3$, $p < .05$], using Tukey's HSD test (Kirk, 1968). That is, for individuals experiencing low equity, the

TABLE 2. Mean Campus Vandalism Scores for Males for Each Level of Perceived Equity and Control

	Control	
Equity	High	Low
High	1.64	1.50
Low	1.25	2.55

Note. 1 indicates never having vandalized; 5 indicates a great deal of vandalism. The highest response indicated by males was a 4. The variables of equity and control were dichotomized using a median split on the data for males.

level of control significantly impacts on vandalism. For those with high equity, the level of perceived control does not affect vandalism scores.

The main effect of perceived control was again significant ($p < .04$). Controlling for perceived equity, males with low perceived control are more likely to vandalize than those with high perceived control. Equity alone was not a significant predictor (see Table 3). The interaction and main effect variables accounted for approximately 22% of the variance (R^2 adjusted).

To parallel the analysis described above, a separate multiple regression analysis was performed for females. Due to the small number of female vandals ($n = 4$), the present study could not adequately test the predictions of the equity-control model for women. However, the pattern of the interaction and the main effects were in the predicted direction.

Included in part two were some items concerning motivations for and targets of vandalism. Some interesting (although not statistically significant) trends were indicated. Specifically, members of the low equity/low control group differed from members of the high equity/high control group in the following ways: Members of the first group were more likely to report that they vandalize "because I get a sense of pleasure from breaking things," "when I feel a sense of despair," "to vent frustration," "to get back at the university, a teacher, or residence hall staff," and finally, "to draw attention to a cause with which I am involved."

DISCUSSION

The major hypothesis addressed in the present study, that vandalism would be predicted by an interaction of perceived equity and control, received support. This manifested itself at several levels: the interaction

TABLE 3. *F* Values and Significance Values for Males as Predicted by Multiple Regression for Campus Vandalism

	F value	*p* value
Interaction	3.576	.07
Control main effect	4.920	.04
Equity main effect	0.108	.75

Note. F values were calculated controlling for all other variables in the equation.

between the two variables occurred as predicted, and the form which it took was highly supportive of the equity-control model. Whether one looks at the entire sample or males only, the pattern of effects is consistent—vandalism is committed by those who perceive low equity and low control via-à-vis the university. The equity-control model predicts exactly this—feeling unfairly treated and perceiving little ability to rectify the situation is associated with vandalism.

Additional support for the model is provided by sex differences in perceived equity, perceived control, and vandalism. Males perceived lower levels of equity and control than females and also committed more vandalism. In a sense then, the model is supported by data from two separate operationalizations of differential equity and control: individual differences on these dimensions, as well as sex differences on them. From either vantage point, lower perceived equity and control are associated with greater vandalism.

Our findings suggest that the equity-control model may compare favorably with other conceptualizations of vandalism. Post hoc tests revealed that the difference between the low equity, low control and the low equity, high control cells was statistically significant. Contrary to the predictions of single factor models which relate control to vandalism (cf. Allen & Greenberger, 1980), in this study control predicted vandalism only under low equity. Thus, it appears that the joint consideration of equity and control, as postulated by the equity-control model, may provide a more powerful means of conceptualizing vandalism than single factor types of conceptualizations.

In addition to moving theory from focusing on a single cause of vandalism (cf. Allen & Greenberger, 1980) to an appreciation of multiple levels of causation, the equity-control model (Baron & Fisher, 1984; Fisher & Baron, 1982) offers other advantages. While other theorists posit environmental conditions as the causes of vandalism (e.g., Newman, 1972) and as determining what targets will be chosen (e.g., Greenberger & Allen, 1980), the equity-control formulation integrates aspects of the physical environment as moderator variables. Along with group variables, environmental conditions are viewed as secondary moderators which are sufficient conditions for vandalism. Although this study does not address the predictions of the model regarding moderator variables, they are corroborated in other research (Cassady, 1985).

While the present data are supportive of the major assertions of the equity-control model, our findings may have certain limitations. First, the data are correlational and share the shortcomings of all correlational studies with respect to causal inference. One could suggest several alternative interpretations of the data. There are two general problems—one is the direction of the effect. Are we simply finding that people who vandalize make up rationalizations after the fact which account for their actions *but* did not actually motivate them? Second, are we simply observing a general response set for certain kinds of people to say negative things about the university?

The plausibility of the above comments may be countered. The fact that we obtained the specific cross-over interaction pattern predicted by our theory mitigates against [*sic*] both possibilities. It is unlikely that rationalizations would take the form of a cross-over interaction fitting our theory. Both alternative interpretations would be plausible only for simple main effect-type correlations, e.g., a finding that people who vandalize more, experience more inequity. The clear sex differences in both perceived equity and control, and tendency to commit vandalism also mitigate against [*sic*] a response set interpretation, particularly since these data fit the general findings of dormitory administrators that physical dormitory vandalism is a male phenomenon.[3]

Other possible limitations relate to the fact that self-reports were used to measure equity, control, and vandalism. Students may have been reluctant to admit that they were not getting fair treatment from the university and could not control such outcomes—these may not have been viewed as socially desirable responses. They may also have been reluctant to admit having vandalized (even though the questionnaires were anonymous), because the experimenter had their names on the experiment registration sheets. However, the impact of these possible limitations is lessened by two kinds of data. First, the construct validity of these instruments is supported by the fact that subject classifications based on the scale provide data supporting the central interaction prediction of the model. Second, there are findings which corroborate the present results in an experimental study which did not employ self-report measures. Cassady (1985) demonstrated that under manipulations of low equity and low control vis-à-vis the experiment and experimenter, subjects engage in more vandalism than under conditions of low equity and high manipulated control.

A final limitation relates to the data for females. Here, the observed patterns of effects were in the predicted direction, but there were too few female vandals to provide an adequate test of the model. A much larger pool of women would be necessary to identify a group of female vandals sufficiently large to permit such a test.

The present study may have implications for how vandalism can be decreased among college students. It suggests that males, in part due

[3]Data from the Department of Residential Life at the University of Connecticut demonstrates that physical campus vandalism is a predominantly male phenomenon.

to lower perceived equity and control, are especially "at risk" for vandalism. To reduce vandalism in both sexes, feelings of low equity and low control might be channeled into constructive behaviors that could restore equity and/or control. For example, student groups could be organized to work toward achieving more satisfactory dormitory living environments, and students could be encouraged to work with administrators to develop new University policies. Here, it is essential that administrators make students feel that their input could make a difference. Under such conditions it appears that favorable results can ensue (cf. Corbett, 1973). Further research may suggest that conceptually-relevant interventions could decrease vandalism in other settings where people feel inequitably treated and perceive that they have little control (e.g., in grammar and high schools, in the workplace, and in government subsidized housing projects).

Finally, the present study also points to the need for future research on vandalism, especially of an experimental or field study nature. Measures of vandalism other than the pencil-and-paper measures used here should be developed. Experiments such as Cassady's (1985) can create a situation in which students are given the opportunity to commit vandalism (which can be coded by the experimenter) after being treated inequitably and having little control to restore equity in a socially acceptable way. Furthermore, most colleges and universities must deal with campus vandals all the time, and keep records on those who are disciplined. Given that it is often difficult to catch a vandal in the act, these campus records can prove a valuable resource to those wishing to study vandalism.

REFERENCES

Allen, V. L. & Greenberger, D. B. (1980). Destruction and perceived control. In A. Baum & J. Singer (Eds.), *Advances in environmental psychology* (Vol. II, pp. 85–109). Hillsdale, NJ: Erlbaum.

Applebaum, M. I., & Cramer, E. M. (1974). Some problems in the nonorthogonal analysis of variance. *Psychological Bulletin*, **81**, 335–343.

Baron, R. M., & Fisher, J. D. (1984). The equity-control model of vandalism: A refinement. In C. Levy-Leboyer (Ed.), *Vandalism* (pp. 63–75). Amsterdam: North Holland Publishing Company.

Clinard, M. B., & Quinney, R. (1973). *Criminal behavior systems: A typology* (2nd ed.). New York: Holt, Rinehart & Winston.

Cohen, S. (1973). Property destruction: Motive and meanings. In C. Ward (Ed.), *Vandalism* (pp. 23–53). London: The Architectural Press.

Corbett, J. A. (1973). Student built housing as an alternative to dormitories. *Environment and Behavior*, **5**, 491–504.

Darley, J. M., & Lantané, B. (1968). Bystander intervention in emergencies: Diffusion of responsibility. *Journal of Personality and Social Psychology*, **8** 377–383.

Einolander, J. C. (1976). Vandalism at Red Rock. In S. S. Alfano & A. W. Magill (Eds.), *Vandalism and outdoor recreation: Symposium proceedings* (pp. 25–26). USDA Forest Service General Technical Report, PSW-17.

Fisher, J. D., & Baron, R. M. (1982). An equity-based model of vandalism. *Population & Environment*, **5**, 182–200.

Greenberger, D. B., & Allen, V. L. (1980). Destruction and complexity: An application of aesthetic theory. *Personality and Social Psychology Bulletin*, **6**, 479–483.

Kirk, R. E. (1968). *Experimental design: Procedures for the behavioral sciences*. Belmont, CA: Wadsworth Publishing Co.

Lavrakas, P. J. (1982). Fear of crime and behavior restriction in urban and suburban neighborhoods. *Population and Environment*, **5**, 242–264.

Newman, O. (1972). *Defensible space*. New York: Macmillan.

United States Senate Judiciary Committee. Subcommittee on Juvenile Delinquency. (1975). *Our Nation's schools—A report card: "A" in school violence and vandalism*. Committee print. Washington, DC.

Ward, C. (Ed.). (1973). *Vandalism* (pp. 13–22). London: The Architectural Press.

Zimbardo, P. (1972, July–August). Vandalism: An act in search of a cause. *Bill Telephone Magazine*.

SHAME AND EMBARRASSMENT AS DETERRENTS TO NONCOMPLIANCE WITH THE LAW

THE CASE OF AN ANTILITTERING CAMPAIGN

HAROLD G. GRASMICK, ROBERT J. BURSIK, JR., AND KARYL A. KINSEY

The Keep America Beautiful campaign and the events surrounding it in the late 1960s and early 1970s generated concern about the problems created by littering not only among the public and government officials but also among behavioral scientists. The past two decades have produced a wealth of research on littering as well as other environmental behaviors (e.g., Casey & Lloyd, 1977; Clark, Burgess, & Hendee, 1972; Durdan, Reeder, & Hecht, 1985; Geller, Winett, & Everett, 1982; Geller, Witmer, & Orebaugh, 1976; Geller, Witmer, & Tuso, 1977; Gendrich, McNees, Schnelle, Beegle, & Clark, 1982; Krauss, Freedman, & Whitcup, 1978; Levitt & Leventhal, 1986; Powers, Osborne, & Anderson, 1973; Reich & Robertson, 1979; Robinson,

AUTHORS' NOTE: Funding for this research was provided by the College of Arts and Sciences, University of Oklahoma, and by the American Bar Association. We wish to thank Mary Baldwin Kennedy for her contribution as a research assistant.

Source: *Environment and Behaviors* (1991) 23(2): 233–251.

1976). While important insights and policy implications have been developed, the research so far has seemed to overlook the fact that littering is illegal. Thus, researchers have not drawn upon theories from the field of criminology concerning determinants of compliance and noncompliance with the law.

On the other hand, despite the enormous costs to our society from widespread littering (Keep America Beautiful, 1970), criminologists interested in social control apparently do not view littering as a serious form of illegal behavior and have excluded it from their research. This is unfortunate since littering is a relatively common form of illegal behavior and affords researchers the opportunity to test hypotheses with an offense for which the proportion of the population who are offenders is fairly high.

The present study draws from the literature in criminology which suggests that threats of shame and embarrassment function in much the same manner as the threat of legal sanctions in generating compliance with the law. Shame, a self-imposed sanction, and embarrassment, a socially imposed sanction, increase the subjective cost of the illegal behavior and, thus, reduce the likelihood that the behavior will occur.

Now common in many states and communities, antilittering campaigns, which appeal to a sense of community pride or moral obligation, rather than threatening legal sanctions, can be viewed as attempts to increase the threats of shame and embarrassment for littering. One such campaign, initiated in Oklahoma in 1987 and continuing today, provides at least a quasi-experimental format for examining the possible impact of such an appeal on citizen reports of whether they would feel ashamed or be embarrassed if they littered and on their inclination to litter. Data concerning these issues were collected in a survey of a sample of the adult population in Oklahoma City in 1982, five years prior to the antilittering campaign. Another sample from the same community was interviewed in 1989, two years after the initiation of the campaign. The sampling procedures in the two surveys were identical, and exactly the same questions concerning littering were asked in 1982 and 1989. Merging these two data sets can indicate if there was a significant reduction between 1982 and 1989 in citizens' inclination to litter and, if so, whether this reduction can be attributed to increases in the community in the levels of shame and embarrassment for littering.

SHAME, EMBARRASSMENT, AND DETERRENCE

Cornish and Clarke (1986, p. vi) argued that the field of criminology and social control would benefit from an explicitly articulated "rational choice perspective" as a unifying theme and Tuck and Riley (1986) suggested that such an approach could begin with a "subjective expected utility" model. Deterrence theory (e.g., Gibbs, 1975) has been one version of a rational choice perspective but has focused on only one factor, the perceived threat of legal sanctions, which might lower the expected utility of noncompliance with the law and, thus, enhance the likelihood of compliance. Meier, Burkett, and Hickman (1984) observed that the concept of deterrence has been unnecessarily restricted to legal sanctions. They suggested that "there is no theoretical reason why the notion of deterrence cannot be extended to other types of sanctions" (p. 68). Deterrence theory has focused on the state, with its threat of fines and incarceration, as an agent of social control. But significant others in an actor's social environment and the actor's own conscience play an analogous role. They pose threats of potential punishment which increase the subjective cost of noncompliance (Grasmick & Brusik, 1990; Grasmick & Green, 1980; Williams & Hawkins, 1986, 1989), and they are precisely the kinds of costs which are the focus of moral appeals as a strategy for increasing compliance with the law.

While the state threatens to fine or incarcerate actors who violate the law, significant others are a potential source of another kind of punishment. When actors violate norms, including legal norms, which are endorsed by people whose opinions they value, they run the risk of being embarrassed or suffering a loss of respect. This idea is closely linked to the concern with interpersonal sanctions in Hirschi's (1969) theory of social bonds and Tittle's (1977) emphasis on informal sanctions. The most immediate consequence of embarrassment is a physiological discomfort, but more long-term consequences, which could further increase the cost of violating the law, might be a loss of valued relationships and perhaps also a restriction in opportunities to achieve other valued goals.

Actors themselves are another source of punishment in the form of guilt feelings or shame (see the discussion of "self-stigma" in Williams & Hawkins, 1989). When actors violate norms they have internalized, they incur the risk of guilt feelings, or feeling ashamed. While embarrassment is a socially imposed sanction, shame is a self-imposed or reflective punishment, which can occur even if the state and significant others do not detect the transgression. As is the case for embarrassment, the most immediate adverse consequence of shame is probably a physiological discomfort. More long-term adverse consequences might include depression, anxiety, or damaged self-concept, which could impede normal functioning in one's social environment. While some might argue that internalization of a norm eliminates the motivation to violate it, others (see Blake & Davis, 1964) maintain that, in deciding whether or not to engage in a particular behavior, individuals take into account whether they would feel ashamed if they did. The risk of shame is one of the costs that actors weigh against potential gains in deciding whether or not to engage in the behavior.

THE OKLAHOMA ANTILITTERING CAMPAIGN

From a social control perspective, appeals to conscience or to a sense of community spirit as a strategy for enhancing compliance with the law are attempts to increase the threats of shame and embarrassment in a community.[1] Their function, whether latent or explicit, is to make people feel guilt if they do not comply with the law and/or to convince citizens that noncompliance is condemned by other people in the community. This is precisely the agenda of the Oklahoma antilittering campaign.

Prior to 1987, Oklahoma had no organized effort to encourage citizens not to litter.[2] Beginning in 1987, the state adopted a twofold campaign, the Adopt-a-Highway program and the "Don't Lay That Trash on Oklahoma" program.[3]

Texas was the first state to develop an Adopt-a-Highway program, and Oklahoma and Missouri followed its lead. Currently, over half the states in the United States have such a program, and these are concentrated in the Midwest and South. In Oklahoma, a volunteer group (consisting of at least two people over the age of 11) and the State Department of Transportation sign a contract. The groups tend to be voluntary organizations as well as various businesses. The group agrees to pick up trash along a stretch of highway, usually a mile or two, at least four times a year for at least two years. The state agrees to provide trash bags and safety training and to post a sign along that stretch of highway noting the name of the group and acknowledging its contribution. Currently, over 1,300 contracts are in force. While one obvious function of the Adopt-a-Highway program is to remove litter from the particular designated areas, the signs along the highways are evidence to other citizens that some people in the community are concerned about the problem of littering and are devoting time and effort to it.

The second component of Oklahoma's antilittering effort is a media campaign centered around the slogan "Don't Lay That Trash on Oklahoma," which is incorporated into a song. The comparable slogan in Texas is "Don't Mess with Texas."[4] The state purchases commercial time from radio and television stations to promote this theme, which stresses the citizen's moral obligation to keep the state clean. Bumper stickers containing the slogan also are available at no cost, as are litter bags for vehicles. From a social control perspective, this effort is aimed at increasing the likelihood that citizens will feel ashamed if they litter.

Objective indicators in Oklahoma revealed a significant reduction in litter during the first full year of this antilittering campaign. Based on visual surveys of a sample of 105 sites along urban and rural streets, highways, and interstates and in state recreation areas, the Oklahoma Department of Transportation (1989) estimated that the number of "litter items" in the state decreased by 22.8% from February/March 1988 to February/March 1989. This figure includes corrections for changes in weather and in traffic and pedestrian volume, and the research was conducted by Daniel Syrek from the Institute for Applied Research (Sacramento, CA) who has conducted similar studies in other states.

The goal of the research described below was to determine first if there has been a reduction in citizens' inclination to litter, corresponding to the objective measure, since the initiation of the antilittering campaign. If so, can the change in inclination to litter be attributed to an increase in the levels of shame and embarrassment for littering? Thus, we have focused not just on the outcome of the antilittering campaign but also on the process by which that outcome might have been achieved.

RESEARCH PROCEDURES

Since 1979, the Department of Sociology, University of Oklahoma, has conducted an annual survey of adults (18 and older) in Oklahoma City. Questions concerning littering were included in the 1982 survey as part of a more general study of compliance with the law. The littering questions were repeated verbatim in 1989. Since the survey methodology, including the sampling procedure, has remained constant over time, it was possible to compare the results from the 1982 survey, five years prior to the initiation of the state's antilittering campaign, to the results from the 1989 survey conducted almost two years after the beginning of the campaign.

Sampling

Data for the Oklahoma City surveys are collected in face-to-face interviews with a random sample of adults. The target sample size in any one year is primarily a function of availability of funds. The total sample size was 350 in 1982 and 330 in 1989. A simple random sample of names and addresses was drawn from the *R. L. Polk Directory* for Oklahoma City. Initial contact was in the form of a letter briefly describing the nature of the survey and indicating that a member of the research team would soon try to schedule an appointment with the person. Attempts to schedule appointments were made in person by trained field supervisors and interviewers. Members of the target sample who refused to participate were replaced by random selection until the target sample size was attained.[5] The 1982 and 1989 samples were compared to 1980 census data for percent female and percent non-White. None of these comparisons showed that the samples differed significantly from the population. Cases with missing data on any of the variables (four cases in 1982 and six in 1989) were excluded from the analysis that follows.

Measures

To measure the risk of shame or guilt feelings for littering, respondents in the two surveys were presented with the statement, "Generally, in most situations I would feel guilty if I were to litter the highways, streets, or a public recreation area." They were asked to respond on a 4-point scale ranging from a low of *strongly disagree* (coded 1) to a high of *strongly agree* (coded 4). The threat of embarrassment was measured in a similar manner. Respondents were asked, "Would most of the people whose opinions you value lose respect for you if you were to litter the highways, streets, or a public recreation area?" Answers were given on a 4-point scale ranging from a low of *definitely would not* (coded 1) to a high of *definitely would* (coded 4).

Following the strategy used by Tittle (1977), the dependent variable was respondents' estimates of whether they would commit the offense in the future. Respondents were asked, "In the future, will you ever litter the highways, streets, or a public recreation area?" Such a measure is similar to the concept of behavioral intention in the work of Fishbein and Ajzen (1975). Answers of yes or no were recorded on a separate answer sheet, which the interviewer did not see, in an attempt to minimize social desirability bias. This measure of inclination to litter is preferable to reports of past littering because it avoids the causal order problem of examining the effects of present threats of shame and embarrassment on past behavior. Instead, the analysis examined the effect of present threats on present inclination to commit the offense.

It should be noted that the dependent variable was a self-report measure rather than an objective observation of behavior in a natural setting. In past research, these two methods sometimes have yielded different conclusions concerning at least some of the correlates of littering. (For a summary, see Durdan et al., 1985.) Hopefully, other researchers will expand the kind of analysis described below to incorporate additional measures of littering.

Controls

Previous self-report research (Keep America Beautiful, 1968) as well as observational studies (e.g., Durdan et al., 1985) indicated that among adults, littering is more common in the younger age brackets. Furthermore, self-report research has suggested that men are more likely to litter than are women. While some observational studies (e.g., Durdan et al., 1985) have found an effect for gender, others (e.g., Finnie, 1973) have not. Because of these previous findings, age and gender were controlled in the analysis. The 1982 and 1989 samples were not expected to differ significantly in the distribution of gender, but, because of the aging of the population, the 1989 sample should be older than the 1982 sample. In addition to gender and age, years of formal education and race were included as controls because of possible sampling fluctuations between the two years and because of possible links between these variables and the threats of shame and embarrassment and the inclination to litter.

Obviously, the before-after comparison of the 1982 and 1989 samples was not a true experiment. There was no control community that did not experience an antilittering campaign. Thus, any reduction in the inclination to litter over the two sample periods, or any increases in the threats of embarrassment and shame, do not necessarily suggest that the antilittering campaign has had an effect. We can, however, address the possibility that any reduction in inclination to litter or increase in threats of shame and embarrassment for littering are part of a more general trend toward increased compliance with the law, not just the law against littering, and increased threats of shame and embarrassment for noncompliance in general. The 1982 survey contained questions about petty theft ("In the future, will you ever take something from someplace worth less than $20 that does not belong to you?") identical to those for littering. Between 1982 and 1989, petty theft was not the target of any particular compliance campaigns. If there had been a reduction in inclination to litter but not to commit petty theft, and if the risks of shame and embarrassment for littering but not for theft had increased between 1982 and 1989, the trends for littering could not be attributed to a more general trend across other offenses. This would provide stronger though still not conclusive evidence of a compliance-enhancing effect of the antilittering campaign.

RESULTS

Table 1 depicts one-tailed *t* tests to compare the 1982 and 1989 samples on all variables. The percent male, percent White, and mean years of

TABLE 1. Comparisons of 1982 and 1989 Samples on All Variables

Variable	1982 (N = 346)	1989 (N = 324)	t	p
Percentage male	45.95	51.54	1.45	>.050
Percentage White	82.95	81.79	−.39	>.050
Mean years of formal education	14.43	13.81	−1.27	>.050
Mean age	42.51	46.12	2.74	.003
Mean risk of shame for littering	3.10	3.52	6.60	<.001
Mean risk of embarrassment for littering	2.26	2.60	5.00	<.001
Percent who will litter in the future	39.02	30.56	−2.30	.011

Note: Data based on one-tailed tests.

education did not differ significantly across the two samples. However, as expected, the mean age was significantly higher in the 1989 sample than in the 1982 sample.

For both shame and embarrassment, the mean perceived risks were significantly higher in 1989 than in 1982. On a 4-point scale, the mean for shame was 3.10 in 1982 and 3.52 in 1989, and the difference was significant beyond the .001 level. Inspection of the full range of answers to this item revealed that in 1982, only 37% of the respondents "strongly agreed" that they would feel guilt if they littered. By 1989, the figure had increased to 67%. For the 4-point embarrassment measure, the mean increased from 2.26 in 1982 to 2.60 in 1989. This difference also was significant beyond the .001 level. At the extreme, in 1982, only 8% of the sample indicated that most of the people whose opinions they value "definitely would" lose respect for them if they littered. This increased to 21% in the 1989 sample.

Finally, Table 1 reveals a significant (p = .011) reduction in the percent of respondents who indicated they will litter in the future. In 1982, 39.02% said they would, compared to 30.56% in 1989. Thus, the increases in the risk of shame and embarrassment, as well as the increase in the average age, between 1982 and 1989 have been accompanied by a reduction in the proportion of respondents who reported that they would litter.

To consider the possibility that the trends observed for littering reflect a more general trend toward compliance with the law rather than the impact of the antilittering campaign, questions concerning petty theft in the two surveys also were analyzed. In contrast to littering, the percent who said they would "take something from someplace worth less than $20" that did not belong to them actually *increased* between 1982 and 1989, from 4.91% to 10.49% (t = 2.73, p = .006). Furthermore, for petty theft, the mean scores for shame (3.74 versus 3.80) and embarrassment (3.29 versus

3.27) did not change significantly between 1982 and 1989. Thus, the tendency observed toward increased risks of shame and embarrassment for littering and reduced inclination to commit the offense were not matched by comparable trends for petty theft.

In Table 2, the two surveys were merged, and the year was treated as a dummy variable coded 0 for 1982 and 1 for 1989. The Ordinary Least Squares (OLS) regressions for shame and embarrassment as dependent variables consider the effect of year on these threats, with controls for the other variables. Standardized coefficients are reported. The control for age is especially important since, as anticipated, the 1989 sample was significantly older than the 1982 sample and since in the combined sample (N = 670) age is positively correlated with both the threat of shame ($r = .288$, $p < .001$) and threat of embarrassment ($r = .340$, $p < .001$). The increases in the threat of shame and embarrassment observed in Table 1 might simply reflect changes in the age distribution of the population rather than the effect of the antilittering campaign. In Table 2, male and White were the dummy variables for gender (coded 1 for males) and race (coded 1 for Whites). Age and education were internal variables measured in years.

As expected, age had a significant positive effect on both shame (beta = .245, $p < .001$) and embarrassment (beat = .318, $p < .001$). But the direct effects of year were positive and also significant beyond the .001 level. In other words, even with the controls, respondents in 1989 tended to score significantly higher than respondents in 1982 on the threats of shame (beta = .229) and embarrassment (beta = .158). For the threat of shame, gender and race also had significant effects. The beta of −.066 for male (p = .034) indicated that males scored significantly lower than females on the perceived risk of shame. The beta of .171 for White indicated that Whites scored

TABLE 2. Effects of Year and Control Variables on Threats of Shame and Embarrassment

	Shame			Embarrassment		
Independent variable	beta	t	p	beta	t	p
Year	.229	6.39	<.001	.158	4.35	<.001
Age	.245	6.82	<.001	.318	8.73	<.001
Male	−.066	−1.84	.034	−.010	−0.27	>.050
White	.171	4.77	<.001	.052	1.43	>.050
Education	.023	0.64	>.050	.000	0.01	>.050
	$R^2 = .162$	$p < .001$		$R^2 = .142$	$p < .001$	

Note: In one-tailed tests, 0 = 1982, 1 = 1989; N = 670.

significantly higher than non-Whites ($p < .001$). For the risk of embarrassment, no other variables besides year and age had significant direct effects.

Finally, Table 3 examined the extent to which the reduction in inclination to litter from 1982 to 1989 was the result of increases in risk of shame and embarrassment rather than changes in the age distribution of the population. In the various equations, the dependent variable was a dichotomy coded 1 for respondents who said they would litter in the future (34.9% of the combined samples) and 0 for respondents who said they would not. The standardized coefficients reported are those from OLS regressions. Because the distribution of the dependent variable was not extremely concentrated into either of the two categories, OLS procedures yielded the same conclusions concerning significance levels as did logistic regressions (not reported). The OLS estimates are reported to facilitate discussion of direct and indirect effects and comparisons of the magnitudes of the effects of independent variables.

Equation 1 indicated that, with controls for gender, race, and education, year had a significant effect of $-.096$ ($p = .007$) on inclination to litter. In other words, respondents in 1989 were less inclined to litter, because of the negative sign, than respondents in 1982.

Equation 2 added age to the control variables to consider the possibility that the effect of year in Equation 1 was simply an artifact of the increased age of the population. With age in the equation, the effect of year was reduced to $-.069$, a reduction of about 30% from Equation 1. Thus, the higher average age of the 1989 sample, coupled with the inverse relationship between age and inclination to litter, accounted for about 30% of the effect of year on inclination to litter. Nevertheless, as Equation 2 indicates, even with the additional control for age, the inclination to litter was significantly lower in the 1989 sample ($p = .034$).

Equation 3 added the threats of shame and embarrassment to the variables in Equation 2. Now the inverse effect of year on the dependent variable vanished, and, in fact, the coefficient for year became slightly positive although not significant (beta = 0.49, $p > .05$). Thus, the part of the effect of year which was not due to age differences between the two samples (i.e., the best of $-.069$ in Equation 2) was explained by the higher levels of shame and embarrassment in 1989 compared to 1982 and the effects of shame and embarrassment on the inclination to litter. In Equation 3, both shame and embarrassment had significant inverse effects on the dependent variable, although the effect of shame (beta = $-.449$) was much greater than the effect of embarrassment (beta = $-.094$).

Several other features of Table 3 are worth noting. First, in Equations 1 and 2, men were significantly more likely than women to say they will litter

TABLE 3. Effects of Year and Other Independent Variables on Inclination to Litter

	Equation 1			Equation 2			Equation 3		
Independent variable	beta	t	p	beta	t	p	beta	t	p
Year	−.096	−2.49	.007	−.069	−1.83	.034	.049	1.40	>.050
Male	.086	2.20	.014	.078	2.07	.020	.048	1.41	>.050
White	−.009	−0.23	>.050	.017	0.45	>.050	.099	2.89	.002
Education	−.051	−1.31	>.050	−.042	−1.11	>.050	−.031	−0.94	>.050
Age	—	—	—	−.245	−6.48	<.001	−.105	−2.91	.002
Shame	—	—	—	—	—	—	−.449	−12.01	<.001
Embarrassment	—	—	—	—	—	—	−.094	−2.54	.006
	$R^2 = .018 \quad p = .022$			$R^2 = .076 \quad p < .001$			$R^2 = .269 \quad p < .001$		

Note: Data based on one-tailed tests, $N = 670$.

in the future. But in Equation 3, the effect of gender was insignificant. Table 2 indicated that males perceived a significantly lower risk of shame than females, and this difference, therefore, accounts for the greater inclination of males to litter.

The findings concerning race also are interesting. Table 2 suggested that Whites score significantly higher than non-Whites on the measure of shame. In Equations 1 and 2 of Table 3, race did not have a significant effect on inclination to litter. But in Equation 3, which includes shame, the effect of White was positive and significant (beta = .099, $p = .002$). In other words, were it not for the greater threat of shame experienced by Whites, Whites actually would be *more* inclined to litter than non-Whites.

Table 2 revealed a significant positive effect of age on both shame and embarrassment. In Equation 2 of Table 3, the direct effect of age, controlling for year, gender, race, and education, was −.245. But in Equation 3, when shame and embarrassment are added as controls, the effect of age was reduced to −.105, a reduction of over 50%. Thus, the greater threats of shame and embarrassment experienced by older people accounted for over half of the effect of age on inclination to litter.

DISCUSSION

Two years after Oklahoma initiated its antilittering campaign based on moral appeals rather than threats of legal sanctions, Oklahoma City residents in a sample were significantly less inclined to litter than were residents interviewed five years before the campaign began. To some extent, this difference was a function of the aging of the population, with older people being less likely than younger people to report that they would litter. But the sample interviewed two years after the campaign began also scored significantly higher on the threats of shame and embarrassment than did the earlier sample. These differences accounted for that portion of the reduction in inclination to litter which was not due to the aging of the population.

We cannot, however, unequivocally attribute the increased threats of shame and embarrassment and resulting reduction in inclination to litter to the state's antilittering campaign. In the absence of a control community that did not experience such a campaign, we cannot rule out the possibility that these trends were part of national trends concerning littering rather than the result of specific efforts in the state of Oklahoma. The changes might have occurred even in the absence of Oklahoma's antilittering campaign. We did, however, reject the possibility that the trends for littering reflected more general trends encompassing other offenses. The analysis of similar variables concerning petty theft suggested that inclination to commit theft actually increased from 1982 to 1989 and that the threats of shame and embarrassment did not significantly change.

Although in the absence of a controlled experiment we cannot be certain that the antilittering campaign has had its intended effect, it is apparent from our analysis that the threats of shame and embarrassment significantly reduce the reported inclination to litter. The research offers evidence supporting policies aimed at these social control variables as a means to address the problem of littering.

As other states and jurisdictions develop and implement programs to reduce the amount of litter, we hope they will design evaluation studies that build upon and improve upon our own. Our own study was not a planned evaluation because the initial 1982 survey was conducted long before Oklahoma's antilittering campaign was envisioned by planners. Our dependent variable, reported inclination to litter, could be supplemented with alternative and perhaps better indicators in future studies. We used face-to-face interviews in a single community in the state in 1989 because that was the method used in 1982. But the growing availability of research capabilities for relatively inexpensive telephone surveys, using random-digit dialing as a sampling technique, should facilitate more carefully planned and controlled research designs to evaluate and monitor programs intended to reduce littering. Such designs should include not only the jurisdiction in which the campaign against littering is conducted but also a control jurisdiction that is not the target of such a campaign.

While the kinds of "litter counts" conducted in many states by the Institute for Applied Research might provide indicators of the *outcome* of antilittering programs, they cannot determine whether that outcome was achieved through the intended *process*—in the case of Oklahoma, through an increase in the threats of shame and embarrassment. The kind of process evaluation we have offered can be especially important where the antilittering campaign has many components. Texas, for example, has a campaign similar to Oklahoma's but has also placed an increased emphasis on legal sanctions as a deterrent. From the perspective of fiscal policy, it is worth knowing the extent to which any observed reduction in littering can be attributed to any one component of the overall program. If, for example, the perceived threat of legal sanctions changes very little as a result of an antilittering campaign and contributes very little to the reduction in littering, it would seem wise to shift resources away from that component to other compliance-enhancing components of the campaign.

NOTES

1. See Schwartz and Orleans (1967) for an experiment on the effect of a moral appeal and taxpayer compliance and Tittle and Rowe (1973) on the effect of such an appeal on classroom cheating.
2. We wish to thank Joanne S. Orr, beautification coordinator, Oklahoma State Department of Transportation, for providing information about the antilittering campaign in Oklahoma and in other states.
3. Initially there was a third major component, an increase in the severity of penalties for littering. In 1988, the State Legislature set the maximum fine for littering at $1,000 and provided for the possibility of a jail sentence of up to 30 days. A few citations have been issued, but the courts have refused to enforce this law, maintaining that they have more important things to do. In effect, therefore, there has been no increase in Oklahoma in the threat of legal sanctions for littering. In contrast, Texas is experimenting with a litter-officer program, which has assessed $62,000 in fines and has a 98% conviction rate.
4. These prompts in Oklahoma and Texas are negatively worded (i.e., *don't* do something). Research by Geller et al. (1976) and Durdan et al. (1985) suggests that positive prompts might be more effective.
5. This sampling procedure has been used in the annual Oklahoma City Survey since 1979. Approximately 60% of the names drawn from the *Polk Directory* result in completed interviews. Among the other 40%, about a fifth result in undeliverable letters, and the remainder cannot be located or refuse to participate. Replacements are chosen at random until the target sample size is achieved.

REFERENCES

Blake, J., & Davis, K. (1964). Norms, values, and sanctions. In R. Fairs (Ed.), *Handbook of modern sociology* (pp. 456–484). Chicago: Rand McNally.

Casey, L., & Lloyd, M. (1977). Cost effectiveness of litter removal procedures in an amusement park. *Environment and Behavior, 9*, 535–546.

Clark, R., Burgess, R., & Hendee, J. (1972). The development of antilitter behavior in a forest campground. *Journal of Applied Behavior Analysis, 5*, 1–5.

Cornish, D., & Clarke, R. (1986). Preface. In D. Cornish & R. Clarke (Eds.), *The reasoning criminal: Rational choice perspectives on offending* (pp. v–viii). New York: Springer-Verlag.

Durdan, C., Reeder, G., & Hecht, R. (1985). Littering in a university cafeteria: Demographic data and the use of prompts as an intervention strategy. *Environment and Behavior, 17*, 387–404.

Finnie, W. (1973). Field experiments in litter control. *Environment and Behavior, 5*, 123–144.

Fishbein, M., & Ajzen, I. (1975). *Beliefs, attitudes, intentions and behavior*. New York: Addison-Wesley.

Geller, E., Winett, R., & Everett, B. (1982). *Preserving the environment: New strategies for behavior change*. New York: Pergamon.

Geller, E., Witmer, J., & Orebaugh, A. (1976). Instructions as a determinant of paper-disposal behaviors. *Environment and Behavior, 8*, 417–439.

Geller, E., Witmer, J., & Tuso, M. (1977). Environmental interventions for litter control. *Journal of Applied Psychology, 62*, 344–351.

Gendrich, J., McNees, G., Schnelle, J., Beegle, G., & Clark, H. (1982). A student-based anti-litter program for elementary schools. *Education and Treatment of Children, 5*, 321–335.

Gibbs, J. (1975). *Crime, punishment and deterrence*. New York: Elsevier.

Grasmick, H., & Bursik, R. (1990). Conscience, significant others and rational choice: Extending the deterrence model. *Law and Society Review, 24*, 837–861.

Grasmick, H., & Green, D. (1980). Legal punishment, social disapproval and internalization as inhibitors of illegal behavior. *Journal of Criminal Law and Criminology, 71*, 325–335.

Hirschi, T. (1969). *Causes of delinquency*. Berkeley: University of California Press.

Keep America Beautiful, Inc. (1968). *Who litters and why: Summary of survey findings concerning public awareness and concern about the problem of litter*. New York: Author.

Keep America Beautiful, Inc. (1970). *Fact sheet: Litter is a national disgrace*. New York: Author.

Krauss, R., Freedman, J., & Whitcup, M. (1978). Field and laboratory studies of littering. *Journal of Experimental Social Psychology, 14*, 109–122.

Levitt, L., & Leventhal, G. (1986). Litter reduction: How effective is the New York State bottle bill. *Environment and Behavior, 18*, 467–479.

Meier, R., Burkett, S., & Hickman, C. (1984). Sanctions, peers, and deviance: Preliminary models of a social control process. *Sociological Quarterly, 25*, 67–82.

Oklahoma Department of Transportation. (1989). *Oklahoma visual litter survey and analysis: 1988–1989*. Unpublished report.

Powers, R., Osborne, J., & Anderson, E. (1973). Positive reinforcement of litter removal in the natural environment. *Journal of Applied Behavior Analysis, 6*, 573–578.

Reich, J., & Robertson, J. (1979). Reactance and norm appeal in antilittering messages. *Journal of Applied Social Psychology, 9*, 99–101.

Robinson, S. (1976). Littering behavior in public places. *Environment and Behavior, 8*, 363–384.

Schwartz, R., & Orleans, S. (1967). On legal sanctions. *University of Chicago Law Review, 13*, 73–89.

Tittle, C. (1977). Sanction fear and the maintenance of social order. *Social Forces, 55*, 579–596.

Tittle, C., & Rowe, A. (1973). Moral appeal, sanction threat, and deviance: An experimental test. *Social Problems, 20*, 488–498.

Tuck, M., & Riley, D. (1986). The theory of reasoned action: A decision theory of crime. In D. Cornish & R. Clarke (Eds.), *The reasoning criminal: Rational choice perspectives on offending* (pp. 156–169). New York: Springer-Verlag.

Williams, K., & Hawkins, R. (1986). Perceptual research on general deterrence: A critical review. *Law and Society Review, 20*, 543–572.

Williams, K., & Hawkins, R. (1989). The meaning of arrest for wife assault. *Criminology, 27*, 163–181.

A SEARCH FOR THE ELUSIVE SETTING EVENTS OF SCHOOL VANDALISM

A CORRELATIONAL STUDY

G. ROY MAYER, MARY NAFPAKTITIS, TOM BUTTERWORTH, AND PAM HOLLINGSWORTH

"Crime and violence threaten the viability of our public schools," said United States Attorney General William French Smith (Nicholson, 1981). Speaking during June, 1981, Smith called for a crackdown on violence and vandalism in the schools, stating that more than 250,000 students and 5,000 teachers are physically assaulted in a typical month. In addition, the National School Resource Network and the California Safety Center (Nicholson, 1981) report that more than $600 million is spent annually on school property repair, security devices, insurance, and guards.

Amidst a great public outcry to address the problems of violence and vandalism, school districts have responded with so-called "hard" measures (Reaves, 1981). The Los Angeles Unified School District developed a security force of more than 325 agents and placed intrusion alarms in many schools. Other districts have developed means of identifying violence-prone youngsters to all concerned agencies (i.e., juvenile court officials, the district attorney's office, and local police departments) or have implemented stringent student disciplinary programs (Reaves, 1981).

Source: *Education and Treatment of Children* (1987), *10*(3):259–270. Reprinted by permission of the Pressley Ridge Schools.

However, one of the consistent factors alleged to be associated with high levels of school violence and property loss is a hostile and authoritarian attitude on the part of school staff toward students (Scrimger & Elder, 1981). Yet, research is showing that today's schools are emphasizing more punitive measures in managing student behavior. For example, results from a survey by the American Association of School Administrators (Brodinsky, 1980) indicated that personnel in school districts spend more time and energy in implementing punitive measures than in positive or preventive measures. Similarly, teachers, on the average, have been observed to use disapproval approximately three times more frequently than approval when they respond to student behavior (Heller & White, 1975; Thomas, Presland, Grant, & Glynn, 1978; White, 1975).

This reliance on heavy security arrangements and punitive discipline strategies may actually aggravate school-related violence and vandalism (Greenberg, 1969, 1974). Likewise, Mayer and Butterworth (1979, 1981) and Mayer, Butterworth, Nafpaktitis, and Sulzer-Azaroff (1983) have suggested that relying on punishment as a school-wide and classroom management procedure is a condition in the school environment that can actually promote school disruption and vandalism. Findings from the experimental analysis of behavior have taught us that extinction and punishment tend to provoke aggression and destruction by laboratory animals (Azrin, Hutchinson, & Hake, 1963). Research with humans also provides "mounting evidence that aversive stimulation generates an instigation to aggression in our species as well as in lower orders" (Berkowitz, 1983, p. 1139). Even frustrations and failures to attain a desired goal "can produce aggressive inclinations because of their aversive nature" (Berkowitz, 1983, p. 1143). It would seem reasonable to hypothesize, then, that some proportion of the aggression and destruction that takes place in public schools is a reaction to aversive school environments.

Mayer and his colleagues (1979, 1981, 1983) also suggest additional factors that may contribute to the punitive nature of the school discipline environment resulting in increased vandalism. These include vague rules, inconsistency, lack of appropriate follow-through, and little or no allowance made for individual differences. The last problem mentioned is exemplified by a lack of individualized consequences so that everyone receives the same punishment for the same infraction. Such misuse of behavior management procedures can result in an increase, rather than a decrease, of aggressive behavior (Mayer & Butterworth, 1979).

Several investigators (Mayer & Butterworth, 1979; Mayer, Butterworth, Nafpaktitis, & Sulzer-Azaroff, 1983) have attempted to eliminate or reduce some of the hypothesized conditions or setting events that produce aggression. By doing so, they were able to obtain significant reductions in vandalism. However, their interventions were complex staff development packages and individual factors possibly contributing to the reduction in vandalism were not isolated.

In an attempt to establish more clearly the direction of future research, the present correlational study was carried out to determine specific characteristics of the school environment that are related to vandalism. Prior research in applied behavior analysis has emphasized the immediate antecedents and consequences of behavior. However, Wahler and Fox (1981) have pointed out that socially important behaviors, such as disruptive school behavior, truancy, and property destruction, may be under the control of temporally remote stimuli or setting events rather than immediate antecedents and consequences. To help provide descriptive analyses of these setting events, Wahler and Fox advocate the use of correlational analyses. This study uses correlational analyses in an attempt to identify possible setting events to school vandalism.

METHOD

Selection of Schools

Twenty-eight intermediate schools (grades 6, 7, and 8; 7 and 8; or 7, 8, and 9) in Los Angeles County participated in the study. These schools represented communities with a wide range of socioeconomic levels as indicated by the percentage of students in each school receiving aid to families with dependent children (0% to 64%). The schools' student enrollments ranged from 402 to 1,639.

In most instances, letters were sent to school principals soliciting their participation. In some cases, such solicitation occurred at a district principals' meeting. Follow-up telephone calls were made with each principal to confirm participation. Of 64 Los Angeles County schools contacted, 28 were selected due to their willingness to participate and their having readily available vandalism data.

Selection of Teachers

In each school, three teachers were picked randomly from a list of staff members using a table of random numbers. Only teachers of academic subjects were selected. Special education teachers were ineligible. If a teacher selected by a random number did not teach an academic subject, the next random number was taken. All teachers selected agreed to participate in the study.

Data Collection Procedures

Vandalism

Vandalism data were obtained from each school and furnished by the principal or his or her secretary. The data of each incident of vandalism and the cost of repairing and replacing vandalized property were recorded in the format shown in Figure 1. If more than one entry was recorded for a particular date, the school custodian was interviewed to determine if the entries represented more than one incident. All vandalism that resulted in any cost to the school was counted as an infraction. These events included graffiti, breaking of glass, equipment theft, fire, and other property damage.

The cost and frequency of vandalism were calculated in units per 100 students to account for differences in school size. Vandalism cost, then, was calculated by dividing the total cost of repairing or replacing property vandalized during a 9-month school year by the student enrollment. This result was then multiplied by 100 to give a figure for each school. Vandalism frequency per 100 students was obtained by dividing the total number of incidents reported during a 9-month school year by the student enrollment. This result was then multiplied by 100 to give a comparative figure for each school.

School Discipline Survey

The School Discipline Survey (SDS) (Mayer, Butterworth, Spaulding, et al. 1983) was used as a measure of the school discipline environment (see Figure 2). Three major areas contributing to a punitive school discipline environment were identified based on previous research (Mayer & Butterworth, 1979; Mayer, Butterworth, Komoto, & Benoit, 1983; Mayer, Butterworth, Nafpaktitis, & Sulzer-Azaroff, 1983). The first included clarity of both school and classroom rules and discipline policies. It was assumed that appropriate stimulus control, or rule following, cannot be developed unless discipline policies and rules are clearly communicated (Sulzer-Azaroff & Mayer, 1986). Further, a lack of rule following behavior tends to result in more punishment being used in the school environment. The second area involved administrative support for staff in student discipline (i.e., consistency and follow-through). If administrative support were weak or inconsistent, it certainly would not be reinforcing enough to support staff efforts aimed at school-wide discipline programs (Mayer, Butterworth, Komoto, & Benoit, 1983). Such a lack of support or reinforcement is also aversive. The third area included allowances made for individual student differences in carrying out discipline policies. It was assumed that when individual differences are recognized and addressed, the envi-

	CLASSROOM BUILDING		CAFETERIA		WASHROOM		OTHER (please specify, e.g., library, playground, administrative building, bus)	
	Date of occurrence(s)	Cost*	Date of occurrence(s)	Cost*	Date of occurrence(s)	Cost*	Date of occurrence(s)	Cost*
BROKEN GLASS								
EQUIPMENT THEFT								
FIRE DAMAGE								
PROPERTY DAMAGE (Graffiti, smashed furniture, fixtures torn off wall, carved desks, miscellaneous ruination)								

*Be sure to include labor cost. If precise dollar figures are not immediately available, estimate cost in pencil. When accurate figures are available, indicate in ink.

FIGURE 1. Recording sheet for occurrence and cost of vandalism.

The growing problems of school violence, vandalism, and absenteeism, are serious concerns of the office of the Los Angeles County Superintendent of Schools. We are asking your help in a research project releated to these problems. We need to know how student discipline is handled at your school. Most items in this survey pertain to what is actually being practiced in your school, except for specific questions that request your personal opinion.

Responses will be grouped to give an overall picture of your school, but your independent judgement is essential. The form should not take longer than fifteen minutes to complete.

PART I

Please read each item and place an "X" on the line corresponding to your answer.

	Yes	No
1. Our school has a written discipline policy. (If answered "no," proceed directly to item 2.)		
a. I have read or referred to the school discipline policy within the past year.		
b. A copy of the discipline policy is given at least on an annual basis to each student.		
c. A copy of the discipline policy is given on at least an annual basis to the parents of each student.		
2. I have a written set of standards for classroom discipline that I use. (If answered "no," proceed directly to Part II.)		
a. I have read or referred to my written classroom standards within the past year.		
b. A copy of my classroom standards is given at least on an annual basis to each student in my class.		
c. A copy of my classroom standards is given at least on an annual basis to the parents of each student in my class.		

PART II

Following is a series of statements describing student discipline and staff relationships. Place a check in the column below the word or phrase which best indicates how closely the statement describes your school or your opinion.

	Rarely	Some-times	More often than not	Consistently
3. Instructional materials to meet individual student differences are provided when I request them.				
4. Action is taken promptly by school authorities when I make a disciplinary referral.				
5. In my opinion, disciplinary action taken by school authorities is appropriate.				
6. Good teaching is recognized and appreciated by the administration.				
7. I confer with other teachers regarding instructional activities occurring in my classroom.				
8. I confer with other teachers regarding how I maintain discipline in my classroom.				
9. Faculty requests and suggestions regarding discipline policy are acted upon promptly.				
10. When disciplining students, it is easy for me to follow the school-wide discipline policy				
11. When I follow the discipline policy, I receive administrative support for my actions				
12. When I follow my own judgement in administering discipline, I receive support for my actions.				
13. As far as I know, other teachers follow the school discipline policy.				
14. I am in agreement with the discipline practices of counselors and administrators				

FIGURE 2. The School Discipline Survey.

(Continued)

	Disagree	Somewhat	Somewhat	Agree
15. In my opinion, the school discipline policy is effective.				
16. In my opinion, the school discipline policy is overly punitive.				
17. Every student who engages in a suspendable offense should be suspended.				
18. Every student who engages in an offense for which expulsion can be applied should be expelled.				

	Rarely	Some-times	More often than not	Consistently
19. I start to formulate an individual plan for improving a student's behavior when the usual methods of classroom discipline fail.				
20. An individual plan for improving a student's behavior is formulated when the usual methods of school discipline fail.				
21. Students who have not been attending schoool regularly are rewarded for improved attendance.				
22. Students receive school-wide recognition for behaving as they should.				
23. Students receive recognition in my classroom for behaving as they should.				
24. I consider using positive incentives to assist students who need to improve their behavior in my classroom.				
25. I consider using changes in assignments and materials to assist students who need to improve their behavior in my classroom.				
26. School authorities consider using positive incentives to assist students who need to improve their school behavior.				
27. School authorities consider using program or class changes to assist students who need to improve their school behavior.				
28. I make allowances for specific students when applying the school discipline policy.				

ronment would become less punitive and more positive (Mayer & Butterworth, 1979; Mayer, Butterworth, Nafpaktitis, & Sulzer-Azaroff, 1983).

The original pool of items for the SDS was generated within the above three categories. These items were analyzed and revised according to their relevance to each specific area, and also according to their adherence to basic criteria such as grammar, difficulty, ambiguity, and overlap.

Through a series of conferences, the final list was shaped in preparation for a logical or content validation process. In this process, a panel of four behavioral and measurement specialists reviewed the item pool for content validity. All panel members had to agree to each item; items not agreed upon were discarded or revised. Their efforts resulted in a 28-item instrument assessing school staff perceptions of discipline policies and practices.

Of the items included on the questionnaire some items require a "yes-no" response, while most items require responses on a Likert-type scale on which the respondent must answer, "Rarely," "Sometimes," "More Often Than Not," or "Consistently." Four items require a response of "Disagree," "Somewhat Disagree," "Somewhat Agree," or "Agree."

The survey was administered to the three randomly selected teachers in each school. They were given the survey form individually and were asked to return it approximately one week later. They also were told that their responses were anonymous and confidential and that each school's scores would be treated as a unit.

Scoring of the Survey

The maximum possible total score on the survey is 136 points, indicating a positively reinforcing environment with clear discipline policies, good administrative support, and maximum allowance for individual differences. Maximum score on the Clarity section (items 1–2) is 32. Maximum score on the Administrative Support section (items 3–16) is 56. Maximum score on the Individual Differences section (items 17–28) is 48.

For items 1a, b, c and 2a, b, c, four points are given for a "Yes" response and zero points are given for a "No" response. For items 3 through 14 and items 19 through 28, four points are given for the response "Consistently," three points for the response "More Often Than Not," two points for "Sometimes" and one point for "Rarely." For item 15, four points are given for the response "Agree," three points for "Somewhat Agree," two points for "Somewhat Disagree," and one point for "Disagree." For items 16 through 18, four points are given for the response "Disagree," three points for "Somewhat Disagree," two points for "Somewhat Agree," and one point for "Agree."

Reliability and Validity of the School Discipline Survey

In order to assess the test–retest reliability of the survey, a second group of 69 teachers from three of the intermediate schools was requested to complete the questionnaire twice at an interval of two to four weeks. A Pearson correlation coefficient was calculated. A high reliability coefficient of .87 was obtained for the total survey, .83 for Clarity, .82 for Administrative Support, and .62 for Individual Differences.

In addition to its use in this correlational study, the SDS was administered to the staffs of six schools, four junior high schools and two high schools, at the beginning of a comprehensive staff development project (Nafpaktitis, Mayer, Hollingsworth, & Butterworth, 1982). On the 198 com-

TABLE 1. School Discipline Survey Mean Total Score, Vandalism Frequency and Vandalism Cost for 28 Schools

School	School Enrollment	Survey Mean Total Score	Vandalism Frequency	Vandalism Cost ($)
1	808	120	20	904
2	348	118	8	960
3	857	110	2	752
4	483	109	6	175
5	576	107	18	3,845
6	588	107	11	1,574
7	791	106	2	2,800
8	587	103	9	1,097
9	660	102	28	3,185
10	1,639	102	12	1,103
11	853	102	35	2,571
12	452	101	39	3,116
13	764	101	11	4,730
14	467	101	15	961
15	543	100	10	2,369
16	429	98	20	4,040
17	547	98	7	1,735
18	841	98	6	2,985
19	807	97	46	1,965
20	471	96	16	1,180
21	1,424	96	33	1,502
22	720	94	4	345
23	582	91	21	2,360
24	512	91	8	931
25	782	89	22	1,322
26	448	81	26	9,130
27	426	71	22	1,446
28	402	69	23	3,093

pleted surveys, additional support for statistical validity was provided by data on internal consistency. Pearson product–moment correlation coefficients were calculated for the three sub-section scores and for the total score of the SDS. The intercorrelations between the three sub-sections were sufficiently low to indicate construct validity. The correlation between Clarity and Administrative Support was .45; the correlation between Clarity and Individual Differences was .23; and the correlation between Administrative Support and Individual Differences was .39. These correlations suggest that each sub-section is measuring a different construct related to discipline policies and practices. Furthermore, Clarity and Administrative Support each correlated with the total score at .80 and Individual Differences correlated with the total score at .65.

RESULTS

Table 1 presents the results of the School Discipline Survey and the vandalism data for each school. The number of incidents of vandalism reported for the 9-month period ranged from 2 to 46. The cost of vandalism to a school for the 9 months ranged from $175 to $9,130. Table 2 lists the ranges, means, and standard deviations for all the variables. Table 3 displays a correlation matrix of measures of the school discipline survey, vandalism frequency, and vandalism cost. While no significant relationship was found between any of the survey's subscores and vandalism, the total score obtained from the school discipline survey was found to be related significantly to both vandalism frequency ($r = -.43$) and cost ($r = -.39$).

DISCUSSION

A major factor was found to relate significantly to vandalism: a punitive school discipline environment, as measured by the school discipline survey. The school discipline environment includes several areas: clarity of

TABLE 2. Ranges, Means, and Standard Deviations of Scores and Variables for All 28 Schools

Score of Variable	Range			
	Minimum	Maximum	Mean	SD
Vandalism frequency/100 students	0.2	8.6	2.9	2.0
Vandalism cost/100 students	$36	$2,038	$392	396
School Discipline Survey Mean total score	69	120	98	11

TABLE 3. Intercorrelations for the School Discipline Survey and Vandalism

	1	2	3
1. School Discipline Survey	1.00	−.43*	−.39*
2. Vandalism frequency/100 students		1.00	.54**
3. Vandalism cost/100 students			1.00

*$p < .05$.
**$p < .01$.

rules, administrative support (i.e., consistency and follow-through), and the allowance for individual differences (i.e., appropriate selection of academic materials, reinforces, and punishers). No one of these areas by itself was found to correlate significantly with vandalism, but the combination of the three areas did.

Because correlations indicate strength of association only and are not evidence of a cause and effect relationship, it might be concluded that these findings have little relevance to the problem of school vandalism. However, research evidence strongly suggests that when the predictor variables in the SDS scale are manipulated as treatment variables, vandalism is indeed affected. For example, when the punitive school environment and other variables were treated in two different experimental studies (Mayer & Butterworth, 1979; Mayer, Butterworth, Nafpaktitis, & Sulzer-Azaroff, 1983), vandalism costs decreased an average of 73.5% for 23 elementary and junior high schools. These findings complement those of Gold and Mann (1982), who also concluded that "poor scholastic experience are significant causes of delinquent and disruptive behavior" (p. 313). They found that when curriculum was more individualized and the environment was made more reinforcing, students behavior and scholastic performance improved.

Perhaps, then, a punitive school discipline environment is a major factor contributing to school vandalism. The correlational evidence of this study, combined with the experimental evidence of other studies (Mayer & Butterworth, 1979; Mayer, Butterworth, Nafpaktitis, & Sulzer-Azaroff, 1983), would appear to support such a conclusion. Certainly, evidence is accumulating to suggest that the discipline environment, as measured in the School Discipline Survey, may be a setting event for school vandalism. Perhaps, then, by making the school environment more reinforcing, by reducing the frequent misuse of behavioral procedures, and by maintaining appropriate behavior through an increased use of positive reinforcement, the amount of vandalism in our schools can be significantly decreased.

In our opinion, the importance of the impact of setting events on vandalism has been overlooked by educators. The emphasis instead has been placed on security arrangements and punishment. School staff need to be educated as to the relevance of setting events. "Because setting events can function powerfully, they all must be identified and dealt with effectively if we are ever durably to prevent, rather than just temporarily suppress, violence and vandalism in our schools" (Sulzer-Azaroff & Mayer, 1986, p. 342).

Additional support for the utility of the School Discipline Survey is suggested by reactions of administrators in the study. They generally reported that they found information on the scale to be helpful in evaluating their discipline policies and in planning policy changes.

Finally, it should be recognized that even though the correlations obtained between the School Discipline Survey and vandalism were statistically significant, they were not extremely high. Additional research studies certainly are warranted to identify and substantiate the existence of setting events for vandalism in order to help us to better understand and prevent this pervasive problem. More precise measurement of vandalism, for example, might improve our identification and understanding of its setting events. Even though it appears impossible to measure acts of vandalism directly, future studies might attempt to assess the reliability of vandalism frequency and cost statistics by using two independent reporters or observers.

Inter-rater reliabilities of the School Discipline Survey also should be studied. Factor analysis of the items of the survey might lend additional support to the theoretically derived categories. Studies of student and parent responses to the survey and correlations of the survey with aggressive or assaultive behavior on the campus would further strengthen the survey's validity.

In the final analysis, however, despite the low correlations, the predictors in the survey as setting events constitute a major departure from the tradition of measuring school climate with vague, highly subjective categories. The concept of setting events with objective statements of environmental variables presents great potential for programmatic utility. More interventions to reduce vandalism also need to be experimentally tested. These include studying the effect on vandalism of a clear discipline policy and studies comparing individualized and standardized approaches.

REFERENCES

Azrin, N. H., Hutchinson, R. R., & Hake, D. F. (1963). Pain-induced fighting in the squirrel monkey. *Journal of the Experimental Analysis of Behavior, 6*, 620.

Berkowitz, L. (1983). Aversively stimulated aggression: Some parallels and differences in research with animals and humans. *American Psychologist, 38,* 1135–1144.

Brodinsky, B. (1980). *AASA critical issues report: Student discipline, problems and solutions* (Report No. 021-00334). Arlington, VA: American Association of School Administrators.

Gold, M., & Mann, D. W. (1982). Alternative schools for troublesome secondary students. *The Urban Review, 14,* 305–316.

Greenberg, B. (1969, October). *School vandalism: A national dilemma.* Palo Alto, CA: The Stanford Research Institute Research and Development Program.

Greenberg, B. (1974). School vandalism: Its effects and paradoxical solutions. *Crime Prevention Review, 1,* 105.

Heller, M. C., & White, M. A. (1975). Rates of teacher verbal approval and disapproval to higher and lower ability classes. *Journal of Educational Psychology, 67,* 796–800.

Mayer, G. R., & Butterworth, T. W. (1979). A preventive approach to school violence and vandalism: An experimental study. *The Personnel and Guidance Journal, 57,* 436–441.

Mayer, G. R., & Butterworth, T. W. (1981). Evaluating a preventive approach to reducing school vandalism. *Phi Delta Kappan, 62,* 498–499.

Mayer, G. R., Butterworth, T. W., Komoto, T., & Benoit, R. (1983). The influence of the school principal on the consultant's effectiveness. *Elementary School Guidance and Counseling, 17,* 274–279.

Mayer, G. R., Butterworth, T., Nafpaktitis, M., & Sulzer-Azaroff, B. (1983). Preventing school vandalism and improving discipline: A three year study. *Journal of Applied Behavior Analysis, 16,* 355–369.

Mayer, G. R., Butterworth, T. W., Spaulding, H. L., Hollingsworth, P., Amorim, M., Caldwell-McElroy, C., Nafpaktitis, M., & Perez-Oserio, X. (1983). *Constructive discipline: Building a climate for learning* (Available from the Office of the Los Angeles County Superintendent of Schools, 9300 E. Imperial, Downey, CA 90242).

Nafpaktitis, M., Mayer, G. R., Hollingsworth, P., & Butterworth, T. W. (1982). *Constructive discipline: Improving attendance and reducing disruption and vandalism costs.* (End of year report. Project No. 5867). Downey, CA: Los Angeles County Superintendent of Schools.

Nicholson, G. (1981). Pursuing school safety in the 80's: An opinion from the attorney general's office. *Thrust, 11,* 26–27.

Reaves, A. (1981). We let it happen—We can change it. *Thrust, 11,* 8–10.

Scrimger, G. C., & Elder, R. (1981). *Alternatives to vandalism: Cooperation or wreckreation.* Sacramento: School Safety Center, California Department of Justice.

Sulzer-Azaroff, B., & Mayer, G. R. (1986). *Achieving educational excellence using behavioral strategies.* New York: Holt, Rinehart and Winston.

Thomas, J. D., Presland, I. E., Grant, M. D., & Glynn, T. (1978). Natural rates of teacher approval in grade-7 classrooms. *Journal of Applied Behavior Analysis, 11,* 91–94.

Wahler, R. G., & Fox, J. J. (1981). Setting events in applied behavior analysis: Toward a conceptual and methodological expansion. *Journal of Applied Behavior Analysis, 4,* 327–338.

White, M. A. (1975). Natural rates of teacher approval and disapproval in the classroom. *Journal of Applied Behavior Analysis, 8,* 367–372.

ENVIRONMENTAL CORRELATES OF SCHOOL VANDALISM

PAVEL PABLANT AND JAMES C. BAXTER

In the last decade, school vandalism has become a critical educational and social problem. The problem includes various forms of illegal entry, defacement, damage, theft, arson and other violent and destructive acts directed against school property. Grieder has defined the crisis as taking "epidemic proportions" and has observed that "vandalism is one of the toughest subjects" that school administrators are faced with today. He states that

> two things seem to be sure. There is no way to police schools or any other kind of property so effectively as to eliminate vandalism and other sorts of violence. Nor will more and more rules do the job. None of us can write a prescription for the solution of this problem, but we must try to understand it, foster understanding by citizens, school personnel, and students, and exercise leadership in improving educational services and ameliorating bad community (social) conditions (1970: 10).

The problem exists in large and small school districts, in schools of economically deprived areas such as centrally located schools, and in "schools of the best caliber, affording the finest opportunities," such as those located in wealthy suburban areas (Grieder, 1970).

The costs of vandalism impose a heavy burden on our educational institutions. Although the total financial loss due to school vandalism has not been determined, a conservative estimate for the year 1969, made by the United States Office of Education, was over $100 million, and several

Source: *Journal of the American Institute of Planners* (1975), *41*:270–279. Reprinted by permission.

insurance companies have estimated the losses for the same year at more than $200 million (Grieder, 1970). This financial toll reflects such items as repair and maintenance of school property and replacement of stolen or damaged equipment. Nevertheless, these estimates constitute a small percentage of the total expenditures associated with vandalism, because they do not include the enormous increase in insurance premiums across all schools (which penalizes nonvandalized schools), expenditures for antiburglary equipment, fences, protective devices, school security personnel, city police patrols, and expensive architectural material and design, which have been used as preventive measures. O'Grince's (1968) discussion of preventive measures used in the Baltimore City school system offers a glimpse of the expenditures incurred by one school district. He reports that in the year 1967 alone, 60,000 broken windows were reported with a total loss of approximately $150,000, and that to prevent this exorbitant damage the school system resorted to the protection of windows with metal guards at an approximate cost of $1.50 per square foot, and the replacement of glass with other expensive nonbreakable material such as plastic polycarbonate glazing. The head of the Maintenance and Operation Division commented that "while the cost of this material at approximately $2.10 per square foot is somewhat high compared to $.45 per square foot for plain glass, you can see that its high cost is justified, especially when you have to replace plain glass four or five times a month" (O'Grince, 1968: 30–31).

Despite increased use of architectural, electronic, and mechanical devices, as well as security manpower as preventive measures, the evidence suggests that crime against school property is on the increase. For example, the Houston Independent School District reports that during the academic year 1969 to 1970, a total of $262,340 was lost in equipment and material, and in the 1970 to 1971 academic year the reported losses went up to $280,871. By 1971 to 1972 the costs had risen to $423,721. Early estimates for 1972 to 1973 reflect a decline in losses, $359,412 although the total number of illegal entries increased from 1,155 in 1971 to 1972 to 1,257 in 1972 to 1973.[1]

The prevention of vandalism is of paramount importance, not only because of the financial losses incurred but because vandalism causes doubt, suspicion, and fear among students, personnel, and the community. These consequences may be assumed to have deleterious effects on the total education process.

Community or societal problems are frequently considered to be at the root of vandalism. Some view vandalism as a symptom of emotional maladjustment, rebellion against authority, a breakdown of personal restraint, or a growing contempt for custom and law (Grieder, 1970).

That vandalic acts grow from psychological or sociological problems may well be so. After all, not all schools are vandalized; some are more vulnerable to vandalism than others. Hoerlein (1968), for example, has observed that the fewest cases of vandalism and the lowest losses of dollar value occur in the center city area, while schools in the suburbs are found to have the highest vandalism rates.

Scattered evidence provided by urbanists and school principals adds to the suggestion that environmental attributes of the school and its neighborhood may be important factors in fostering or deterring vandalism. Jane Jacobs (1961) has argued that neighborhood activity levels, diversification of building usage, pathway utilization, and population density, among other indices, are very important factors in street crime deterrence. Jacobs' hypothesis may be readily extended to crimes against the school, in that neighborhood activity, diversity, and the like may be important variables influencing vandalism rates.

School administrators have observed that the aesthetic characteristics of school buildings and surrounding grounds promote a sense of pride and concern for the school in the community. Because the concern of the community for its schools has been assumed to be an important factor in the protection of school property, the aesthetic characteristics of school buildings may have an effect on the safety of the school and on its protection from crimina acts. Lloyd made the following observation on the remarkable selective effect of new relocatable, aesthetically appealing buildings on vandalism frequency:

> These air conditioned buildings have exterior walls made of bright-colored and beautifully finished porcelain-enamel steel paneling and windows made of colored plexiglass.
>
> Although the relocatable schools stand on the grounds of existing schools built with conventional brick and mortar, the permanent buildings have been heavily vandalized while the others, only 10 or 15 yards away, have hardly been touched. Apparently the beauty and colorfulness of the new buildings, which are attractively landscaped, have aroused genuine community pride (1968: 31).

A second example has been offered by a beautification program of school property undertaken by a Washington, D.C. elementary school. The principal, W. B. Thomas, has reported encouraging success in dealing with vandalism.

> We at Walker Jones School have developed our own secret weapon for fighting school vandalism—*student pride*. Our aim is to make people aware of the importance of conservation and beautification in the school community and in the city. We base our philosophy on the following objectives:
>
> To develop in students and parents a pride in the upkeep of their property.
>
> To let participants share in planning and realizing the aesthetic needs of the schools and the community.

> To bring about an awareness that consistent care of surrounding areas—of plants, shrubbery, and flowers—is the prime factor in a successful beautification program (1968: 29).

At the end of the project's first year in which students, parents, neighbors, and teachers participated, W. B. Thomas reported that

> because of our positive approach, we had only a few broken windows during the school year and when school opened this fall, we had only one.... Our beautification project isn't finished, say the students. It never will be, for "beauty is a demanding mistress" and pride is catching (1968: 30).

After careful consideration of Jacobs' arguments and the reported success of school beautification programs in deterring vandalism, it was hypothesized that environmental variables such as the aesthetic quality of school property, activity level and habitation density of the immediate neighborhood surrounding the school, and related variables may be important factors differentiating highly vandalized schools from schools with lower vandalism rates. Therefore, the relationship between such environmental variables and vandalism rates was explored in the present study.

The following main hypotheses were tested:

1. Schools with low vandalism rates will be characterized by a higher level of esthetic appeal and maintenance of the properties, while schools with high vandalism rates will be characterized by lower aesthetic appeal and inadequate upkeep.
2. Schools with low vandalism rates will be surrounded by highly diverse and active neighborhoods with high habitation density and land coverage, while schools with high vandalism rates will be surrounded by less active neighborhoods with lower habitation density and land coverage.
3. Unimpaired visibility of school property will function as a deterrent to vandalism, such that high visual accessibility of school property by neighbors and passersby will be found to be associated with low vandalism rates, while the reverse will characterize schools with high vandalism rates.

METHOD

An examination of the distribution of heavily vandalized and relatively nonvandalized schools in the Houston Independent School District revealed that such schools were dispersed throughout the city, and that schools in close geographic proximity were observed to have high or low vandalism frequencies. Thus, an interesting opportunity for relatively controlled environmental research was available.

The amount of vandalism directed toward a particular school was operationally defined as the number of forcible entries with consequent theft of or damage to school property or equipment as reported to the security office of the district. Such reports were regularly made by individual schools in the district. Overall records were assembled and disseminated by the security office. Figures for the 1970 to 1971 school year were used for present purposes, because they provided the most recent data available at the time of the investigation.

An effort was made to control for potentially confounded variables, such as neighborhood income level, proportion of students from various ethnic backgrounds, school size, and elementary versus secondary level. To do this, pairs of high vandalism (HV) and low vandalism (LV) schools were matched on these four characteristics. A school having at least twice the frequency of reported vandalism of a paired LV school was defined as a HV school.

Matched pairs were selected from the 235 schools which were then included in the district. An effort was made to include schools from all areas of the district. The pairs were located in close geographic proximity and were of comparable size, as measured by total enrollment; of comparable proportion of Black, Mexican-American, and White pupils; and the same grade level, elementary of secondary.

The matching criteria for the sixteen pairs obtained in this manner are presented in Table 1. The matched schools are distributed widely throughout the district, representing higher and lower socioeconomic sections, and interior and suburban areas of the city. As can be seen in Table 2, none of the differences between the matching criteria for the two groups of schools reached conventional significance levels, with the exception of the dependent variable, vandalism frequency.[2]

School–Neighborhood Attributes Scale

As an exploratory procedure, the hypothesized attributes of school buildings and neighborhood characteristics associated with high or low vandalism rates were incorporated into a carefully prepared rating scale. The procedure underwent several refinements before any ratings were attempted. The final form of the School-Neighborhood Attributes Scale (SNAS) is presented in the Appendix. The scale is composed of ten subscales which measure (a) the quality of the school building, its physical characteristics, upkeep, and attractiveness; (b) the quality of the school grounds and immediate neighborhood; (c) the distinctiveness of the school

TABLE 1. Paired HV and LV Schools with Associated Matching Characteristics

Code	Name	Reported entries	Losses $	Enrollment	Blacks	Mexican-American	Whites*	Distance in miles
1	Black Jr.	16	2,601	2,112	141	105	1,866	.75
21	Waltrip Sr.	5	1,108	2,511	128	129	2,235	
2	Washington Jr. Sr.	25	13,235	786	790	10	46	2.75
22	Williams Jr. Sr.	7	915	616	571	12	33	
3	Browning El.	8	964	465	0	198	267	.75
23	Fields El.	0	13	555	4	165	386	
4	Garden Oaks El.	8	362	673	5	52	616	1.30
24	Oak Forest El.	0	822	838	11	72	752	
5	Yates Sr.	11	4,804	1,975	1,940	8	25	.80
25	Ryan Jr.	3	2,489	1,506	1,487	3	16	
6	Dunbar El.	21	3,171	449	441	5	3	.05
26	Jones Will El.	7	1,358	551	464	50	37	
7	Neff El.	5	795	1,296	7	54	1,235	.75
27	E. White El.	1	0	1,181	1	30	1,141	
8	Fondren Jr.	13	3,507	2,072	27	38	2,007	2.00
28	Westbury Sr.	1	245	1,938	15	7	1,906	

9	Lockhart El.	10	1,948	913	856	1	56	.80
29	Southland El.	2	156	936	873	29	34	
10	Wheatley Sr.	27	10,129	1,614	1,293	260	61	1.50
30	Fleming Jr.	7	4,744	1,166	1,053	113	0	
11	Franklin El.	17	2,345	1,674	16	1,513	145	1.25
31	Burnet El.	5	995	1,279	1	1,098	180	
12	Park Place El.	5	485	559	1	68	490	1.30
32	Golfcrest El.	0	21	581	1	130	447	
13	Pleasantville El.	20	4,246	567	406	114	47	.75
33	Port Houston El.	1	411	531	278	193	60	
14	Rucker El.	15	1,627	849	2	136	708	1.75
34	Bonner El.	2	52	726	3	143	580	
15	Scott El.	12	2,028	838	766	71	1	.50
35	Dogan El.	2	802	938	879	59	0	
16	Eliot El.	12	4,138	1,132	380	637	115	.50
36	Scroggins El.	4	897	815	270	434	113	

*Including Orientals and Indians.

TABLE 2. HV and LV School Comparisons

Variables	School means HV	LV	t value
Vandalism entries	14.06	2.94	9.349**
Amount of loss (1970–71)	3,766.66	876.75	3.491*
Number of Blacks	448.19	377.62	1.841
Number of Mexican-Americans	210.87	167.44	1.199
Number of Whites	449.31	495.00	.491
Total Enrollment	1,123.37	1,016.75	1.713

*$p < .05$.
**$p < .001$.

property; (d) the neighborhood's observable activity level; (e) the neighborhood's potential activity level in terms of variety of usage; (f) the density of land usage; (g) the isolation of the school building from the surrounding neighborhood; (h) the visibility of the school building; (i) the penetrability of the school grounds; and (j) the lighting of the school grounds and neighborhood.

To maximize the reliability of the rating scale, an effort was made to define each item of the scale as objectively as possible. Each item was composed of three descriptive levels characterizing the school or neighborhood on the attributes assumed to be related to vandalism. A score of three was assigned to descriptions hypothesized to be associated with high vandalism, a score of one to descriptions assumed to be associated with low vandalism. A score of two was assigned to intermediate values.

Procedure

To assess the reliability of ratings, all schools were rated independently by three judges.[3] Observations and ratings were made only during weekdays, once in the afternoon (after school) and once in the early evening hours. None of the judges knew the schools' vandalism rates. Raters toured the neighborhood surrounding each school and made ratings from all perspectives and approaches to the school. Observations on eight city blocks surrounding the school property were made.

RESULTS

Interrater reliability was established by computing the percentage of agreement between the three judges' ratings on each item of the scale. This was done by dividing the number of agreements by the combined total of agreements and disagreements. Agreement scores were tallied only when all three ratings coincided. Thus, a very stringent criterion of agreement was adopted. The level of agreement obtained for all schools on all scales was 67.7. This seems quite satisfactory in view of the criteria adopted and the type of ratings being made. Data used in the overall analysis are based on median ratings from the raters.

Because the data were ordinal in nature, the Mann-Whitney U-test was used to assess the significance of the differences between the median values of the two groups of schools. Two-tailed tests of significance were considered in this part of the analysis (Seigel, 1956; 116–126).

As can be observed in Table 3, the total SNAS score and all subscales scores significantly differentiated between the HV and LV schools.

Comparisons between HV and LV schools' ratings on individual items show that fourteen of the twenty-nine items reached significant levels of difference at or beyond the .05 level of confidence. Two additional scales achieved significance at the .10 level of significance. The means and significance levels for the comparisons between HV and LV schools on each item of the SNAS are presented in Table 4. Examination of the twenty-nine pairs of means also indicates that the differences obtained were in the expected direction in all cases ($p < .01$ by sign test).

The data were further analyzed in terms of the sensitivity of the SNAS in differentiating between each pair of schools. Table 5 presents the total

TABLE 3. Comparison of HV and LV Schools on Subscales and Total Scores of the SNAS

Subscales	Range*	Means HV	Means LV	U-values	Significance levels
Quality of school building	4–12	9.06	7.25	49.0	.02
Quality of surroundings	3–9	6.75	5.25	11.0	.002
Distinctiveness of school	3–9	5.43	4.25	52.5	.02
Observed activity level	3–9	6.60	5.25	70.0	.05
Potential activity level	3–9	7.12	5.93	55.0	.02
Density of land usage	4–12	9.62	7.75	36.5	.002
Isolation of school building	3–9	6.87	5.57	55.0	.02
Visibility of school building	2–6	4.37	2.93	52.0	.02
Penetrability	2–6	4.31	3.50	69.0	.05
Lighting	2–6	5.56	4.62	56.0	.02
Total SNAS score	29–87	65.74	51.93	31.5	.002

*Minimum and maximum possible scores for each subscale.

TABLE 4. Comparison of HV and LV Matched Pair Ratings on Individual Items

Items	Means HV	Means LV	Significance levels
1 Preservation S property	2.37	1.62	.01
2 S surface form	2.37	1.75	.05
3 S building design	2.37	1.93	.02
4 S structure	2.56	1.93	N.S.
5 Aesthetics of S grounds	2.56	1.93	.02
6 Preservation of N	1.87	1.81	N.S.
7 S/N quality	2.31	1.50	.01
8 S building size	1.62	1.31	N.S.
9 Identification of S	2.00	1.37	.05
10 S/N age	1.81	1.56	N.S.
11 N activity level	1.68	1.18	.05
12 N usage diversity	2.50	1.87	.05
13 Pathways utilization	2.43	2.15	.05
14 N potential activity	2.25	1.43	.01
15 S grounds use	2.62	2.50	N.S.
16 N block size	2.25	2.00	N.S.
17 S/grounds proportion	2.50	2.15	N.S.
18 N habitation density	2.50	1.68	.02
19 N land coverage	2.25	1.50	.01
20 N building's line	2.37	1.81	.01
21 S building's line	2.56	2.15	.05
22 N open space	1.87	1.25	.02
23 S/N continuity	2.43	2.37	N.S.
24 S viewpoint propinquity	1.87	1.31	.05
25 Residents S view	2.50	1.62	.01
26 S fences	1.62	1.25	N.S.
27 S windows	2.69	2.25	N.S.
28 S lighting	2.69	2.25	N.S.
29 N lighting	2.87	2.37	.05

SNAS scores, z-scores, based on a signed-rank analysis of each item, and one-tailed significance levels for the comparison of each matched pair of schools (Seigel, 1956: 75–83). The difference between fourteen paired schools attained significance beyond the .05 level and all sixteen pairs differ in the predicted direction at or beyond the .10 level of confidence. An analysis of this pattern of results by sign test is also statistically significant at the .01 level of confidence.

TABLE 5. Comparison of Matched Pairs of HV and LV Schools on Total SNAS Scores

Matched pairs	Total SNAS scores HV	Total SNAS scores LV	z-scores*	Significance levels
1	64	47	3.1	.001
2	61	57	2.2	.015
3	70	44	2.7	.003
4	72	53	1.6	.05
5	62	54	1.7	.04
6	65	53	2.9	.001
7	67	53	2.3	.01
8	72	54	6.8	.00003
9	64	58	1.5	.06
10	70	49	3.4	.0003
11	62	54	1.3	.09
12	64	57	3.1	.001
13	68	50	2.8	.002
14	62	54	1.7	.04
15	71	44	4.0	.00003
16	68	49	3.3	.0007

*Wilcoxon matched-pairs signed-rank test applied to individual items.

DISCUSSION

The present environmental approach to the investigation of school vandalism offers an encouraging perspective in understanding this growing problem. The results offer support for the hypothesized relationship between vandalism rates and the aesthetic quality and level of preservation of school property. Schools with low vandalism rates were characterized by excellent upkeep of buildings and surrounding school grounds. Building surfaces were well-preserved and the school property was characterized by careful maintenance and evidence of landscaping and beautification efforts. Highly vandalized schools were characterized by neglected maintenance and building upkeep, and the school grounds showed little or no evidence of aesthetic appeal or beautification efforts. In general, highly vandalized schools offered an appearance of abandonment regardless of architectural material or design.

Several other observations emerged from the comparison of HV and LV schools. Contrary to expectation, modernistic architectural designs were frequently encountered among the HV schools and simple architectural designs were frequently observed among the LV schools. The age of the school was found to bear no relationship to vandalism frequency in the present sample, since both old and newly erected school buildings were observed in the high and low categories. Thus, HV and LV schools were consistently differentiated on their building maintenance and upkeep, on the neatness of their grounds, and on landscaping efforts, regardless of age and architecture. The quality of preservation of neighborhood property was not a differentiating characteristic in the present sample. However, it was found that the schools' overall quality was generally superior to the immediate neighborhood in the LV group and inferior in the HV group.

These findings are congruent with the assumption that the quality of upkeep and aesthetic appeal of the school property, although modest, may be instrumental in engendering community concern and pride in the school. This process, then, may be an effective deterrent to criminal acts against the school property. This is an important consideration, because it suggests that beautification efforts such as regularly swept school grounds, modest landscaping, painting of buildings, and maintenance of school grounds may be more effective in deterring vandalic acts than steel fences, electronic sensors, and fortresslike expensive building construction. Indeed, it is important to note that the use of fences, protection of windows, lighting of school grounds and buildings, and electronic alarm systems were found to be undifferentiating features between HV and LV schools in the present sample.

The hypothesized relationship between neighborhood activity level and vandalism rates was also supported. Activity level of the surrounding neighborhood, as measured by observed, incidental, or potential activity, habitation density of surrounding area, and usage diversity was found to significantly differentiate HV and LV schools. The LV schools were generally located in areas characterized by multimodality of usage such as residences, commercial buildings, recreation centers, churches, and so on, while HV schools were frequently surrounded by areas of less usage diversity. Neighborhood diversification of usage appears, therefore, to be an important environmental variable affecting the school's safety.

With respect to habitation density, it was found that 81 percent of HV schools and 25 percent of LV schools faced uninhabited land such as railroad tracks, freeways, parks, sports fields, or vacant land on at least one side. It was also observed that the building lines of residences surrounding HV schools were further removed from the streets than residences surrounding LV schools. Likewise, neighborhood land coverage and habitation density surrounding HV schools was found to be significantly lower than that of LV schools.

These findings indicate that higher vandalism frequencies are encountered in schools which are isolated from the mainstream of the neighborhood's life. It may be assumed that isolated schools, or schools located in low-density areas, have less potential for neighborhood vigilance, and, therefore, are more vulnerable to vandalism.

The assumption of vigilance as a deterrent to vandalism was further supported by results indicating that residents of houses surrounding LV schools had a greater visibility of the school property than residents of houses surrounding HV schools. That is, there were fewer obstacles such as shrubbery, trees, and fences interfering with neighbor's visibility of the school building. It was also found that the streets surrounding LV schools were better illuminated than the streets surrounding HV schools. Perhaps better illumination of areas surrounding the school facilitates the vigilance and activity levels of neighborhoods adjacent to the school property.

The degree of visibility available would appear to be an important factor influencing the level of vandalism directed against a given school. It is important to note that this interpretation of the present results is congruent with the theorizing of Jane Jacobs (1961) and is also consistent with some recent data reported by Newman (1972, 1973). In general, Newman found that crime rates in individual housing projects of the New York Housing Authority could be predicted by analysis of certain architectural design features which favored or impaired visibility. Such findings would appear to have many important implications for both the design and utilization of many types of public facilities.

The conclusions suggested by the present investigation may be summarized in terms of immediate and long-term recommendations which may contribute to alleviating some of the problem of crime against schools and other public property.

Immediate Recommendations

Immediate recommendations are assumed to be well within the means of administrators and maintenance personnel of existing schools.

1. Maximize the aesthetic characteristics and level of preservation of school property by landscaping of grounds; beautification of buildings by painting, modest remodeling, and maintenance; and adequate upkeep of the entire school property and surrounding areas including sidewalks, streets, and vacant adjacent land.
2. Maximize the visibility and potential visibility of the school property by neighbors and passersby by eliminating shrubbery and bushes which cover large areas, trimming low tree branches, removing view-obstructing fences, adjusting landscape to avoid obstruction, and perhaps by encouraging neighbors to remove ob-

structions from potential viewpoints such as doors and windows of residences facing the school.

3. Encourage activity on the grounds or adjacent areas by opening pathways through school property, encouraging the parking of vehicles on school property or adjacent streets, and diversifying the use of the school buildings.
4. Maximize the illumination of streets surrounding the school property.

Long-Term Recommendations

Specific recommendations for long-term land planning measures which may be tentatively drawn from these results appear to include the following:

1. Minimize the isolation of social buildings from the neighborhoods surrounding them by locating new schools in more densely populated regions of diversified usage, perhaps where the greatest proportion of surrounding land is actively used for residences as well as commercial or public buildings such as stores, restaurants, service stations, recreational facilities, and the like.
2. Maximize articulation of the school site with neighborhood property on all sides, perhaps by locating the school building close to streets and surrounding structures, and minimize unoccupied or unused school grounds.
3. Maximize the visibility of the school property from adjacent areas, perhaps by designing structures which afford maximum visibility from the streets and neighborhood on all sides and by planning adequate illumination and landscaping forms to allow unobstructed view of the area.
4. Design the school building with one or a minimum number of enclosing structures.
5. Provide for diversified use of the building after hours as far as possible by emphasizing designs suitable for varied uses by the community.
6. Maximize the aesthetic appeal of the property by simple but attractive characteristics and materials, perhaps with the aim of facilitating building maintenance.

The results and implications of the present investigation are quite provocative and challenging. However, the need for further research in this area cannot be overemphasized because its applied possibilities reach far beyond the problem of school vandalism and show potential for contributing to a deeper understanding of the relationship between land planning and social pathology.

NOTES

1. These figures were obtained from the security division of the Houston Independent School District.
2. It may be noted from Table 1 that the dollar value loss was higher for the HV school in fifteen of the sixteen pairs.
3. The authors would like to express appreciation to Viera Pablant and Thomas Moore for assistance in rating the schools on the SNAS.

REFERENCES

Grieder, C. (1970) "Vandalism Symptomatic of Our Societal Sickness," *Nation's Schools 82* (April): 10, 18.

Hoerlein, P. H. (1968). "How Can Schools Control the Rising Incidence of Damage and Loss of School Property?" in "Ways of Fighting Vandalism Symposium," *Today's Education 57* (Dec): 31–32.

Jacobs, J. (1961) *The Death and Life of Great American Cities*. New York: Vintage Books.

Lloyd, R. C. (1968). "In Fighting Vandalism ... ," in "Ways of Fighting Vandalism Symposium," *Today's Education 57* (Dec): 31.

Newman, Oscar (1972) *Defensible Space*. New York: Macmillan.

——— (1973) *Architectural Design for Crime Prevention*. Washington, D.C.: National Institute of Law Enforcement and Criminal Justice.

O'Grince, S. (1968) "Public School Vandalism—How Baltimore Fights It," *American School and University 40* (July): 30–32.

Seigel, S. (1956) *Nonparametric Statistics for the Social Sciences*. New York: McGraw-Hill.

Thomas, W. B. (1968) "Fighting School Vandalism," in "Ways of Fighting Vandalism Symposium," *Today's Education 57* (Dec): 29–30.

APPENDIX

School–Neighborhood Attribute Scale

I. QUALITY OF SCHOOL BUILDING

1. Preservation of school property
    a. All features of building and surroundings well cared for: painted, washed, clean, trim, tidy, and neat.
    b. Adequate upkeep: presence of at least one neglected feature such as peeling paint or unkept lawn, and so on.

   c. Neglected upkeep: peeling paint, cracks, dirt, weeds, unmowed grass, unwashed windows, dirty walls. Minimum care.
2. School building surface form
   a. Highly differentiated appearance: diverse, contrasting patterns and textures, uniqueness of window and door shape or material, brightly contrasted colors and textures.
   b. Presence of differentiated features: some texture, shape, or form contrast such as the use of two colors or two forms.
   c. Homogeneous appearance: plain, dull colors, repetitive texture, and shape. No ornaments.
3. Building design characteristics
   a. Unique shape, original designs. Aesthetic appeal of building structures, such as columns or building layout. Use of more than two shapes or forms.
   b. Combination of two forms, isolated features of aesthetic appeal.
   c. Simple shape, no form or shape variety, nonappealing.
4. Structure
   a. School composed of only one structure.
   b. Two or three separate structures.
   c. Four or more separate structures even if connected with corridors. Not including stadiums.

II. QUALITY OF SURROUNDINGS

5. Aesthetic quality of school grounds
   a. Evidence of beautification program: careful landscaping, differentiated bushes, flower beds, objects of art, or patterning of bushes and trees.
   b. Isolated instances of aesthetic features, such as casual bushes, plants, trees, or flower beds.
   c. Plain characteristics. No evidence of aesthetic planning, such as uninterrupted grass or concrete or undifferentiated bushes.
6. Preservation of neighborhood property
   a. All neighborhood properties are well preserved.
   b. One-third of the properties are unkept.
   c. Two-thirds of neighborhood properties are neglected in upkeep: dirty, peeling paint, unkept yards, dirty sidewalks, and so on.

7. School-neighborhood property quality
   a. School building noticeably superior to neighborhood in preservation and upkeep.
   b. School building is of comparable quality to neighborhood maintenance.
   c. School building noticeably inferior to neighborhood in preservation.

III. DISTINCTIVENESS OF SCHOOL BUILDING

8. Building size
   a. School building is larger in size and ground coverage than surrounding structures.
   b. School building is larger but of comparable ground coverage to surrounding structures or vice versa.
   c. School building is of comparable height and ground coverage to surrounding structures.
9. Identification of school property
   a. Distinctive and recognizable from any side as a school building: presence of signs, architectural characteristics, view of classrooms, playground, and sports fields, outdoor corridors, or school buses.
   b. Distinguishable only by signs or frontal features or back or side features.
   c. Not obviously distinguishable as a school. Lack of signs, but recognizable as a public building or other nonresidential structure.
10. School building vs. neighborhood age
   a. School building newer than surrounding structures.
   b. Same age.
   c. School building older than surrounding buildings.

IV. OBSERVED ACTIVITY LEVEL

11. Activity level
   a. More than ten people present in surrounding school area during observation period.
   b. Between four and ten people.
   c. Three or less people.
12. Usage diversity of immediate surroundings
   a. At least one store on each side or more than four commercial or public buildings surrounding school grounds. An

assortment of commercial or public buildings: bars, restaurants, recreation facilities, service stations, and so on.
 b. Some diversity of use. Residential plus two or three commercial or public buildings in surrounding area.
 c. Lack of diversity of use. Predominance of only one modality, such as residences. No more than one commercial structure or public building in surrounding area.

13. Usage of surrounding pathways
 a. School grounds delimited by at least two commercial thoroughfares.
 b. Surrounding streets used by residents of other neighborhood areas. At least one commercial street.
 c. School grounds delimited by residential streets; that is, used only by residents of immediate area.

V. POTENTIAL ACTIVITY LEVEL

14. Potential or incidental activity of surrounding area.
 a. Numerous parked cars, more than three commercial buildings, such as theaters, bars, restaurants, stores, service stations visible from school grounds and more than one block away.
 b. Few parked cars on surrounding streets and at least two public buildings visible from the school grounds.
 c. No parked cars on surrounding streets and no public or commercial buildings visible from the school property.

15. School grounds usage
 a. Playground facilities, sports fields, and parking spaces open to public.
 b. At least open spaces available to public.
 c. Playground, sports facilities, and open spaces closed to public.

16. Block size surrounding school
 a. Two hundred feet or less.
 b. Two hundred to 400 feet.
 c. Over 400 feet.

VI. DENSITY OF LAND USAGE

17. Proportion of enclosed space on school grounds
 a. More than 25 percent of school grounds occupied by buildings such as classrooms, gymnasiums, and so on.
 b. Ten to 25 percent of school grounds occupied by buildings.

   c. Ten percent or less of school grounds occupied by buildings.
18. Density of usage of surrounding land
   a. Ten or more buildings or houses, or one apartment complex of more than twenty units in use per 400 feet.
   b. Six to ten buildings or houses or one apartment complex of less than twenty units in use per 400 feet.
   c. Less than six buildings or houses or one apartment complex, with less than ten units in use per 400 feet.
19. Land coverage density
   a. More than 75 percent of surrounding land covered by actively used buildings such as residences and commercial buildings.
   b. Twenty-five to 75 percent of actively used land.
   c. Twenty-five percent or less of surrounding land covered with buildings or 75 percent or more of yards, empty lots, freeway, railroad, and so on.
20. Building lines of surrounding blocks
   a. Average building lines on surrounding streets less than fifteen feet from street.
   b. Average building lines from fifteen to thirty feet from street.
   c. Average building lines more than thirty feet from street.

VII. ISOLATION OF SCHOOL BUILDING

21. School's building line
   a. Three or four sides of school buildings less than thirty feet from street or surrounding structures.
   b. One or two school building sides thirty or more feet from street or surrounding structures.
   c. Three or four school building sides thirty or more feet from the street or surrounding structures.
22. Open space surrounding school
   a. All four surrounding blocks inhabited or actively used, such as residences, commercial, or public buildings.
   b. At least one side facing empty land, such as railroad tracks, parks, empty lots.
   c. All four sides facing uninhabited land more than 100 feet from school.
23. School-neighborhood continuity
   a. Three or more sides of school grounds contiguous to other buildings, such as houses, stores, and so on.

b. At least one side of the school ground contiguous to other buildings.
c. School grounds delimited only by streets.

VIII. VISIBILITY OF SCHOOL BUILDING

24. School visibility
   a. School grounds and landscaping offer no obstruction of view.
   b. Approximately 50 percent of school grounds or landscaping have view obstructing features.
   c. More than 50 percent of the school's grounds or landscaping have view obstructing features.
25. Resident's school view
   a. Surrounding residents' view of the school building is unobstructed by bushes, trees, walls, or fences on all sides.
   b. At least 50 percent of the residents' doors and windows have obstructive features.
   c. Residents' view of school heavily impaired.

IX. PENETRABILITY

26. Fences
   a. Fenced on all four sides (fences over five feet).
   b. Partly fenced or fenced on three sides.
   c. Open entrance to school grounds. No fences.
27. Window characteristics
   a. Protected windows or absence of windows ten feet above the ground.
   b. Lower base of windows five to ten feet above the ground, unprotected.
   c. Lower base of windows less than five feet from the ground, unprotected.

X. LIGHTING

28. Lighting of school property
   a. Flood lighting close to building illuminating school building and/or school grounds. Clear school surface differentiation.
   b. Entrance lighting or lighting of outside passages. Lighting inside building.

c. Incidental lighting from street lights. Scattered lighting. No surface differentiation.

29. Lighting of neighborhood
    a. Very well illuminated. Surface of neighborhood structures are distinguishable on all four blocks. Porch lights and good street lighting.
    b. At least two surrounding blocks are well illuminated.
    c. Poor illumination. Only one light on each corner of block.

THE SPATIAL ECOLOGY OF STRIPPED CARS

David Ley and Roman Cybriwsky

> Environments are invisible. Their groundrules, pervasive structure, and overall patterns elude easy perception.
>
> Marshall McLuhan

An inclination toward the analytical and topical rather than the synthetic and global sometimes obscures from our view parsimonious regularity in the outside world. As an example, consider the geography of crime. Every crime has fixed spatial coordinates, a location. The scale of the location varies widely, from the specific site of a block mugging to broad tracts of territory which may remain under the hold of lawless bands for decades. But, despite this range of scales, might there be particular *types* of locations amenable to crime? Might there exist a common set of spatial ecological conditions favorable to deviant behavior?

Although every crime has a location, inquiry has discarded study of the individual site and shown preference for a descriptive, macro-scale perspective. This tradition does indeed seem to have obscured from our sight behavioral variables, whose contribution to the spatial incidence of deviant activity may be demonstrated as critical at the micro scale. It is quite possible that similar behavioral variables operate across scales and

Source: *Environment and Behavior*, (March 1974), 6(1):53–68. © 1974 Sage Publications, Inc. Reprinted by permission of Sage Publications, Inc. The authors wish to acknowledge the helpful comments of Julian Minghi and Deryck Holdsworth.

strongly influence macro-scale patterns. The aim of this paper is to uncover generic properties of the *behavioral environment* (Kirk, 1963) at the micro scale conducive to criminal activity. The second task, to project these same properties to macro-scale discussion of lawlessness in North American cities, will not be developed here.

The argument might be condensed in the following manner. Crime results from the failure of a local societal system of territorial control. The *local control system* is itself nested within a broader or *national control system* with potentially greater power of discretion, sustainable over a long period. Locations which suffer from weak sociospatial control are locations with an ecology favorable to criminal behavior. The main body of this discussion will be concerned with the role of local control, rather than with the national system. The thrust of this paper is as much conceptual as substantive, though research in progress will be used to illustrate the relationship between local spatial control and one particular form of criminal activity in the North American city.

THE LOCAL CONTROL SYSTEM

The underlying problem is to explain rather than describe the location of crime, and this task requires considerable sensitivity to context. Such an emphasis on environment is not consistent with strong traditions in both geography and psychology. The sterile laboratory of the psychologist has its counterpart in the isotropic plain of the geographer, a surface akin to a billiard table, uniformly flat, with no resource differentiation, and with equal access from every point to every other. From this contrived landscape has been derived some of human geography's most sophisticated theorizing. But such a landscape consists of empty space, an insipid surface. It has no topography, no quality, no meaning. "The meaning of space in the positivist tradition is obvious: space is meaningless" (Samuels, 1972).

In contrast, the local context, a rich and varied social and behavioral environment, is regarded here as a central variable. The environment is never featureless; it assumes meaning as well as form. Neither man nor nature acknowledge vacuous landscapes, and not the least salient of the differentiated attributes of the urban environment consist of the experiential and the perceived (Ley, 1972).

Such attention to fine-grained behavioral variables has not been a characteristic in studies of the geography of crime (Cybriwsky, 1972b). While the environment has rarely been reduced to the status of an isotropic surface, it has taken on the formal structure of socioeconomic variables drawn from the census. A common strategy has been to plot the incidence of metropolitan crime, and then relate incidence to the city's socioeconomic structure. Rather limited conclusions may be derived; the inner city has a higher crime rate than the suburbs, and there is usually a correlation between incidence of crime and income and racial variables. For example, in a recent sociological study of crime rates in 682 U.S. townships (Webb and Clemente, 1972) the researchers undertook a multiple regression of crime rate against population size, population density, and industrial diversification. To increase a low multiple correlation, the sample was partitioned by region. Though the coefficient rose, the interpretation of the results reveals the bluntness of this approach. Thus in the Northeast, a region of large urban areas, high densities, and industrial diversification, the authors detected a correlation between crime and large cities, high densities, and industrial diversity.

A far more promising beginning was made in much earlier studies of urban behavior. The Chicago school of human ecology articulately emphasized the relationship between spatial patterns and the existing social order, minutely exploring the environmental context of forms of deviant behavior (Phillips, 1972; Downey and Hunt, 1972). The painstaking thoroughness with which Thomas and Znaniecki (1927) charted the Polish peasant's encounter with a new environment and the conditions under which deviance evolved, and Thrasher's (1963) long-term contact and sensitivity to the nuances of Chicago's teenage gang culture, are [*sic*] monumental examples of a keen awareness of the influence of local environment in instigating criminal behavior. More overtly spatial themes, also bound within an ecological context including local control systems, run through studies of the distribution of commercial vice (Reckless, 1971), juvenile delinquency (Shaw and McKay, 1969), and in the celebrated schema of the promiscuity triangle, where deviant locations were those outside the range of local control (Park and Burgess, 1968: 147).

The ecological approach emphasized the creation of distinctive subcultural worlds in the metropolis from the linkage of a particular social group and a particular environment (Short, 1971). Each world had its own behavioral norms, a value system and a control system, and these systems had definite territorial bounds; beyond its bounds a local control system was no longer enforceable.

Thus urban space is impregnated with meaning; a given behavior may be appropriate in one setting and totally inappropriate in another (Barker, 1971). This conclusion is supported by more recent participant observation studies; in Italian sections of Boston, both Whyte (1955) and Gans (1962) have commented on the power of regulatory local controls over deviant behavior; Suttles (1968) documented what he labeled an "ordered segmentation of space" in Chicago's multiethnic West Side, which assured residents of each ethnic segment a certain level of security within that space, but offered no assurance of safety beyond its domain. Jacobs (1961) and Newman (1972) have discussed this process at the micro scale; drawing upon a varied urban sample, both argue that certain micro-scale configurations of land use are strongly related to the occurrence of criminal behavior when coupled with a weak local control system.

THE BEHAVIOR SETTING OF STRIPPED CARS

In each of these instances, then, we note the operation of a spatially bound local control system which maintains neighborhood norms and prescribes checks against deviant behavior. The structure of local control is far from monolithic. Besides having formal groups such as neighborhood associations, inner-city locations have quasi-formal groups such as block clubs and the informal control exercised by individual households, all making a claim to local space and the activities pursued within it. The inner-city row house commonly fronts directly onto the street, giving residents a legitimate claim to the space of the adjoining sidewalk and even the roadway, and invoking the effervescent outdoor life of the inner city (Cybriwsky, 1972a). In the daytime and more particularly on summer evenings, whole families empty onto their porches, their stoops, and the sidewalk itself. In this manner, surveillance and territorial control pass beyond the household and onto the street.

We would expect a geographical corollary to this close claim on residential space, to the extension of ownership rights onto the street. The stronger the territorial control of the local society, the more completely will nonsocial and criminal behavior be confined to spaces where there is no surveillance. *Deviant behavior makes its own bid for space; and this bid, we hypothesize, finds its location in the power vacua of socially claimed space.*

It is this hypothesis which will be investigated, rather than formally tested, with crime data from inner-city Philadelphia. For the hypothesis, the exact location of each crime must be known; even reference to the closest intersection admits too much approximation, for it is essential to know whether the site of the crime is under the direct surveillance of the local control system; a difference of five yards can determine whether a location falls under or evades this surveillance. This requirement, and the reticence of the local police department to make public its records, forced us to use only one indicator of deviant activity to constitute a crime index.

The activity selected was the stripping down of abandoned cars; softer data on other crimes will be briefly introduced later. Vehicle-stripping has become a serious problem in the American city (Kessler, 1971; Metz, 1969);

as a crime indicator it has the advantage of a fixed, enduring, and thereby easily recorded location. Criminal activity may be continued over a period of several months from the initial abandonment of the vehicle to its eventual removal by city authorities. A stripped car may indicate two deviant activities, the initial abandonment and the continued process of stripping and vandalism. Thus the site of a stripped car implies that several individuals may have independently perceived the setting as appropriate for deviant activity.

Stripped cars have a variety of histories. Some are stolen and then stripped, some abandoned and stripped, some stripped legitimately by their owners, some legally parked but stripped nevertheless. The particular history is unimportant for present purposes; the interest here is the end state, the stripped vehicle, and the spatial ecology of its immediate location.

Police records of abandoned vehicles (rather than stripped vehicles) allude to a Philadelphia total of over 21,000 for 1971. The metropolitan pattern follows the concentric spatial form typical of urban pathologies. Abandoned car densities range from less than 100 per square mile per year for scattered peripheral districts, to between 800 and 1,000 plus per square mile per year for one police district in the heart of the North Philadelphia ghetto. In the study area of Monroe, densities fell within the median range of 200–500 per square mile per year (Cuff and Young, 1972).

The research task was to relate the location of each stripped car to the physical and social characteristics of the immediate setting. An area was chosen in inner-city Philadelphia for which there was already substantial behavioral data from a detailed community study (Ley, forthcoming). This neighborhood, which will be called Monroe, has a maximum north-south extent of eighteen blocks and a maximum east-west breadth of twelve blocks; in 1970 its population of 60,000 was ninety percent nonwhite. Common to most inner-city neighborhoods, Monroe contains an admixture of nonconforming industrial and institutional land uses among its residential units.

Two one-day partial surveys in the summer and fall of 1972 revealed a total of 138 unambiguously stripped cars in Monroe; the actual total was probably slightly higher as a conservative strategy was adopted in identifying marginal cases.[1] Vehicles were classified as stripped only if they exhibited at least two of such indicators as broken windows, missing body parts, flat tires, a raised hood, heavy graffiti defacement, or otherwise severe physical dilapidation. The spatial distribution at this scale shows no clearly defined pattern, and is probably closer to random than clustered. Following the traditional macro-scale approach to the geography of crime, the attempt at explanation might end here, with a conclusion of no apparent regularity. But we will see that by extending the argument to the microscale and incorporating behavioral variables, a clear relationship does emerge between behavior setting and criminal activity.

The land use and behavior setting of each vehicle were recorded, and the settings eventually collapsed to six categories. Each category reflected both the land use type of the space adjacent to the vehicle, and also the presence or absence of territorial control exerted over that space by the local control system (Table 1).

Institutional land use provided the most frequent location; these sites were occupied by railroad, factory, school, or hospital structures—public facilities making no territorial claim of any strength to adjacent street space. Vacant structures, houses, stores, and empty lots—sites also devoid of an enduring claim on space by a local control system—provided a second group of settings with a meaning encouraging deviant behavior. The third most common type of location occurred near an intersection, beside the doorless and often windowless flank of a residential unit, a setting which was evidently free of immediate surveillance. In most instances the opposite side of the street was also without surveillance; either it too was a corner residential lot or it abutted against an institutional land use. In contrast, settings adjacent to a local territorial control system—private houses, stores, and apartment houses—were less common locations for stripped cars.[2]

These relationships were sharpened by a twenty percent random sample of land use in Monroe. The actual sample size was 74 blocks, randomly drawn from a population of 386 blocks and part blocks. Sample land use proportions were estimated by measuring ground level street frontages. The information was abstracted from a 1972 revision of a federal land use zoning map. The sample showed that stripped car settings did not match actual land use proportions in the neighborhood (Table 2). A number of simplifying assumptions had to be made in the compilation of the table; for example, the land use map did not identify doorless flanks or

TABLE 1. The Behavior Setting of Stripped Cars

Setting	n = 138	%
Doorless flank	28	20.3
Institutional	31	22.5
Vacant house or store	29	21.0
Occupied apartment or store	17	12.3
Vacant/parking lot	18	13.0
Occupied house	15	10.9

TABLE 2. Land Use Proportions in Monroe

Setting	% Street frontage	% Stripped cars
Doorless flank (residential plus commerce)	18.5	20.3
Institutional	16.7	22.5
Vacant house	7.9	20.3
Commerce (functioning and vacant)	14.3	6.5
Vacant/parking lot	1.6	13.0
Occupied house and apartments	41.0	18.1

abandoned structures. The vacant house category in Table 2 was computed from the 1970 U.S. Census block statistics for Philadelphia. Hence the table should be used only as a general guide, but even so there emerges an explicit differential in criminal responsiveness to controlled and uncontrolled settings. Occupied houses in particular present a local social system of territorial control which deters criminal activity in the space to which they lay claim. This property is shared with commercial land use. While unsurveilled doorless flanks attract slightly more than their due proportion of stripped cars, the remaining three categories, institutional land use, vacant houses, and empty lots, are vastly overrepresented as deviant settings. Accounting for 26.2% of street frontage land use, they provide the site for 55.8% of the neighborhood's stripped cars. If the percentage figures were converted to nominal frequencies (with $n = 138$) and tested with chi-square (with five degrees of freedom), the difference between the two data sets in Table 2 would be significant at the .001 level (another test of the hypothesis would be to observe the relative speed of vandalism and deterioration for abandoned vehicles in each of the six settings).

Evidently the absence of a strong private claim on space in certain generic locations, the inferred attribute of weak local control, conspires to present a meaning which is alluring to the potential criminal. If car-stripping is one manifestation of delinquent or criminal activity, we conclude that this form of behavior does indeed make its own distinctive bid for space, and that this bid is located in zones and at points where space is otherwise weakly claimed and poorly surveilled—at the interstices between local control systems. There *are* generic locations which encourage criminal activity.

CONCLUSION

There are several implications here for land use planning. In addition to their known dysfunctional properties (Wolpert et al., 1972), such incompatible classes as institutional and residential land use should be separated because of a spillover effect from the weaker local control systems of many institutions—a control vacuum which encourages criminal bids for space, especially at night and at periods outside normal operating hours. In the same vein, derelict land parcels such as empty lots and abandoned houses indicate a lifting by legitimate powers of strong local control, and present an open invitation to illegitimate users. Clearly, new structures should be designed to maximize occupant surveillance and encourage local territorial control.

A good deal of softer data introduce evidence to support these proposals. Current research on graffiti defacement indicates that similar unclaimed spaces lure the spray painter. A playground, bounded on one side by the railroad and on a second by a derelict apartment building, comes under limited community surveillance and is the most common battleground for gang fights in Monroe. The role of back alleys for minor delinquency such as teenage drinking and acts of nuisance is well known, and some blocks with more enterprising block clubs have sought to seal off the alley behind their homes. Certain generic locations where the local control system is weak, and the risk of mugging ever present, are assiduously avoided by pedestrians. Commonly a pedestrian will take a detour increasing a nocturnal journey by as much as one half to avoid locations such as poorly lit railroad bridges. In short, the meaning of a locale, the strength of its territorial control system, would seem to be central variables in a causal explanation of the geography of crime.

NOTES

1. An untidy element of the research design is that the field data were collected at two different periods, a day in late July for the northern two-thirds of Monroe, and a day in early November for the southern one-third. The southern extension was added after preliminary analysis, to increase the sample size. The episodic nature of data collection means that no statements can be made concerning differential spatial intensities of stripped cars in Monroe. However, no such neighborhood analysis is intended here; the goal is to identify types of locations where stripping occurs, rather than provide a commentary on unclassified distribution over space.
2. It is of course important to be certain that this distribution is not a result of selective removal by the city's caretaker force, the Police Department Tow Squad. In fact the Tow Squad's removal policy ensures that such is not the case. Philadelphia is divided into 22 police districts, and the tow unit follows a cyclic rota moving weekly from one district to the next. Thus each district is visited once every 22 weeks, and during that week *all* removal of abandoned cars in that

district is carried out. During this week, the streets of each district are scoured for cars, which are removed en masse. This schedule is rigidly adhered to; complaints from citizens are noted, but no action is taken earlier than the scheduled time, unless the vehicle is a gross traffic hazard on a main thoroughfare. Letters of complaints to the Philadelphia newspapers of the tow squad's nonresponsiveness to citizen inquires substantiate this position. Thus we can be sure that the locational data on stripped cars are not biased by any selective priorities for removal.

REFERENCES

Barker, R. G. (1971). *Ecological Psychology*. Stanford: Stanford Univ. Press.

Cuff, D. and W. Young (1972) *Personal communication based on unpublished research results*. Temple University Department of Geography.

Cybriwsky, R. A. (1972a) *Social relations and the spatial order in the urban environment: A study of life in a neighborhood in central Philadelphia*. Ph.D. dissertation, Pennsylvania State University.

———. (1972b) *The anomie theory and the geographic study of crime*. Presented at the annual meeting of the East Lakes Division of the Association of American Geographers, Indiana, Pennsylvania.

Downey, G. T. and R. G. Hunt (1972) *The spatial structure of intraurban criminal behavior*. Presented at the annual meeting of the Association of American Geographers, Kansas City, Missouri.

Gans, H. (1962) *The Urban Villagers*. New York: Free Press.

Jacobs, J. (1961) *The Death and Life of Great American Cities*. New York: Vintage.

Kessler, M. Z. (1971) *Abandoned Vehicles: A Selected Bibliography*. Monticello, III.: Council of Planning Librarians Exchange Bibliography 192.

Kirk, W. (1963) "Problems of geography." *Geography* 47: 357–371.

Ley, D. F. (forthcoming) *The Black Inner City as Frontier Outpost: Images and Behavior of a Philadelphia Neighborhood*. Washington, D.C.: Association of American Geographers Monograph Series 7.

——— (1972) *The meaning of space in an inner city context*. Presented at a local meeting of the Canadian Association of Geographers, Vancouver, British Columbia.

Metz, T. (1969) "Auto-age eyesore: abandoned cars litter city streets posing disposal problem." *Wall Street Journal* 173 (June 25).

Newman, O. (1972) *Defensible Space*. New York: Macmillan.

Park, R. E. and E. Burgess (1968) *The City*. Chicago: Univ. of Chicago Press.

Phillips, P. D. (1972) "A prologue to the geography of crime." *Proceedings of the Assn. of Amer. Geographers* 4: 86–91.

Reckless, W. (1971). "The distribution of commercialized vice in the city," pp. 239–251 in J. Short (ed.) *The Social Fabric of the Metropolis*. Chicago: Univ. of Chicago Press.

Samuels, M. (1972) *The meaning of space*. Presented at a local meeting of the Canadian Association of Geographers, Vancouver, British Columbia.

Shaw, C. R. and H. D. McKay (1969) *Juvenile Delinquency and Urban Areas*. Chicago: Univ. of Chicago Press.

Short, J. [ed.] (1971) *The Social Fabric of the Metropolis*. Chicago: Univ. of Chicago Press.

Suttles, G. (1968) *The Social Order of the Slum*. Chicago: Univ. of Chicago Press.

Thomas, W. I. and F. Znaniecki (1927) *The Polish Peasant in Europe and America*. New York: Alfred A. Knopf.

Thrasher, F. M. (1963) *The Gang*. Chicago: Univ. of Chicago Press.

Webb, S. D. and F. Clemente (1972) "Urbanization processes and crime." *Pacific Viewpoint 13*: 87–98.

Whyte, W. F. (1955) *Street Corner Society*. Chicago: Univ. of Chicago Press.

Wolpert, J., A. Mumphrey, and J. Seley (1972) *Metropolitan Neighborhoods: Participation and Conflict over Change*. Washington, D.C.: A.A.G. Commission on College Geography, Resource Paper 16.

ENVIRONMENTAL CUES AND VANDALISM

AN EXPLORATORY STUDY OF PICNIC TABLE CARVING

DIANE M. SAMDAHL AND HARRIET H. CHRISTENSEN

Vandalism and destruction of recreation resources and facilities is a major concern to managers of parks and forests (Alfano and Magill, 1976; Driessen, 1978; Downing and Clark, 1979). The kinds of depreciative behavior that managers report include damage to restrooms, gates, fences, and other facilities; graffiti on picnic tables, walls, rocks, and trees; litter; theft; and general disregard for rules and restrictions. This concern by managers may reflect an increase in the occurrence of such acts and may also stem from the growing dollar demand on meager recreational budgets that must be spent on repair, replacement, education, or other strategies in response to those problems. Effective and cost-efficient methods to reduce depreciative impacts are necessary.

Although the causes of destructive behavior are often difficult to determine, recent literature has offered some important insights into understanding the problems of vandalism in recreation settings. Researchers have begun to document the magnitude of impacts at recreation areas

AUTHOR'S NOTE: This study was conducted under a cooperative research agreement between the USDA Forest Service and the College of Forest Resources, University of Washington, Seattle.

Source: *Environment and Behavior* (July 1985), *17*(4):445–458.

(Clark et al., 1971a). Researchers have also studied perceptions of users and managers to understand better the conflicting definitions of what is proper, and to uncover potential motives for this behavior (Boggs, 1971; Clark et al., 1971b; Downing and Clark, 1979; Roggenbuck et al., 1980). These studies provide baseline information on the dynamics of depreciative behavior.

Yet little is currently known about the effectiveness of alternative practices for the prevention or control of depreciative behavior (Christensen and Clark, 1979). Other than the litter incentive and appeal-to-help programs, no strategies have been systematically tested for their effectiveness (Clark et al., 1972; Clark, 1976; Christensen, 1981; Christensen and Clark, 1983). Consequently, evaluative studies of management practices are needed (Samdahl et al., 1982).

One promising line of research in this direction is drawn from the naturalistic study of human behavior, called *ecological psychology*. In their discussions of ecological psychology, Barker (1965, 1968, 1969), Wicker (1972, 1979), and Willems (1973, 1974, 1977) propose an interaction between environmental conditions, people, and behavior that suggests that the environment provides cues to indicate appropriate behavior for any particular setting. In this sense, the environment guides behavior by subtly altering an individual's actions to fit the setting.

Allen and Greenberger (1978) have applied the theory of ecological psychology to the study of vandalism, supporting the notion that the environment gives discriminatory cues that affect one's behavior, and suggesting that the physical condition of an object may encourage vandalism in certain situations. These environmental cues are called *releasor cues*, implying that they stimulate or encourage the release of otherwise inhibited behavior (Zimbardo, 1973). Releasor cues communicate to an individual the idea that acts such as vandalism may be acceptable in the present context.

Although the environment may give cues that alter or affect an individual's behavior, this alone cannot explain the total incidence of vandalism or other acts. Other factors must exist that influence an individual's behavior.

The sociology of deviance offers a theoretical perspective that addresses the release or inhibition of deviant behaviors. The containment theory of deviance as proposed by Reckless (1961, 1972) describes external and internal mechanisms of control that inhibit inappropriate behavior. External mechanisms of control may include reactions of others in the social group, law enforcement, maintenance practices, and site design. Internal mechanisms of control are the consequences of socialization that might reflect a belief in law and order or the desire to act appropriately.

When these external and internal controls are strong, depreciative behavior has a greater chance of being held in line; when these controls become weakened, depreciative behavior may appear.

The theoretical perspectives of ecological psychology and social control have an important issue in common: the premise that external environmental factors can affect behavior. Ecological psychology proposes that releasor stimuli may encourage acts of vandalism; social control proposes that such acts will occur more often if external control mechanisms are weak. In searching for managerial strategies to mitigate depreciative impacts, both of these notions may become important. External environmental factors are often influenced by managerial policy and practices; controlling these environmental conditions may have the effect of reducing vandalism. Therefore, it was felt important to study the influence of environmental conditions on the occurrence of vandalism in recreation areas. This study was an exploratory attempt to apply these perspectives in explaining one type of vandalism—the carving on picnic tables in campgrounds.

OBJECTIVES

The conceptual model examined in this study was based on the theoretical perspectives of ecological psychology and social control. Drawing from the preceding discussion, it was proposed that certain aspects of the physical condition of a recreation facility might act as releasor cues that trigger or encourage depreciative impacts. The effect of these releasor cues would be expected to be most apparent in conditions of low social control but would become reduced when external social control is increased.

The study focused on carving on picnic tables as a form of vandalism. Specifically, it was proposed that (1) the occurrence of new carving would be related to existing physical features of a picnic table, and (2) the occurrence of new carving would be greatest in situations of low external social control surrounding the location of that picnic table.

PROCEDURES

To minimize the variation in type of recreation use and users, picnic tables at developed or semideveloped campgrounds were chosen for study. Three campgrounds were selected, all located along 20 miles of State Highway 410 in western Washington: (1) Silver Springs, a USDA Forest Service campground with no host or resident ranger; (2) Dalles, a Forest

Service campground with a resident volunteer host; and (3) White River, a USDI National Park Service campground with two resident rangers and a law enforcement officer. In all three campgrounds midweek use was light and weekend use was heavy.

All 190 picnic tables in the campgrounds were included in the study. The tables were observed in early June 1980 and again in September 1980 after the camping season had ended. Depreciative impact was defined as the occurrence of new carving on a table during the study period. Data were also collected on the physical appearance of each table and on the strength of external social controls in that recreation setting.

Variables reflecting the physical appearance of the tables included age (old or new), color (grey or brown), and presence or absence of previous carving on the table. Variables reflecting the strength of external social control included the relative visibility of each table and the presence of a campground host or ranger (salience of authority) at the recreation area. Relative visibility was measured by the percentage of exposure of the table to other sites or to the roadway: a site that was exposed along 50% of its perimeter was determined to have moderate screening; over 75% exposure was considered low screening, and under 25% exposure was considered high screening. The salience of authority at each recreation location was measured by the presence of a campground host or ranger: The campground with no host or ranger had low salience of authority, the campground with a volunteer host living on site had medium salience of authority, and the campground with the resident rangers and law enforcement officer had high salience of authority. Because only three sites were studied, data on the salience of authority must be interpreted with caution. No measure of the content, extent, or frequency of carving was included in this study.

ANALYSIS

Analysis was conducted to determine potential relationships among physical condition, external controls, and the presence or absence of new carving impacts. Chi-square, a test of statistical significance, was used to indicate whether the variations in the data were likely to be due to chance. Because of the exploratory nature of this study, statistical significance was assumed when the probability of chance was 0.10 or less. However, because small cell size in the contingency tables reduces the consistency of a test such as chi-square, it is important to note also the strength of association even in seemingly nonsignificant tables. Gamma was used to indicate the strength of relationships for all tables. Measurement error will reduce the value of any measure of association (Blalock, 1972: 414); therefore, gamma, with a value larger than many other ordinal measures, appeared to be appropriate for an initial exploratory study in which relationships may be confounded by uncontrolled variables. Results of this study will require further verification through more rigorous measurement and experimental designs.

RESULTS

The presence of previous carving and the salience of authority were significantly associated with the occurrence of new carving on picnic tables (Table 1). Of those tables on which previous carving was evident at the beginning of the study, 31.8% were carved on again by late summer. Only 13.7% of the tables with no carving on them in June were found to have new carvings by the end of the summer. Therefore, a table with previous carving was almost two and one-half times more likely to receive new

TABLE 1. Percentage of Picnic Tables with New Carving by Specific Characteristics of the Table

Characteristics	Tables with new carving: Percent	Total *N*	Significance
Presence of previous carving			
No previous carving	13.7	(80)	$\chi^2 = 7.29$, 1*df*
Previous carving	31.8	(110)	$p < 0.01$
			$\gamma = 0.49$
Salience of authority			
Low salience	35.8	(53)	$\chi^2 = 5.45$, 2*df*
Medium salience	20.5	(44)	$p < 0.07$
High salience	19.4	(93)	$\gamma = 0.28$
Screening from road or other sites			
Low screening	22.4	(143)	$\chi^2 = 3.09$, 2*df*
Medium screening	35.3	34	$p < 0.21$, N.S.
High screening	15.4	13	$\gamma = 0.15$
Color of table			
Grey	22.5	(142)	$\chi^2 = 0.54$, 1*df*
Red/brown	29.2	(48)	$p < 0.46$, N.S.
			$\gamma = 0.18$
Age of table			
Old	24.1	(145)	$\chi^2 = 0.001$, 1*df*
New	4.4	(45)	$p < 0.99$
			$\gamma = 0.01$

carving than were tables without previous carving. This association between previous carving and new carving impacts supports the notion that previous carving might be a releasor cue that encourages otherwise inhibited carving behavior.

The salience of authority also appeared to be an important indicator of new carving impacts at each recreation site, although the limited number of campgrounds restricts the interpretation of this effect. In the campground with low salience of authority, 35.8% of the tables received new carving; only 20.5% and 19.4% of the tables received new carving in the campgrounds with medium and high salience of authority. These results suggest that the presence of authority might reduce acts of carvings. Whether this result is indeed due to the salience of authority cannot be positively determined in these data, but the results are suggestive and in line with the proposed effects of external social control.

The age and color of the picnic tables were not associated with new carving. Old or grey weathered tables were just as likely to receive new carving as were the newer tables or those with brown paint. Screening also was not significantly related to new carving. However, both color and screening had measures of association that were high enough to suggest that nonsignificance was related, in part, to the effect of small cell size on the calculation of the chi-square statistic.

If environmental conditions are indeed effective mechanisms in inducing vandalism or depreciative behavior, it is possible that the above relation between new and previous carving is spurious. That is, both acts of carving might have been influenced by environmental cues that were salient and inducing each time carving (new or old) occurred. If this were so, the relation between new and previous carving would be significantly reduced when that factor was controlled.

Table 2 presents the relationship between new and previous carving when the factors of salience of authority screening, or color are controlled. If the initial relationship had been spurious relative to any of these three conditions it would be expected to disappear in these tables. However, as shown, the relationship between new and previous carving remains strong; indeed, it has been enhanced with the controls on screening and color.

This second analysis suggests that the relation between new and previous carving is not spurious relative to any of these three control factors. It is likely that other factors are indeed involved in the occurrence of carving impacts, but these results are supportive of the interpretation that previous carving does have the effect of a releasor cue to encourage new carving impacts.

TABLE 2. Percentage of Picnic Tables with New Carving by Presence of Previous Carving, Controlling for Salience of Authority, Screening, and Color

Characteristics	No previous carving	Previous carving
Salience of authority		
Low	27.8 (18)	40.0 (35)
Medium	14.3 (28)	31.3 (16)
High	5.9 (34)	27.1 (59)
	Pooled $\chi^2 = 8.80$, 3 *df*	
	$p < 0.02$	
	Pooled gamma = 0.53	
Screening		
Low screening	16.9 (59)	26.2 (84)
Medium screening	5.9 (17)	64.7 (17)
High screening	0.0 (4)	22.2 (9)
	Pooled $\chi^2 = 15.04$, 3 *df*	
	$p < 0.01$	
	Pooled gamma = 0.44	
Color		
Red/brown	9.3 (43)	28.3 (99)
Grey	18.9 (37)	36.4 (11)
	Pooled $\chi^2 = 14.39$, 2 *df*	
	$p < 0.01$	
	Pooled gamma = 0.63	

DISCUSSION AND CONCLUSIONS

The data support the proposition that carving impacts are related to environmental conditions surrounding the picnic table. The occurrence of new carving on tables was significantly related to the presence of previous carving, for tables with previous carving had two and one-half times more new carving than did tables without previous carving. This relationship did not disappear under controls for salience of authority, screening, or color of the table, suggesting that the relationship is not spurious. Previous carving was viewed as a releasor cue that defined carving as an acceptable action for that particular setting.

An alternative interpretation of the effect of the released cue is that the marginal impact of new carving is reduced on a table that already displays previous carving. As with the case of litter, the additional degradation of one more act is not as great as the impact of the initial act. This interpretation of marginal impact, however, still assumes an inhibition of such acts when the relative impact is high. This is not discordant with the premise that previous carving, acting as a releasor cue, defines when new carvings will be acceptable.

The data are mixed relative to the potential effect of external social controls in preventing vandalism. In this study, screening (which represented visibility of the table to the roadway or to other sites) was not significantly related to the occurrence of new carving impacts, but salience of authority *was* related. The small number of campgrounds means that the effects of salience of authority must be interpreted with caution.

It might have been expected that screening (by reducing the chances of getting caught) would have been a more powerful social control than salience of authority, but the data did not show this. One interpretation of this result is that fear of getting caught was not an inhibiting factor affecting carvings. An alternative explanation might be that the presence of external controls (the salience of authority) has acted as an environmental reminder of societal values and proscriptions, thereby reinforcing the internal controls (attitudes, values) already present within each individual. Perhaps an increase in the salience of these external reminders acts to stimulate internal control mechanisms indirectly, rather than directly control behavior through external forces. This may explain why the presence of a relatively powerless authority (the volunteer campground host) was related to a significant reduction in depreciative impacts but screening was not.

If one were apprehensive about viewing the campground effect as a measure of salience of authority, it still can add an important dimension to this analysis. Viewed conservatively, each campground can be seen as an independent replication of the test of association between new and previous carving. The appearance of this effect in all three campgrounds thereby supports the interpretation of previous carving as a releasor cue for new carving.

With further verification, these results suggest that the removal or reduction of existing impacts may be important for the prevention of similar impacts in the future. If true, this would stress the value of maintenance as a preventive strategy that can act to protect recreation facilities from vandalism or other forms of destruction. Moreover, the presence of an authority may prevent some depreciative impacts at recreation areas. If supported, this finding would encourage managers to keep personnel on site in recreation areas as often as possible. Host programs and maintenance crews may be as effective as enforcement officers in providing this deterrence.

Application of the principles of ecological psychology offers many new strategies for prevention and control of depreciative impacts in recreation areas. The present study is suggestive of the relevance of this research approach; it will be important to replicate these findings in other recreation settings, to explore the effects of other types of external control, and to determine the applicability of these results to other types of impacts. If behavior is influenced by environmental cues, as suggested here, managers of recreation areas may have an easy and accessible solution to some of their problems, for environmental conditions are often under the control of park management.

REFERENCES

Alfano, S. S., and W. Magill (eds.) (1976) *Vandalism and outdoor recreation: Symposium proceedings* (General Technical Report PSW-17). Berkeley: U.S. Department of Agriculture, Forest Service, Southwest Forest and Range Experiment Station.

Allen, V. L. and D. B. Greenberger (1978) "An aesthetic theory of vandalism." *Crime and Delinquency 24*: 309–321.

Barker, R. G. (1969) "Wanted: an eco-behavioral science," pp. 31–43 in E. P. Willems and H. L. Raush (eds.) *Naturalistic viewpoints in psychological research*. New York: Holt, Rinehart & Winston.

——— (1968) *Ecological psychology: Concepts and methods for studying the environment of human behavior*. Stanford, CA: Stanford University Press; 1968.

——— (1965) "Explorations in ecological psychology." *Amer. Psychologist 20*: 1–14.

Blalock, H. M., Jr. (1972) *Social statistics*. New York: McGraw-Hill.

Boggs, S. L. (1971) "Formal and informal crime control: an exploratory study of urban, suburban and rural orientations." *Soc. Q. 12*: 319–327.

Christensen, H. H. (1981) *Bystander intervention and litter control: Evaluation of an appeal-to-help program* (Research Paper PNW-287). Portland, OR: U.S. Department of Agriculture, Forest Service, Pac. Northwest Forest and Range Experiment Station.

——— and R. N. Clark (1983) "Increasing public involvement to reduce depreciative behavior in recreation settings." *Leisure Sciences 5*, 4: 359–379.

——— (1979) "Understanding and controlling vandalism and other rule violations in urban recreation areas," pp. 63–84 in *Proceedings of the National Urban Forestry Conference*, November 13–16, 1978. Washington, DC: Government Printing Office.

Clark, R. N. (1976) *How to control litter in recreation areas: The incentive system* (GPO 997-150). Portland, OR: U.S. Department of Agriculture, Forest Service, Pacific Northwest Forest and Range Experiment Station.

———, J. C. Hendee, and R. L. Burgess (1972) "The experimental control of littering." *J. of Environmental Education 4*, 2: 22–28.

Clark, R. N., J. C. Hendee, and F. L. Campbell, (1971a) *Depreciative behavior in Forest Campgrounds: An exploratory study* (PNW-161). Portland, OR: U.S. Department of Agriculture, Forest Service, Pacific Northwest Forest and Range Experiment Station.

——— (1971b) "Values, behavior, and conflict in modern camping culture." *J. of Leisure Research 3*, 3: 143–159.

Downing, K. B. and R. N. Clark (1979) "Users' and managers' perceptions of dispersed recreation impacts: a focus on roaded forest lands," pp. 18–23 in R. Ittner et al. (eds.) *Recreation Impact on Wildlands Conference Proceedings*, October 27–29, 1978. Seattle, WA: U.S. Department of Agriculture, Forest Service and U.S. Department of Interior, National Park Service, Pacific Northwest Regions.

Driessen, J. (1978) *Problems in managing forest recreation facilities: A survey of field personnel*. Missoula, MT: U.S. Department of Agriculture, Forest Service, Equipment Development Center.

Reckless, W. C. (1972) "A new theory of delinquency and crime," pp. 161–168 in R. Giallombardo (ed.) *Juvenile delinquency: A book of readings*. New York: John Wiley.

——— (1961) *The crime problem*. New York: Appleton-Century-Crofts.

Roggenbuck, J. W., J. D. Wellman, and A. C. Smith (1980) *Specialization, displacement and definitions of depreciative behavior among Virginia canoeists*. Final report to U.S. Department of Agriculture, Forest Service, North Central Forest and Range Experiment Station. Blacksburg, VA: Dept of Forestry, Virginia Polytechnic Institute and State University.

Samdahl, D. M., H. H. Christensen, and R. N. Clark (1982) *Prevention and control of depreciative behavior in recreation areas: managerial concerns and research needs*," pp. 52–54 in *Forest and river recreation: Research update*. Agriculture Experimental Station Miscellaneous Publication 18. University of Minnesota.

Wicker, A. W. (1979) *An introduction to ecological psychology*. Monterey, CA: Brookes/Cole.

——— (1972) "Processes which mediate behavior-environment congruence." *Behavioral Science 17*: 265–277.

Willems, E. P. (1977) "Behavioral ecology," in D. Stokols (ed). *Perspectives on environment and behavior: Theory, research, and applications*. New York Plenum Press.

——— (1974) "Behavioral technology and behavioral ecology." *J. of Applied Behavior Analysis 7*: 151–165.

——— (1973) "Behavioral ecology as a perspective for man-environment research," pp. 152–166 in W. F. E. Preiser (ed.) *Environmental design research*, Vol. 2. Stroudsburg, PA: Dowden, Hutchison & Ross.

Zimbardo, P. G. (1973) "A field experiment in auto shaping," pp. 85–90 in C. Ward (ed.) *Vandalism*. London: Architectural Press.

INCREASING PUBLIC INVOLVEMENT TO REDUCE DEPRECIATIVE BEHAVIOR IN RECREATION SETTINGS

HARRIET H. CHRISTENSEN AND ROGER N. CLARK

INTRODUCTION*

A range of depreciative behaviors, such as vandalism, theft, and other rule violations, occurs in recreation settings. Managers and users have expressed concern about the occurrence of these problems and their impacts on the natural environment, public and private property, and the recreationists' enjoyment of the area (Driessen, 1978; U.S. Department of the Interior, 1978; Downing and Moutsinas, 1978; Alfano and Magill, 1976; Clark et al., 1971b). Some recent estimates indicate the costly impact of some of these problems on agency budgets. The USDA Forest Service, for example, reports that vandalism and littering in the National Forests cost taxpayers over $7 million in 1974 (USDA Forest Service, 1975). The Bureau of Land Management, with fewer and more widely dispersed facilities, reports that vandalism costs $250,000 per year (Alfano and Magill, 1976). The Seattle, Washington, Parks and Recreation Department estimated that

*This report has been abstracted from a research paper published by the USDA Forest Service (Christensen, 1981), which evaluated a program to increase involvement of campers in the management of depreciative behavior by reporting violations they witness.

Source: *Leisure Sciences* (1983), *5*(4): 359–379.

vandalism cost $236,000 during 1976 (U.S. Department of the Interior, 1977). The problems of vandalism and other violations of rules permeates the entire recreation opportunity spectrum from urban parks to Wilderness Areas (Clark, et al., 1971b; Boston Parks and Recreation Commission, 1978; Hendee et al., 1978; Shafer and Lucas, 1978).

To protect resources and maintain area appeal, managers use a variety of programs and strategies to mitigate and prevent crime, vandalism, and other rule violations (Christensen and Clark, 1978; Clark, 1976a). Current approaches include site planning, architectural design, appropriate construction material and specifications, user education, fees, increased surveillance and detection, frequent maintenance, and public involvement, as well as adding more rules and regulations. Other than the litter incentive program, no strategy has been tested adequately and evaluated for its effectiveness in reducing problem behaviors (Clark et al., 1972a; Clark et al., 1972b; Burgess et al., 1971; Clark, 1976b; Kohlenberg and Phillips, 1973; Powers et al., 1973).

Involving the public in the management of depreciative behavior has been identified by users, managers, and researchers as a potential solution to the problem. Ways must be found, however, to identify how and under what conditions users will become involved (Clark, 1976a; Clark et al., 1971a; Flickinger, 1976). Recreationists, when asked why they would do if they witnessed a rule violation, often say they would do nothing. For instance, Flickinger's (1976) survey in Ohio State campgrounds found that campers said they would do nothing if they observed littering; however, they would report theft or vandalism. Yet another self-report study in Washington State campgrounds indicated that campers would report witnessed rule infractions immediately (Clark et al., 1971b). Regardless of the act, a norm of noninvolvement has been found when behavior is actually observed; that is, people normally do not become involved. What people say they will do is not necessarily what they actually do (Campbell et al., 1968). In a study of campers in a developed campground, Clark et al. (1971a) found that 90 percent of the depreciative acts produced little or no reaction from witnesses. Although there may be many legitimate explanations for this noninvolvement, there is little likelihood of completely controlling rule violations until this behavior is changed.

BYSTANDER INTERVENTION

Clinard (1974:35) observed that, "Where only the general public or the government is a victim, private citizens are less likely to report the offenses." Noninvolvement is a factor in our social system (Latané and Darley, 1970), as evidenced two decades ago in the notorious Kitty Genovese murder; 38 people witnessed the incident, yet police were not called for half an hour.

Although people often say they will intervene, research has shown that they usually do not. Why is this? Some may be afraid of retribution; others may not know how or believe that others will report the problem. In some cases, bystanders may not understand the act is illegal or a problem. Witnesses may also feel they do not have the time to get involved, or that it will not make any difference if they do (Bickman and Green, 1977). Early socialization also seems to play a role—as a society, we teach our children not to "tattle" or "snitch" on others. Ways must be found to change this norm of noninvolvement into prosocial behavior (also called altruism, bystander intervention, or helping behavior) to reduce depreciative behavior.

Latané and Darley (1970) suggested that the witness to an illegal act goes through a process of questioning and decision making that asks, "What's going on? What should I do? Should I take responsibility?" Five distinctive steps characterize this process: (1) person notices something; (2) person interprets the situation; (3) person decides to assume personal responsibility and do something; (4) person decides what to do; and, finally, (5) person engages in the behavior decided upon. The authors assert that people may not decide against acting, but rather that they refrain from making any decisions. They are in a state of conflict over steps 2, 3, and 4.

Baron and Byrne (1976) point out that minimizing ambiguity may cause users to intervene, which could help to mitigate or reduce rule violations in recreation areas. Perhaps users would intervene—for example, by reporting the act or speaking to an offender—if they were aware of problems in a campground. Would bystander behavior change if users were told that everyone should take personal responsibility and were informed about how to do it? Heberlein (1971) found that people littered less if they were aware of the potential consequences of littering and felt responsible for these consequences.

This study is based on the concept that nonintervention is caused by uncertainty and ambiguity, not by indifference. We further assume that an "appeal to help," which asks the recreation user to report witnessed offenses, could reduce the problem, litter in this case. Users, when confronted with depreciative behavior, should be encouraged to ask three questions: What is going on? Who is responsible for redirecting the antisocial action? What can I do to help?

STUDY OBJECTIVES

The objective of this study was to evaluate the effectiveness of using bystander intervention procedures to control and prevent littering in a recreation setting. Specific objectives were to:

1. Determine the response to an appeal to help.
2. Determine the nature and extent of different types of reactions, such as recreationists reporting the offense to the Ranger, intervening directly with the offender, or picking up the litter.
3. Evaluate two types of reporting: filling out a card and dropping it in the fee box, and reporting directly to authorities.
4. Determine the response of users to different appealers (Ranger, volunteer, and campground Host) and different types of appeal media (oral appeal and a printed flier).
5. Examine the effects of social, situational, and rule-violation characteristics on bystander intervention patterns.

The thrust of this study was to find ways to control witnessed rule violations (after the infraction was committed) through user intervention and reporting of illegal acts to authorities. Preventing the infractions from occurring was not a focus of this study. We an only speculate that a potential offender may be discouraged from committing an infraction after observing some users confronting violators.

METHOD

This study was conducted during 1977 at the Lake Kachess campground on the Wenatchee National Forest in Washington State. It focused on users and their reactions to littering. During the past decade this area has been the site of other studies of depreciative behaviors (Clark et al., 1971a, b, 1972a). The campground is intensively developed, has heavy use, on-site Rangers and campground Hosts, and opportunities for water-related activities. It has a nature trail and swimming area, day-use areas with picnic tables and fire grills, and six overnight camping areas with a total of 200 campersites.

Littering was selected as the illegal act to study, because it is relatively innocuous and nonthreatening. Further, most people perceive littering as illegal. Littering was also selected because of the considerable number of other studies on the subject.

While camping, groups at randomly selected campsites received an "appeal to help" message asking them to report illegal acts they witness to the campground Ranger. The message was delivered either by a campground Ranger, volunteer, or the campground Host. The message was delivered either orally or as a printed cartoon. Control groups did not receive the message.

Two hours after the appeal, littering was simulated in view of the subjects by a man and woman driving past the selected campsite. Two observers in a second car measured three specific responses by witnesses—direct intervention, picking up the litter, and no reaction. Littering was simulated because measuring the reactions to the unpredictable occurrence of natural littering was considered impractical.

Ten minutes after the littering, a Ranger walked through the campground to measure reporting behavior. The major dependent variable (witness response) was classified as reporting, direct intervention with the litterers, picking up the litter, or no reaction. The experimental design varied depending on who delivered the appeal (Ranger, volunteer, or Host), and the way the appeal was delivered (orally or as a printed cartoon). Camp area and type of litter dropped (beer or soft drink cans), however, were assigned to clusters of campsites. Social characteristics and response of campers were measured by the appeal deliverers, the litterers, the observers in the second car, and the Ranger patrol. The study was conducted on weekends, beginning August 6 and ending September 5, 1977.

The study was conducted in public areas of the campground only so as not to invade the privacy of campers; only activity that was in view of other campers was observed.

Definition of Terms

Four reactions to the witnessed illegal act of littering were possible: doing nothing (nonintervention); picking up the litter, which was also referred to as antilittering (indirect intervention); reporting, where campers comply with a request for help and submit a written or oral report to an authority (indirect intervention); and dealing with the offender (direct intervention).

Selection of Subjects

A random sample of campsite clusters and of campsites within a cluster was selected. A cluster included campsites that were visible and adjacent to one another. After campsites were selected within a cluster, they were randomly assigned to the experimental conditions. Experimental units (campsites) were assumed independent of each other, even though samples were drawn in clusters. The subjects were camping parties at campsites.

Experimental Variables

Three variables were manipulated in the experimental condition: type of appeal deliverer, type of message, and type of response form.

Deliverer Type

Ranger as an Appeal Deliverer

Some of the appeals were delivered by a uniformed Ranger. She approached subjects at their campsites, said "Good Morning" (or "Good Afternoon"), and gave her name. She provided Smokey Bear fire prevention handouts to the youngsters, determined group composition, and delivered the appeal.

Volunteer and Campground Host as Appeal Deliverers

Sometimes a volunteer or resident campground Host delivered the appeal to determine the tenability of using volunteers and campground Hosts. The volunteer was dressed as a camper with a Forest Service volunteer patch on his shirt. Both the Host and the volunteer were males wearing nametags that included their title, "Forest Service Volunteer" or "Host." They said "Good Morning" (or "Good Afternoon"), gave their names, and announced they were helping out the Ranger by contacting campers. They gave handouts to the children, gathered data on group composition, and delivered the appeal.

Message Type

Printed Message

Subjects chosen for the printed message received a cartoon flier which included two major messages: (1) The area has a few problems with rule violations such as litter and nails hammered into trees; and (2) witnesses should report violations to the authorities. After informal conversation and recording group composition, the appeal deliverer handed the subjects a litter bag with the flier on top without commenting on the flier.

Spoken Message

An oral message was given by an authority figure—Ranger, Host, or volunteer. The message consisted of the following components, although actual wording may have varied slightly:

(The problem) We're having problems with rule violations—people on motorbikes, nails in trees, littering, campfires left burning—and we need your help.

(Reporting) If you see any of these activities or others that concern you, we would really appreciate your letting us know so that we can talk to these individuals, tell them about the problem, and ask for their cooperation.

(Personal responsibility) We would like to encourage everyone to take personal responsibility for reporting problems to us so that we can get a handle on the kinds and frequency of problems and talk with the individuals concerned.

(Commitment) So if you see a violation, will you tell me or someone designated who did it by reporting the campsite number or license number and where they went?

Subjects were asked to spread the work to the rest of their parties, thanked for their help, and provided with a litter bag.

Response Form Type

Report Cards

Subjects selected to receive cards were given 3 × 5 in. preprinted cards on which to report offenses anonymously. Campers were told they could drop the cards in the campground fee box or give them to the Ranger.

No Card

Subjects without cards could only report rule violations orally, unless they provided their own paper or card.

Subjects with and without cards were randomly assigned to oral, printed, or no appeal groups; the appeal deliverers were also varied. Oral response was tested the first half of the summer and written response the second half.

Control Group

Subjects in the control group were contacted by the authorities as outlined above, but no appeal was made. For further information regarding procedures, readers are referred to Christensen (1981).

Pretest

A training session and pretest were held the weekend prior to the actual study. It involved training the research team, sampling the sites, selecting the subjects, delivering the appeals, staging littering, and measuring subjects for reactions.

Data Base

At the completion of the study a total of 128 usable observations were obtained out of 215 (Table 1). Eighty-seven trials were discarded because the subjects did not witness or receive all three stages of the experimental manipulation—the appeal, simulation, and patrol.

Campers who received an appeal may not have been the same ones who witnessed the littering or the patrol. For instance, two people in a party might have received the message while the third person was out of camp. The third person could have seen the littering and said nothing or witnessed the patrol and done nothing., while the other two people were out of camp. The oral message attempted to deal with this possibility by asking campers to spread the message to the rest of the party, but this did not guarantee that others would be informed.

Reliability

Reliability checks for data collection by the appeal deliverer and patrol observer were conducted on one weekend. Interobserver agreement was 97 percent for the appeal deliverer and 95 percent for the patrol observer.

RESULTS AND DISCUSSION

Effect of the Appeal to Help

The major objective of this study was to determine the effect of an "appeal to help" on campers' reactions to a rule violation. It was expected that cueing the camper by explaining problems with rule violations and suggesting that campers could help by reporting them would increase involvement, although it was uncertain by how much.

The appeal-to-help treatment had a substantial effect on response to littering. In 83 percent of the trials, campers who received an appeal to help responded or reacted in some way to the act, while 61 percent of the control reacted without a cue. This finding suggests that appealing for the help of campers does have a significant effect and demonstrates that a new behavior pattern can be stimulated for some people by a specific appeal suggesting how they can help.

The 22 percentage point difference between experimental and control groups demonstrates that defining the situation and explaining the prob-

TABLE 1. Number of Cases in Each Experimental Condition ($N = 128$)[a]

Appeal deliverer	No card condition: Verbal appeal	No card condition: Printed appeal	Reporting issued card condition: Verbal appeal	Reporting issued card condition: Printed appeal
Ranger	20	21	15	12
Forest Service volunteer	5	10	0	0
Forest Service campground Host	0	9	0	0
Control (no message)	36	0	0	0

[a]A Case was defined as a camping party at a campsite.

lem and how to deal with it will increase campers' involvement. Other studies have found similar results. Bickman and Green (1977), in their study of shoplifting and reporting behavior, also found that intervention increased when witnesses were cued to take action. Moriarty (1975) and Shaffer et al. (1975) were able to increase theft observation intervention by providing definitional cues to subjects. Similar results were found by Bickman (1971, 1976), Clark and Word (1972, 1974), and Muth and Clark (1978). It is not known which of the components in the appeal-to-help message were effective in changing behavior. The 22 percent change may result from any one or a combination of cues to the problem, commitment, or personal responsibility, or to the influence of the Ranger, Host, or volunteer.

A direct comparison between the oral and printed (cartoon) message treatment failed to show any statistically significant differences; campers who received the printed message reacted to the simulated littering as much as those who received an oral appeal.

The role figures who delivered the appeal to campers (Ranger, Forest Service volunteer, and campground Host) were expected to affect the behavior of camping groups. No significant differences were found between the type of appeal deliverer and percentage of trials in which campers reacted to littering, which adds legitimacy to the potential of volunteers and Hosts in working with the public.

Type of Reactions

Three types of responses by campers to the littering were observed: (1) antilittering behavior indicated by campers immediately picking up the littered can and placing it in the garbage can; (2) direct intervention during the act of littering or immediately thereafter, indicated by campers overtly intervening with the litterers; and (3) reporting behavior indicated by campers reporting the act of littering to the Ranger.... Campers could react in more than one way; they may have picked up a can and reported the violator, or they may have picked up the can and dealt directly with the litterer. Significant differences were found between the control and experimental groups for antilitter behavior and reporting behavior.

Anti-Litter Behavior

Picking up the litter was the primary reaction of the most campers. The appeal to help resulted in a 17 percent increase in the antilittering behavior compared to the control group (73 versus 56 percent). It is not surprising that so many people helped without prompting, because millions of taxpayers dollars have been spent on litter education and other types of programs to prevent and control littering. To what extent this same response would hold for other types of depreciative behaviors is uncertain at this time.

Direct Intervention

Twenty-six percent of the treatment subjects intervened directly with the litterers, representing a 7 percent increase over the control group (26 versus 19 percent), a difference not found to be statistically significant. Some interesting patterns were observed about people who did intervene. Three types of direct intervention were observed: (1) the camper made a physical gesture such as point a finger, placing hands on hips, or nodding head; (2) the camper responding verbally with expressions such as "Somebody threw a can," or "Pick that up," or (3) the camper left his/her campsite, followed the litterer to the camp entrance and interacted with him or her. It was possible for campers to react in more than one way. Although both men and women intervened, men responded more frequently and usually verbally. Children intervened infrequently.

The type of can used in the simulated littering was found to have a statistically significant relationship to direct intervention (Table 2). More intervention occurred when beer cans were used (33 percent) than when soft drink cans were used (12 percent). Campers evidently perceive beer cans as more objectionable litter than soft drink cans.

Intervention was also influenced by style of camping and whether campsites were single or double occupancy (Table 2). More intervention was observed in trials at sites with multiple camping styles (39 percent) than at sites with one type of recreational vehicle or tent (21 percent). Trials

TABLE 2. Relationship between Intervention by Users and Characteristics of the Littering Violation

A. Type of Can			
Reaction	Beer	Soft Drink	Total
Did not intervene	67	88	76 (97)[a]
Intervened	33	12	24 (31)
Total	100 (72)	100 (56)	100 (128)[b]
B. Style of Camping			
Reaction	Single	Multiple[c]	Total
Did not intervene	79	61	76 (92)
Intervened	21	39	24 (29)
Total	100 (103)	100 (18)	100 (121)[d]
C. Design of Campsite			
Reaction	Single Campsite	Double Campsite	Total
Did not intervene	79	59	76 (97)
Intervened	21	41	24 (31)
Total	100 (106)	100 (22)	100 (128)[e]

[a]Numbers in parentheses indicate the number of cases on which the percentages are based.
[b]Tau$_b$ = ×.24 significant at .003 level.
[c]"Multiple" implies more than one type of equipment and may also imply increased group size.
[d]Tau$_b$ = .15 significant at .05 level.
[e]Tau$_b$ = .18 significant at .02 level.

at double campsites produced significantly higher intervention rates (41 versus 21 percent). Both of these variables (style of camping and site design) are related to the number of people at the site, which may increase the security for someone who chooses to intervene with offenders.

Reporting Behavior

[Results] show that in 128 trials, 16 percent of the subjects receiving the appeal reported the litterers, an increase of 10 percent over the control group. The appeal to help was an attempt to increase responses that some could interpret as snitching or tattling, a practice inhibited by early socialization practices. This does not suggest that reporting behavior cannot be produced; results of this study demonstrate that campers sometimes will report a violation if encouraged. Further research is needed to discover the best ways to increase such reporting.

Size of camping party and time of offense were found to be statistically significant to reporting behavior (Table 3). In contrast to direct intervention where larger groups increase the likelihood of involvement, when the size of the camping party was small more people chose to report the act. It may be that small groups turn problems over to the authorities, rather than deal

TABLE 3. Relationship between Reporting Behavior and Size of Party and Time of Offense

A. Size of Camping Party (persons)				
Reaction	0–2	3–5	6 or more	Total
Did not report	70	87	95	87 (111)[a]
Reported	30	13	5	13 (17)
Total	100 (23)	100 (63)	100 (42)	100 (128)[b]
B. Time of Offense				
Reaction	Morning	Afternoon	Evening	Total
Did not report	81	89	94	87 (111)
Reported the act	19	11	6	13 (17)
Total	100 (53)	100 (44)	100 (31)	100 (128)[c]

[a]Numbers in parenthesis indicate the number of cases in which the percentages are based.
[b]Tau_c = ×.17 significant at .003 level.
[c]Tau_c = ×.11 significant at .05 level.

with the problems themselves. Or peer pressure within larger groups may decrease reporting.

An analysis of time of the offense revealed that 19 percent of the morning trials were reported, whereas only 11 percent of the afternoon trials and 6 percent of the evening trials were reported (Table 3). Higher response rates in the morning might be expected, because campers were generally in camp; activities were usually quiet and passive—eating breakfast, drinking coffee, or playing table games. In the afternoon, however, most people were at the beach, hiking, or boating. Still fewer trials were reported during the evening, when there were competing activities such as socializing, eating, and playing.

Two types of reporting strategies were tested in this study. Campers could report the littering to the Ranger on patrol immediately following the violation, or they could fill out a card and either drop it in the campground fee box or hand it to the Ranger on patrol. The most successful method for reporting was for campers to report personally to the Ranger or campground Host (89 percent), rather than provide written responses (11 percent).

Why don't more people intervene directly? Perceived costs of intervention, such as embarrassment, verbal abuse, and physical abuse to the witness, may be an explanation for the low rate of this type of response. The cost–reward model of intervention (Piliavin and Piliavin, 1972:353) stats: "As costs for helping increase the probability of direct intervention decreases and the probability of indirect help increases." Bleda et al. (1976) suggested that reporting shifts responsibility for corrective action to someone who holds a position of authority. Direct intervention requires a much greater degree of personal involvement. The data reported here imply that campers perceived direct intervention as less costly than reporting, although direct intervention would appear to be more risky. Possible explanations are that reporting to the Ranger was not sufficiently convenient, or that direct intervention against littering was not considered a high risk action. It may also be that in this case, the couple who littered was not perceived as threatening.

CONCLUSIONS

Previous research has suggested a norm of noninvolvement by recreation visitors who witness rule violations. This study was founded on the bystander intervention theory, which suggests that cueing the recreation visitor to report witnessed offenses should increase user involvement. The present study demonstrated that some campers will become involved when an appeal to help is delivered asking users to report any violations that they witness.

The most frequent reaction by users was to pick up the litter followed by directly intervening with the litterer. Reporting the act to the authorities was the least frequent reaction. Involvement is probably related to the perceived consequences of intervention to the user. Previous research has indicated that reactions may depend on the nature of the offense, age of the reactor, appearance of the offender, and number of offenders.

This study showed that if the offense is fairly innocuous, as in the case of littering, campers prefer to pick up the litter or intervene directly.

Educating the public to intervene or report a violation is not a new idea. Reporting programs began in the early 1960s. Some examples of current campaigns are: "Next time you see someone polluting, point it out" (Keep America Beautiful), "Report Vandalism" (Washington State Highway Department); and "Rat on a Rat" (Washington Bankers Association and Washington Savings League). Similar reporting programs may be found that relate to hunting and fishing violations.

A bystander involvement program has several benefits. First, it may deter a potential rule violator from following through with an infraction, possibly out of fear of being caught, or reported by a witness, or simple embarrassment.

Second, a reporting program may control some current problems and prevent others. It directs management contact to individuals who may not, in fact, recognize a behavior as being depreciative. A Ranger can contact a party who has been reported, explain the nature of the problem, and ask for cooperation. In fact, it may be largely a matter of educating the user. This type of strategy could contribute to socializing an individual or group to the appropriate skills and behaviors needed in recreation settings.

Third, it may control and prevent problems and impacts by individuals or groups who purposely commit rule-violating behaviors. They can be detected through the reporting system and removed from the area, if necessary, by the authorities.

Fourth, a bystander program informs managers of some offenses that previously went unreported, giving them a better understanding of the amount and nature of depreciative behavior occurring in their area.

Fifth, such reporting reduces impacts on the natural environment and on both public and private property; it reduces the impact on fiscal resources and increases users' satisfaction and enjoyment of an area, the ultimate goal of recreation management.

No single strategy has been found to control effectively littering, vandalism, or other rule violations in recreation areas, and it is doubtful that a single solution will be developed. Consequently, it is important that mangers of recreation areas use a variety of approaches for minimizing the effects of depreciative behaviors.

Preventing and controlling litter using many procedures is a good example of a comprehensive approach that has been evaluated. Research has shown the relative effectiveness of education, litter cans and bags, using incentives, and involving the public (Clark, 1976a, b; Clark et al., 1972a, b; Burgess et al., 1971; Christensen, 1978, 1981). Others have evaluated the effectiveness of penalties and signs (Heberlein, 1971). None of these approaches provides a complete solution, but taken together a fairly complete solution may be possible. Similar strategies need to be developed for other problems.

Prevention programs should focus on the various social, political, and physical-environmental factors to reduce nonconforming behavior and increase conforming behavior. We know little about how all the possible controlling factors interact, and research is necessary to identify the important factors and evaluate their relative advantages and disadvantages in a variety of conditions.

Some rule violations may be controllable; others may not. In the absence of severe restrictions on use and users, we may have to accept some forms of antisocial behavior, because the controls may be worse than the problems they are meant to solve.

REFERENCES

Alfano, Sam S., and Arthur W. Magill, ed. 1976. *Vandalism and outdoor recreation: Symposium proceedings.* U.S. Department of Agriculture Forest Service General

Technical Report PSW-17, 72 pp. Pacific Southwest Forest and Range Experiment Station, Berkeley.

Baron, Robert A., and Donn Byrne. 1976. *Social psychology, understanding human interaction*; 2d ed. 588 pp. Boston: Allyn and Bacon, Inc.

Bickman, Leonard. 1972. Social influence and diffusion of responsibility in an emergency. *Journal of Experimental Social Psychology*, *8*: 438–445.

Bickman, Leonard. 1976. Attitude toward an authority and the reporting of a crime. *Sociometry*, *39*(1):76–82.

Bickman, Leonard, and Susan K. Green. 1977. Situational cues and crime reporting: Do signs make a difference? *Journal of Applied Social Psychology*, *7*(1):1–18.

Bleda, P. R., S. E. Bleda, D. Byrne, and L. A. White. 1976. When a bystander becomes an accomplice: Situational determinants of reactions to dishonesty. *Journal of Experimental Social Psychology* 12:9–25.

Boston Parks and Recreation Commission. 1978. *Managing vandalism—a guide to reducing damage in parks and recreation facilities*. Parkman Center for Urban Affairs, Boston, 58 pp.

Burgess, Robert L., Roger N. Clark, and John C. Hendee. 1971. An experimental analysis of anti-litter procedures. *Journal of Applied Behavior Analysis*, *4*(2): 71–75.

Campbell, Fred L., John C. Hendee, and Roger N. Clark, 1968. Law and order in public parks. *Parks and Recreation* (December):28–31, 51–55.

Christensen, Harriet H. 1978. *Bystander intervention and litter control: An experimental analysis of an appeal to help program*. U.S. Department of Agriculture Forest Service Research Paper PNW-287, Pacific Northwest Forest and Range Experiment Station, Portland, 25 pp.

Christensen, Harriet H., and Roger N. Clark. 1978. Understanding and controlling vandalism and other rule violations in urban recreation areas. *Proceedings of the National Urban Forestry Conference*, Vol. 1, November 13–16, 1978, Washington, D.C.

Clark, R. D. III, and L. E. Word. 1972. Why don't bystanders help? Because of ambiguity? *Journal of Personality and Social Psychology*, *24*(3):392–400.

Clark, R. D. III, and L. E. Word. 1974. Where is the apathetic bystander? Situational characteristics of the emergency. *Journal of Personality and Social Psychology*, *29*(3): 279–287.

Clark, Roger, N. 1976a. Controlling vandalism in recreation areas—fact, fiction, or folklore? In *Vandalism and outdoor recreation: Symposium proceedings*, pp. 62–72, S. S. Alfano and A. W. Magill, eds. U.S. Department of Agriculture Forest Service General Technical Report PSW-17, Pacific Southwest Forest and Range Experiment Station, Berkeley.

Clark, Roger N. 1976b. *How to control litter in recreation area: The incentive system*. U.S. Department of Agriculture Forest Service Information Leaflet, 10 pp., Pacific Northwest Forest and Range Experiment Station, Portland.

Clark, Roger N., John C. Hendee, and Fred L. Campbell. 1971a. *Depreciative behavior in forest campgrounds: An exploratory study*. U.S. Department of Agriculture Forest Service Research Paper PNW-161, 12 pp., Pacific Northwest Forest and Range Experiment Station, Portland.

Clark, Roger N., John C. Hendee, and Fred L. Campbell. 1971b. Values, behavior, and conflict in modern camping culture. *Journal of Leisure Research*, *3*(3): 143–159.

Clark, Roger N., Robert L. Burgess, and John C. Hendee. 1972a. The development of anti-litter behavior in a forest campground. *Journal of Applied Behavior Analysis*, *5*(1):1–5.

Clark, Roger N., John C. Hendee, and Robert L. Burgess. 1972b. The experimental control of littering. *Journal of Environmental Education*, *4*(2):1–7.

Clinard, Marshall B. 1974. *Sociology of deviant behavior*, 4th ed. New York: Holt, Rinehart and Winston, 685 pp.

Downing, Kent, and Cynthia M. Moutsinas. 1978. Manager's views of dispersed recreation along forest roads. *Journal of Forestry*, *76*(9):583–585.

Driessen, Jon. 1978. *Problems in managing forest recreation facilities: A survey of field personnel*. U.S. Department of Agriculture Forest Service Equipment Development Center, 106 pp. Missoula, Montana.

Flickinger, Theodore B. 1976. *Crime and law enforcement in Ohio's State Parks*. Ph.D. thesis, Ohio State University, Columbus.

Heberlein, Thomas A. 1971. Moral norms, threatened sanctions, and littering behavior. Ph.D. thesis, University of Wisconsin, Madison, 253 pp.

Hendee, John C., George H. Stankey, and Robert C. Lucas. 1978. *Wilderness management*. Miscellaneous Publication 1365, U.S. Department of Agriculture Forest Service, Washington, D.C.

Kohlenberg, Robert, and Thomas Phillips. 1973. Reinforcement and rate of litter depositing. *Journal of Applied Behavior Analysis*, *6*:391–396.

Latané, Bibb, and John M. Darley. 1970. *The unresponsive bystander: Why doesn't he help?* New York: Appleton-Century-Crofts, 131 pp.

Moriarity, Thomas. 1975. Crime, commitment, and the responsive bystander: Two field experiments. *Journal of Personality and Social Psychology*, *31*(2):370–376.

Muth, Robert M., and Roger N. Clark. 1978. *Public participation in wilderness and backcountry litter control: A review of research and management*. U.S. Department of Agriculture Forest Service Research Paper PNW-75, 12 pp. Pacific Northwest Forest and Range Experiment Station, Portland.

Piliavin, J. A., and I. M.Piliavin. 1972. Effect of blood on reactions to a victim. *Journal of Personality and Social Psychology*, *23*(3):353–361.

Powers, Richard B., J. Grayson Osborne, and Emmett G. Anderson. 1973. Positive reinforcement of litter removal in the natural environment. *Journal of Applied Behavior Analysis*, *6*:579–586.

Shafer, Elwood L., Jr., and Robert C. Lucas. 1978. Research needs and priorities for dispersed recreation management. *Journal of Leisure Research*, *10*(4):311–320.

Shaffer, D. R., M. Rogel, and C. Hendrick. 1975. Intervention in the library: The effect of increased responsibility on bystanders' willingness to prevent a theft. *Journal of Applied Social Psychology*, *5*(4):303–319.

U.S. Department of Agriculture, Forest Service, 1975. *Recreation information management system*, RIM Center, Washington, D.C.

U.S. Department of the Interior 1977. *National urban recreation study: Seattle, Everett, and Tacoma*. Heritage Conservation and Recreation Service, and National Park Service, Seattle, 363 pp.

U.S. Department of the Interior. 1978. *National urban recreation study*. Executive Report, Heritage Conservation and Recreation Service, Washington, D.C., 184 pp.

FIELD AND LABORATORY STUDIES OF LITTERING

ROBERT M. KRAUSS, JONATHAN L. FREEDMAN, AND MORRIS WHITCUP

The idea that a great deal of individual behavior is regulated by social norms is something of a sociological homily. In virtually any social aggregate it is necessary that individuals adhere to a set of rules specifying what each properly may and may not do, especially as their actions affect others.

It is useful to distinguish among three somewhat different types of normative rules. First, there are rules whose violation has immediate serious consequences for others and whose precise form is nonarbitrary. Norms prohibiting theft and murder are examples of this type of rule. The particular form of such rules is nonarbitrary, that is, they are not merely a matter of convention, because in a very real sense they specify what most members of a culture agree upon as the necessary conditions for social life. Such rules permit little or no deviation and their violation will usually result in the application of severe sanctions.

A second sort of rule is one whose violation may have equally serious consequences for others, but whose specific form is arbitrary or conventional. Rules regulating vehicular traffic are an example. Most people would agree that it makes little difference whether cars keep to the left or right side of the road or whether the stop signal is a red or green light, so long as all drivers adhere to the same convention. But if one person drives on a different side of the road from everyone else, the consequence can be

---

Source: *Journal of Experimental Social Psychology* (1978), *14*: 109–127.

disastrous. The point is that in the absence of such conventions orderly traffic would be impossible and so some rule must be adopted and enforced by the application of formal sanction.

There is a third type of rule that plays a pervasive role in everyday life. Such rules are nonarbitrary in form, but the consequences of their violation (both for the violator and for others affected by the violation) are not particularly serious. Sanctions are seldom applied and, when they are, tend to be both mild and informal. In general such rules relate to the amenities of everyday life rather than issues of survival and because of this a wide range of behaviors can be tolerated. Even widespread violation tends to make life unpleasant or inconvenient, rather than impossible. Rules regulating such minor antisocial behaviors as littering and noisemaking are examples.

One interesting aspect of such rules is that their violation becomes a matter of consequence only when reasonably large numbers of people are involved or when people are so densely clustered that one person's actions begin to impinge upon the living space of others. If a small fraction of the pedestrian traffic on a quiet suburban street litters, the result will probably go unnoticed. But if the same proportion of people litter the densely trafficked street of a city, the result will be an unsightly mess. Similarly, on a beach with a density of 10 people per acre, the playing of a portable radio is likely to bother no one. The same radio played on a more densely populated beach might be a source of considerable annoyance.

The particular behavior to be considered in the studies reported here is environmental littering. Littering and its consequences are interesting in their own right. At best, litter is unsightly and annoying; at worst, it gives rise to a sanitation problem of some magnitude and helps create the unwholesome and dispiriting atmosphere many associate with large urban centers. But this is not the only, or even the primary, reason for wanting to study littering. As a behavior more or less representative of a large class of minor antisocial behaviors it has much to recommend it. In the first place, it is generally agreed to be an undesirable act; few, even among those who litter, would argue that it is a good thing. Second, it is an easily defined overt act and so may be readily observed unobtrusively, without the use of questionnaires or special instruments. Third, it can be manipulated and studied both in the field and in more controlled laboratory situations, making for a potentially fruitful interplay between these two data collection settings.

SOME THEORETICAL CONSIDERATIONS

In this section we will sketch out some theoretical notions relevant to the processes of compliance with and violation of minor norms. The specific sort of normative behavior we will study is littering, and so our theoretical development will reflect that interest.

Why does littering occur? The most obvious explanation, and the one most likely to be offered by laymen, is based on an appeal to individual differences: Some individuals litter because, somehow, they are litterers. Although the tautologous nature of such an explanation requires no comment, the notion that individuals differ in their propensity to litter is probably to some extent true. In order for individual behavior to be affected by social norms, three conditions must be satisfied: First, the individual must have learned the normative rule. Second, he must perceive the salience of the rule visà-vis a particular situation (i.e., he must recognize that the rule is applicable to the situation in which he finds himself). Third, he must be affected by the sanctions contingent upon rule violation. Such sanctions may either derive from external sources or be administered by the individual himself, as when one feels anxiety or guilt for having done something he "knows he should not have done." If for a particular individual one or more of these conditions do not exist, the likelihood is great that he will consistently violate the norm. One would, therefore, expect children to be more likely to litter than adults, either because they have not yet learned the normative rule or because they do not recognize the relevance of the rule to the circumstances in which they find themselves. Similarly, the individual who knows the rule and its applicability but for some reason is exempt from or impervious to the sanctions which attach to it (e.g., is not embarrassed by the censure of others) also will be less likely to comply.

Assuming that the three conditions specified above are satisfied, we would still expect an individual's propensity to litter to be influenced by situational factors that affect the strength and salience of the norm. It is clear that in most situations normative rules are relevant only to some part of the concurrent behaviors in which the individual is engaged. That is to say, in a particular situation more than one set of motives may be engaged and the form of behavior prescribed by normative rules may conflict with behaviors deriving from other motives. When the strength of contranormative motives is great, one would expect the likelihood of norm violation to be commensurately great despite the individual's knowledge of the rule and its applicability and the sanctions associated with violation. We would expect a person to be more likely to discard a candy wrapper when fleeing a subway fire than when taking a leisurely stroll.

In addition, various factors can make normative rules more or less salient in any given situation. If other people are seen transgressing the rule, it is likely to increase transgression. This has been demonstrated with a minor transgression such as jaywalking (Lefkowitz, Blake & Mouton, 1955) and would probably hold for other rules of this sort. A similar effect would be expected if the individual has evidence that the rule has been broken even if he does not witness the actual transgression. This effect can come about both through a direct modelling effect (Bandura & Walters, 1963) and because any norm violation that is observed tends to weaken the norm by detracting from its social validity. For many, the idea that "everyone does it" is sufficient justification for engaging in a behavior that they might agree in principle was undesirable. With regard to littering, this is to some extent sensible. If everyone litters in a particular area, the contribution of an additional bit of litter is relatively minor compared to the effect of the same bit of litter in a pristine spot.

Another possible factor that is often mentioned as the cause of rule-breaking in urban areas is stress. The argument is that people under stress are less likely to obey rules, perhaps because the stress distracts them from the norms, produces deliberate counternormative behavior as a response to stress, or for some other unspecified reason. While the logic of such an argument is not clear, it does seem as if stress might contribute to the breaking of norms.

This is by no means an exhaustive list of factors that determine the extent to which people obey norms. Obviously, the ease of obeying the rule (how close is the wastebasket; how messy is the litter; etc.) plays a role, as does the likelihood of being exposed to sanctions. And there are, no doubt, many other relatively nonpsychological factors of this type. For the present, however, it seems most interesting to focus on the factors described above. To summarize: We would expect littering to be affected by the strength and salience of the social norm against it, the presence of litter as an indication that others have broken the rule, and perhaps by the arousal of stress. These expectations were tested in the four studies reported below.

EXPERIMENT 1

Experiment 1 was an exploratory field experiment designed to ascertain some of the demographic and situation correlates of littering and to determine the relationship between the size of an unwanted object and the likelihood of its being improperly discarded. As one experimenter distributed an innocuous handbill varying in size to passersby by several urban locations, an observer recorded how the handbill was disposed of.

Method

Procedure

One of two male experimenters was stationed at a street corner in the metropolitan New York area, distributing to passerby a handbill exhorting them to register to vote in an upcoming primary election. Three handbills of different size were randomly distributed: 20.3 × 35.6, 20.3 × 27.9, and 20.3 × 12.7 cm. Approximately 100 m away, a second experimenter unobtrusively noted whether the subject retained the handbill (i.e., put it in a pocket, handbag, shopping bag, etc.), deposited it in a trash basket, or disposed of it improperly (i.e., littered). Subjects were observed for the entire length of the block. Those who left the block while still retaining the handbill were classified as nonlitterers. Subjects who entered a building on the block while holding the handbill were dropped from the sample and their data are not included in the results. Subjects who neither traversed the block nor entered a store were observed for 2 min. Those who retained the handbill for that time were classified as nonlitters. (This latter situation typically arose with subjects waiting at a bus stop.)

The first experimenter recorded his estimate of the subject's age, race, and sex, as well as the size of the leaflet received. Also recorded was a rating of the cleanliness of the area during the time data were collected.

A total of 1,765 subjects was observed at nine different locations in the Greater New York metropolitan area. The locations spanned a wide range of socioeconomic variation, but in all cases the specific streets sampled were primarily commercial rather than residential or industrial. Each location was sampled on more than 1 day and between 121 and 252 observations were made at each.

Results

Handbill Size

No significant differences in littering rate were observed as a function of handbill size. Consequently, data from the three handbill conditions were combined in the results presented below.

Demographic Variables

Overall, males were found to litter somewhat more frequently than females, 7.4 vs. 5.3%, respectively, a difference that is of marginal statistical significance [$\chi^2(1) = 3.19, p < .10$].[1] No significant differences in littering rates were found for white subjects compared to nonwhites [$\chi^2(1) = .88, p > .50$]. However, a subject's estimated age was strongly related to the likelihood that he would litter. Subjects whose estimated age was 20 years or less were more than three times as likely to litter than the remainder of the sample [$\chi^2(1) = 35.60, p < .001$]. Although subjects' ages were estimated and probably subject to considerable error, the estimates were made prior to the

[1]This and all other χ^2 tests reported have been adjusted for continuity by the application of Yates' correction.

subjects' littering (or not) and therefore are not contaminated by experimenter bias.

Environmental Variables

Considerable variation in littering rates was observed among the nine locations studied. These data are shown in Table 1. It will be noted that littering occurs nine times more frequently at the highest rate location (Brooklyn) that at the lowest (Scarsdale). We cannot account for these differences in any straightforward fashion, but we can eliminate some obvious possibilities. For example, it is not the case that variations in littering rates are a consequence of differences in the age or sex distributions found at the nine locations. Nor does it seem to be the case than differences in rate are directly related to socioeconomic level of the area sampled. Although the three locations with the lowest littering rates (Scarsdale, Bronxville, and Madison & E. 81st St.) are among the most affluent sampled, the two highest rate locations (Broadway & 181st St. and Brooklyn) are by no means the poorest. None of the variables correlated with littering rate seems to explain the striking differences observed among locations. Nor is it likely that the rates are simply random fluctuations; a field experiment run at the two high rate areas 1 year later (see Experiment 4 below) found comparably high rates.

The one variable that was strongly related to littering was the rated cleanliness of the sampled areas on the days data were taken. Subjects at locations rated 1.0 or 1.5 (extremely clean) littered 3.7% of the time, compared to subjects at locations rated 2.0 or worse, who littered 12.3% of the time [$\chi^2(1) = 50.12$, $p < .001$].

Discussion

The finding that younger subjects have a greater propensity to litter is consistent with a normative interpretation of littering behavior. In this interpretation it is assumed that normative controls develop as a result of the socialization process and it would be expected that younger subjects would be less likely to have acquired both the internal controls and the cognitive information (knowledge of the norm, the ability to recognize the applicability of the norm to a particular situation) that the assumed to deter the transgression of social norms.[2]

[2]In retrospect it is clear that registering to vote was a poor choice of topic for our handbill. It could be argued that our under-20 subjects littered at a disproportionately high rate because they were less interested in the handbill's contents than were the older subjects. Our best guess is that this was not an important factor, but it is a question that could easily be resolved by an additional experiment.

TABLE 1. Littering Rates at Nine Locations in the New York Metropolitan Area[a]

	Manhattan				Queens	Brooklyn	New Rochelle	Scarsdale	Bronxville	
	Broadway & 102nd St.	Broadway & 80th St.	Madison Ave. & E. 81st St.	Broadway & 181st St.	Queens Blvd. & 64th Ave.	Kings Hwy. & E. 15th St.	Main St.	Main St.	Main St.	Total
Subject littered	14 (5.8)	11 (4.4)	6 (2.5)	33 (18.8)	7 (3.8)	25 (20.7)	6 (3.3)	3 (2.1)	4 (2.4)	109 (6.2)
Subject did not litter	226	240	237	206	178	96	173	140	160	1,656
Total	240	251	243	239	185	121	179	143	164	1,765

[a]Figures in parentheses are percentages.

The finding that littering occurs less frequently in relatively clean areas is suggestive, but no clear interpretation can be offered on the basis of the present data. Since the finding is correlational in nature, the direction of causality is impossible to ascertain. Conceivably, people who live, shop, or work in relatively clean areas tend to be nonlitterers and would be wherever they happened to find themselves. Nevertheless, the most plausible interpretation is that clean environments deter littering and dirty ones encourage it. In addition, and despite the substantial differences in littering rates between the "extremely clean" and other areas, it should be noted that the observed range of cleanliness ratings among locations was really quite small. The "dirtiest" locations were rated 2.5 (on a five-point scale). No really filthy locations were included in our sample.

EXPERIMENT 2

To examine under controlled conditions the effect of the cleanliness of an area on the likelihood that it will be littered, a laboratory experiment was conducted in which subjects, after participating in a cover experiment, were presented with an opportunity to litter in an area that was either littered or clean.

METHOD

Subjects

A total of 30 male and 30 female undergraduate students at Columbia University participated as subjects. They received either extra credit in one of their psychology courses, experimental credit to fulfill a course requirement, or simply "the opportunity to participate in interesting psychological research." They were recruited by phone and told only that the experiment involved "a study of creative thinking."

Procedure

The experiment was conducted in an experimental cubicle which opened onto a small waiting room. Aside from the subject and experimenter, no other persons were present. The subject was ushered into the experimental room, which contained a desk, a wastebasket, and a small table holding two 20.3 × 30.5-cm Plexiglas sheets, a box of tissues, cotton swabs and a variety of bottles containing colored liquids. The experimenter told the subject that the study was concerned with the physiological correlates of creative thought. He said that the procedure was to measure autonomic activity by taking palm prints before and after creative work. Thereupon the experimenter asked the subject whether he or she was left or right handed, swabbed the palm of the dominant hand with a greenish oil, and placed it carefully on one of the Plexiglas plates. After 15 sec (carefully timed for the subject's benefit) the experimenter removed the subject's hand from the plate, swabbed it with an ointment he called a "solvent" (actually Vaseline) and instructed the subject to allow the solvent to "work" for 60 sec. After this time had elapsed, the experimenter handed the subject some tissues to wipe away the solvent. The used tissues were deposited in the wastebasket.

The subject was then given the "creativity task" consisting of 40 anagrams to be solved in 20 min. When 20 min had elapsed, the experimenter, who had left the cubicle, returned, examined the subject's answer sheet, remarked that his or her performance was slightly below average, and proceeded to take a second palm print. This time, however, after applying the "solvent," the experimenter excused himself, explained that he had to rush to set up for the next subject, and instructed the subject again to allow the "solvent" to remain on the palm for 1 min before removing it. After giving him or her some tissues, the experimenter rather abruptly ushered the subject into the waiting room with instructions to leave after the solvent had been removed. The experimenter then reentered the cubicle closing the door behind him and remained there until the subject had left the waiting room.

Experimental Manipulation

Subjects were randomly assigned to either a littered or unlittered environment. In the "littered" condition, the waiting room floor was strewn with two crushed paper cups, candy bar wrappers, a newspaper, a paper bag, a crushed soft drink can, some string, and some bits of cellophane. In the nonlittered condition, the waiting room floor had been swept clean. No tissues or similar objects were included among the mess in the littered condition and in neither condition did the waiting room contain anything resembling a proper trash receptacle.

Behavioral Measure

The sole datum recorded was whether the subject left the used tissues in the waiting room or took them with him. Since there was no proper trash receptacle in the waiting room, all subjects who left tissues there were classified as litterers. In pilot work it was found that all subjects who took the tissues with them subsequently disposed of them properly. Because of this, and because of the difficulty of controlling subjects' routes and observing them unobtrusively after they left the waiting room, all subjects who took the tissues with them were classified as nonlitterers.

Results

Male and female subjects did not differ appreciably in their littering rates. However, significant differences were found as a function of the cleanliness of the environment. Thirty percent of the subjects exposed to the littered environment and only 6.7% of subjects exposed to the nonlittered environment disposed of their tissues in the waiting room [$\chi^2(1) = 4.01$, $p < .05$].

This finding clarifies the earlier field observation that an individual is less likely to litter a clean street than a dirty one. In some sense, litter begets more litter. The mechanism that accounts for this, however, is not completely clear. It may be that the presence of litter simply mitigates the presence of the norm against littering by presenting evidence of its failure to control the behavior of others. Alternatively, subjects' behavior may have been controlled by the not unreasonable notion that an additional piece of litter "makes less difference" in an already dirty environment than in a clean one.

In any case, it is clear that the cleanliness of the environment is one factor that controls littering but hardly the only one. It will be recalled that even in the cleanest environments (both in the field and in the laboratory) at least some subjects littered. It seemed reasonable to suppose that some intrapersonal variables would affect litter rate and a second laboratory experiment was conducted to explore this possibility.

EXPERIMENT 3

Although we assume normative controls to be an important factor affecting individual behavior, it also seems likely that other predispositional and situational factors may concurrently operate to moderate normative controls. One such factor that seems particularly relevant to urban environments is stress. It is certainly true that such major norm violations as delinquency and crime occur more frequently in urban than in rural areas (National Commission on Violence, 1970). While this is probably due mainly to socioeconomic factors, the noise, congestion, and rapid pace of life that typify much of urban life are potentially severe stressors, at least for some people, and this stress may contribute to norm violations.

One stressor that has been extensively studied, and which is particularly pertinent to any consideration of urban life, is loud, unpredictable noise. Glass and Singer (1972) have demonstrated in laboratory experiments that such stimulation produces a greater impairment in performance on a cognitive task (proofreading) than either soft unpredictable noise, soft predictable noise, or loud predictable noise. Interestingly, the greatest impairment was observed subsequent to (and in the absence of) stressful stimulation.

In order to assess the effect of noise on littering and to replicate the effect of the cleanliness of the environment, the present study employed the procedure of the previous one with the addition of two noise conditions. Some subjects were exposed to loud, aperiodic noise during the anagram task while others were not.

METHOD

Subjects

Thirty-five (32 male and 3 female) undergraduate students at Columbia University served as subjects. They were paid $2.00 each for their participation. As in the previous experiment, they were recruited by telephone and told only that the experiment involved a "study of creative thinking."

Procedure

The experimental procedure was identical to that employed in the previous study except for modifications necessitated by the introduction of the stress condition. Subjects were informed that the study concerned the effect of urban environments on creativity and that they would be assigned to work on a "creativity task" in either a noisy or a quiet environment. The cover story for the palm prints was also made relevant. The "creativity task" consisted of 40 anagrams in four 10-trial blocks. Subjects worked for 5 min on each block of anagrams. They worked alone in the experimental cubicle, paced by tape-recorded instructions that signaled them when to begin work and when to move on to the next block of anagrams.

Half of the subjects were randomly assigned to a "noisy" condition and half to a "quiet" condition. The stimulus in the "noisy" condition consisted of a loud broadband signal delivered aperiodically during the 20-min experimental session. The signal had a frequency range of 150–6000 Hz with its mode at about 600 Hz and was delivered through a horn speaker at 110 db (C weighting) or 108 db (A weighting).[3] No extraneous noise was presented in the "quiet" condition.

Again, a ruse was employed to rush the subject out of the experimental cubicle into the waiting room after the second palm print was taken but before he or she had an opportunity to remove the "solvent." As in the previous study, for approximately half of the subjects the waiting room was littered and for half it was clean.

Results

Anagram Performance

The ability of subjects to adapt to the stressor is evidenced by the increase in the number of anagram solutions by subjects in the "noise" condition from block one to subsequent blocks, relative to control ("quiet") subjects. In the first block, subjects in the "noisy" condition solved an average of 2.93 anagrams compared to 4.30 for "quiet" subjects [$t(33) = 1.75$, $p < .10$]. For the remaining three trial blocks the differences were small and nonsignificant (all t's < 1).

Littering

The finding of the previous experiment, that a higher rate of littering is found in a littered environment than in a clean environment, was replicated. The proportions of subjects who littered were 32% for the littered environment and 6% for the clean ($p = .07$ by Fisher's exact test). However, no support was found for the hypothesis relating littering to stress. Indeed, there was somewhat more littering in the "quiet" condition (28 vs. 12%), although the difference was quite far from achieving an acceptable level of statistical significance ($p = .22$ by Fisher's exact test).

Clearly, stressful stimulation did not induce a higher rate of littering in our experiment. Apart from the possibility that littering is unrelated to stress, there are a number of possible reasons for our failure to find such a relationship. The most plausible of these is that the degree of stress induced was insufficient to moderate the strong and salient normative controls that regulate littering behavior. We cannot reject this possibility, but it should be borne in mind that a stressor identical to the one employed in the present experiment is sufficient to induce substantial and reliable postadaptational decrements in performance on a cognitive task (see Glass & Singer, 1972).

[3]For a more complete description of the stimulus tape see Glass and Singer (1972). We gratefully acknowledge the generous aid of Dr. David C. Glass, who made the tape available to us and instructed us in its proper use.

Of course, a 20-min exposure to even a quite noxious stressor such as we employed is probably not comparable to chronic exposure to the variety of stressor experienced by many urban dwellers. Below we report some additional results for more "natural" environmental stressor that replicate our failure to find a relationship between littering and stress.

EXPERIMENT 4

The research reported thus far has examined the demographic and situational factors associated with littering. However, if littering behavior is affected by normative controls, it should be possible to reduce the rate of littering by a number of methods, e.g., increasing the salience of the norm, increasing the magnitude of the sanctions attached to violation or the likelihood that transgression will be punished, etc. These seem to be the main methods that municipal governments employ in their attempt to control littering. In New York City, where these studies were conducted, a variety of signs are posted which proclaim that littering is a violation of law and punishable by a $50 fine. And in previous years, extensive media campaigns have stressed such themes as "A Cleaner New York Is Up to You" and "Vote Here [a litterbasket] for a Cleaner New York." Despite this, there is general (albeit informal) agreement that such campaigns have had little effect on littering rates and we know of no evidence to support the conclusion that they do. Of course, one may argue that the forms such normative influence attempts typically take are particularly ineffectual and that other methods might be more successful. Certainly the pedestrian's eye in a city like New York is assaulted by so large a variety of signs and notices that it is possible that a sign reading "Don't Litter—$50 Fine" never even enters into awareness. Moreover, despite the Draconian nature of the threatened sanction, no one we have asked has ever seen or heard of anyone receiving a summons for common littering. As criminologists point out, even severe sanctions will not act as deterrents when the subjective probability of apprehension and punishment is low.

Experiment 4 attempted to affect the level of littering in a field situation by experimentally increasing the salience of more or less relevant norms.

Method

Procedure

The general procedure for the present experiment was similar to that employed in Experiment 1 except for the manipulations necessary to increase the salience of social norms. Subjects received a handbill and were observed to determine the method by which they disposed of it. However, prior to receiving the handbill, some subjects were stopped and asked to sign a petition. Three different petitions, varying in their relevance to antilittering norms, were employed. All were addressed to the (then) Governor of New York, Nelson Rockefeller. The first ("Clean Streets") asked for increased state aid so that the Sanitation Department could do a better job of street cleaning. This petition was assumed to be most directly relevant to antilittering norms. The second petition ("Antipollution") asked for more stringent enforcement of laws against industrial atmospheric pollution in order to protect the environment. This petition was assumed to be relevant to environmental concerns, but not specifically to littering. The third petition ("Highway Safety") called for better maintenance of roadways to promote safer travel. This petition was assumed to be least relevant to concerns about littering. Two additional conditions were run as controls. The first ("Time") was viewed as a control for merely being stopped and asked to perform a common courtesy. An experimenter simply approached the subject and politely asked the correct time. A final sample of subjects ("Control") was not stopped at all by the first experimenter but simply received the handbill, replicating exactly the procedure of Experiment 1.

Subjects, alone or in groups, were approached randomly by the first experimenter and asked to sign one of the three petitions or to tell the time. In his approach, the experimenter simply stated the contents of the petition. For groups of subjects, he attempted to include all members of the group in his approach. In the Control condition, the first experimenter simply indicated unobtrusively to the second experimenter which individual or group was to be included in the sample.

Approximately 100 ft further down the block, subjects were handed a handbill containing information about registering to vote by the second experimenter, who was blind to which of the three petitions the subject had been asked to sign. The subject was then observed to determine his or her method of disposing of the handbill.

Subjects

To minimize the problem of a "floor effect" it was decided to sample subjects only at the two locations which in Experiment 1 showed the highest littering rates. Brooklyn and Broadway & 181st St. Otherwise, criteria for inclusion in the sample were the same as those employed in that experiment.

Results

Stability of Littering Rates

The present study, conducted approximately 1 year after Experiment 1, afforded an opportunity to determine the stability of the rates of littering previously observed. The rates for control subjects in this experiment were quite similar to the rates found at the same locations a year earlier. There was somewhat less littering in the Brooklyn area than there had been and slightly more at Broadway & 181st St., but neither difference approached significance.

Demographic Factors

Again, males littered more frequently than females [13.3 vs. 8.2%, respectively, $\chi^2(1) = 7.30$, $p < .01$]. Younger people (10–30) littered significantly more than the rest of the sample [$\chi^2(1) = 5.44$, $p < .02$]. Unlike the previous study, we did find a difference between whites and nonwhites in the rate at which they littered. A higher percentage of whites than nonwhites dropped their leaflet on the ground [11.7 vs 5.1%, $\chi^2(1) = 6.00$, $p < .02$].

Environmental Variables

Again, littering rate was affected by the cleanliness of the location at the time the observations were made. However, probably because we observed only two locations (though at various times), the difference did not attain an acceptable level of significance [$\chi^2(1) = 2.44$, $p < .20$].

In Experiment 3 we hypothesized, but failed to find, a relationship between experimentally induced stress and littering. In the present experiment we attempted to pursue this question further by examining correlations between littering rate on a particular day and the average temperature, humidity, and temperature—humidity index (widely regarded as a measure of discomfort in summer) on that day. None of these correlations approached significance. Certainly these indexes are exceedingly gross measures of stress and the failure to find a relationship between any of them and littering is not surprising. Hence we are unwilling to discard the hypothesis on the basis of the data we have examined thus far, but our enthusiasm for it has been tempered somewhat.

Modelling Effects

To the extent that littering is a behavior under normative control, it would be expected that the rates of littering among members of groups would differ from the expected values for such rates derived from individual subjects. More specifically, in dyads we would anticipate fewer than the expected number of dyads in which only one person littered and more than the expected number of dyads in which both littered.[4] The data support such an expectation. Although, under the assumption of independence, we would have expected 34.5 dyads with one litterer, the number actually observed was only 15. Conversely, the expected value for dyads in which both members littered was 2.0; the observed frequency was 7. These results are consistent with a modelling hypothesis, but we cannot with certainty reject the possibility that one of the criteria by which individuals choose their companions is characteristics (e.g., social responsibility) that are related to littering.

Effect of Petition

Littering rates for subjects in the three petition conditions and the two control conditions are shown in Table 2; the overall χ^2 statistic computed for this table is of marginal significance [$\chi^2(4) = 8.24$, $.10 > p > .05$]. However, subjects approached to sign the Clean Streets petition littered less than half as often as Control subjects [$\chi^2(1) = 5.77$, $p < .02$]. Although less littering was observed in all of the other conditions relative to the Control, none of these pairwise comparisons is statistically reliable. It would be tempting to conclude that any approach to a subject that induces him to perform a prosocial act (giving the time or signing a petition) reduces littering, but our data do not permit us to draw such a conclusion with very much confidence.

DISCUSSION

We have found that young people litter more than older people, that more littering occurs in an area that is already littered, and that people asked to sign a petition relevant to clean streets litter less than those not approached. All of these results are consistent with the notion that littering is affected by the strength and salience of norms against littering. We found no evidence that stress induced by exposure to loud aperiodic noise increases littering or that there is more littering on days when the weather is uncomfortable. These negative results certainly do not indicate that stress can be ruled out as a factor, but clearly it did not play a role in our studies.

Although research on littering is in an early stage, our findings suggest some reasons that public campaigns against littering may be unproductive.

[4]Two-person groups were examined because it was the only size that occurred with sufficient frequency to permit analysis.

TABLE 2. Littering Rates in Five Experimental Conditions

	Experimental condition					
	No petition	Asked time	Highway safety	Antipollution	Clean streets	Total
Percentage of subjects who littered	14.5	10.2	8.5	11.5	7.1	10.4
N	228	196	201	200	227	1,052

Attempting to reduce littering by changing people's attitudes or by exhorting them on television not to litter is unlikely to be effective. To begin with, virtually everyone agrees that littering is bad, but some people litter despite this. Relatively few adults in our sample littered and very likely it would be difficult to reduce this number very much. Most of the littering that we observed was done by young people, who are probably least likely to be influenced by mass media campaigns. To the extent that such campaigns are used, it would make sense to concentrate them in classrooms and children's television programs, where they will reach those who do most of the littering.

In contrast, situational variations appear to have powerful effects on littering. In particular, there is less littering when streets are clean, and there is some indication that littering is reduced if the individual is made aware of environmental concerns at about the time he has a chance to litter. The latter condition may be difficult to achieve, but the former is not. Instead of blaming littering on a lawless public and trying to change deep-seated attitudes, public officials might do well to accept the fact that some amount of littering is one of the costs of urban living. By diverting money from ineffectual media campaigns to street cleaning, government might reduce the rate of littering substantially.

These studies focused on littering, but presumably these generalizations apply to other, similar behaviors. Compliance with any rules of this sort, nonarbitrary in form but not of great consequence, should be affected by the strength and salience of the rule. We would expect this to hold for rules of courtesy, sharing, queueing, and other minor social behaviors that help make the difference between pleasant, civilized living and its opposite.

REFERENCES

Bandura, A., & Walters, R. H. *Social learning and personality development*. New York: Holt, Rinehart and Winston, 1963.

Glass, D., & Singer, J., *Urban stress*. New York: Academic Press, 1972.
Lefkowitz, M., Blake, R. R., & Mouton, J. S. Status factors in pedestrian violation of traffic signals. *Journal of Abnormal and Social Psychology*, 1955, **51**, 706–708.
The National Commission on the Causes and Prevention of Violence. *To establish justice, to insure domestic tranquility*. New York: Praeger, 1970.

INDEX